MEDIEVAL
ENGLISH GARDENS

Medieval
English Gardens

TERESA McLEAN

COLLINS
St James's Place, London
1981

William Collins Sons & Co. Ltd
London · Glasgow · Sydney · Auckland
Toronto · Johannesburg

First published 1981
© Teresa McLean, 1981
ISBN 0 00 216535 X

Set in Garamond
Made and Printed by T. J. Press (Padstow) Ltd
and Bound by Robert Hartnoll Ltd, Bodmin

FOR MY PARENTS

Contents

Acknowledgements

The people who have helped with the research for this book are, like the sources they have helped me track down, too numerous for individual mention. I would like to assure them all of my warmest thanks, and to thank just a few of the most outstandingly kind of them by name. Above all, I would like to thank my dear friend Robert Ombres, O.P., for his tireless encouragement and initiative; Clare Coleman, Oliver Rackham, Douglas Webb and Greta Gorse, for their generous help with the unexciting chores of authorship; Richard Cohen, for bringing the book into existence, and my editor, Elizabeth Walter, for using her skill and understanding to make it what it is; Edward Miller and Anil Seal for giving me time and support to write it, and Seriol and Selina for keeping me and the book alive.

Illustrations

LINE DRAWINGS IN TEXT

Introduction

This book is about English gardens in the period between the Norman Conquest and the Renaissance. It makes occasional forays into the other countries of the British Isles and into the pre-Conquest period, but is basically concerned with the gardens of medieval England. These are among the most varied, colourful, fragrant and neglected delights of English history, and are overdue for redemption from the obscurity into which the better-documented still-surviving gardens of later centuries have plunged them.

Medieval gardens are not easily accessible to the historian, being only very fragmentarily recorded in account rolls, charters, surveys and registers, written in drastically, often eccentrically, abbreviated medieval Latin, French and English on decaying scraps of paper and parchment. This book is an exploration of the wealth of secrets about English medieval gardens contained in such documents.

Gardening was already old in England by the time the Normans came. It had been influenced and expanded by the Romans and the Anglo-Saxons, but the Normans influenced and expanded it still more, and in more recorded detail. Medieval English gardening records effectively begin with the Normans, so Norman England is the natural beginning for this book, just as Tudor England is the natural end.

It is not a history book so much as a book set in a period of history, and it is only chronological in so far as the gardens it explores developed chronologically. The first four chapters deal with the location, ownership, purpose, layout, overall appearance, fashions and workmanship of English gardens, the last five with their contents and detailed appearance.

It is a book about the comparatively unrecorded time known as the Middle Ages, which was in fact a brilliantly coloured era. In that sense it is historical, though it is also timeless, as all books on gardening are. It is a book for those who like gardening and for those who are homesick for the pre-industrial world of harvesting, gardening Christendom. It is about a world which has long since vanished, but is there for any gardener, and anyone with a willing imagination, to recreate.

I

The Monastic Garden

According to the Old Testament, the Lord God made a garden in Eden, where he walked in the cool of the day. He created Adam and Eve to dwell there with him, and let Adam name all the different trees and plants for him. When Adam and Eve were cast out of this Paradise they were condemned to cultivate the earth by the sweat of their brow in order to live; medieval pictures of the expulsion from Eden usually show Adam carrying a spade, and Eve a hoe or a distaff. From then on, man had to work the land to live. The purest and most divinely aspirational way of doing this was gardening, because it recreated the paradise he had once shared with God.

It was therefore the perfect occupation for Christian monks and nuns, who devoted themselves to a life of prayer, supported by manual work. Thus medieval monastic gardens are the obvious starting point for this book, and their English history the obvious subject of its opening chapter. In order to appreciate these gardens it is necessary to look back to the origins of the monastic life and the place of gardening within it. The principles of monastic gardening were established right at the start of the monastic movement.

The First Christian Gardens

The first Christians to devote themselves entirely to the religious life were the third-century Egyptian cenobites, who retired to the desert to live solitary lives of prayer. They were also the first recorded Christian gardeners, so that Christian religious gardening is as old as the oldest form of Christian religious life. The Egyptian cenobites lived off bread brought to them by villagers, water, a supply of which was the only material requirement they made of their cave homes, and a few plants which they grew in the enclosures they made outside their caves. This is how St Jerome (AD 342-420), a desert cave dweller of long standing, began his instruction of a young man about to take up the same life: 'Hoe your ground, set out cabbages, convey water to the conduits.'

It was another desert hermit, St Antony, who founded the first Christian monastery, and it is no surprise to find that he was also a gardener. He was born in lower Egypt in AD 251, of wealthy parents who died when he was about twenty years old, leaving him to take care of his younger sister. He decided that the best way to do this was to put her in a house of maidens, perhaps the first Christian nunnery, and then he retired to the desert outside his village and devoted himself to a life of prayer and spiritual reading. When he was thirty-five he cut himself off still further from his home, crossing the Nile to live high up on the slopes of a remote mountain, where he stayed for twenty years, alone but for a man who came to bring him bread every six months.

Yet it was while he was here, in his most austere retreat, that he made a little garden, which has been described for us by the Palestinian hermit and friend of St Antony, St Hilarion: 'These vines and these little trees did he plant himself; the pool did he contrive, with much labour for the watering of his garden; with his rake did he break up the earth many years.' Antony probably gardened to give himself some physical occupation rather than to grow food, which he seems to have regarded as an unavoidable necessity. One day, when he was feeling depressed, an angel appeared to him in a vision, plaiting mats out of palm-tree leaves, and said to Antony: 'Do thus.'

In this way the balance between prayer and work which characterizes Christian monasticism was born, and it was brought into the world when St Antony founded the first Christian monastery in the Fayum in AD 305. At first the monastery was a handful of scattered cells which he visited periodically. Later, he brought them together into one place, though the monks continued to live in individual cells, engaged in a combination of prayer and work, particularly gardening, that has never been displaced as the monastic ideal. Significantly, the two men venerated as the patron saints of gardening were both early Christian hermits who lived out that combination.

The earlier of the two is St Phocas, a contemporary of the Egyptian cenobites, who lived outside the gates of Sinope, on the Black Sea, in his little garden, where he grew vegetables for the poor, and flowers. One day he was visited by some strangers, whom he invited to stay the night. A savage persecution of Christians had recently been raised, and Phocas's guests told him that they were soldiers and had been sent to find the Christian, Phocas, and slay him. Late that evening, when he had said his prayers, Phocas went out into his garden and dug a grave. The next morning he told his guests that he was Phocas, took them out into his garden, and stood by the grave he had dug. They cut off his head and buried him there, amid his flowers. St Phocas is always portrayed with a spade.

The Middle East was the first area to which the monastic movement founded by St Antony spread. Within a century it had reached Europe, where an Italian nobleman named Benedict gave up his studies at Rome and retired to the solitude of Subiaco to become a monk. There the roseto – little rose garden – of St Benedict, whose flowers delighted his senses and whose thorns he used to mortify his flesh, is still preserved. Eventually he withdrew to the heights of Monte Cassino, on the borders of Campania, and in AD 530 founded a monastery there.

It was at Monte Cassino that St Benedict wrote the first monastic Rule, which for 600 years was the one and only Rule of western monasticism, except for the Celtic. The Rule was written for one monastic house, governed by an abbot whom the monks elected for life, and independent of all control save that of the Rule and of God. The monastery was a spiritual family living apart from the world in order to serve God without distraction, under the leadership of its father abbot. It extended hospitality, medical help, teaching and alms to those nearby, but it was essentially self-contained and self-sufficient.

The necessaries of its life were the familiar ones: water, a mill to make grain, and a garden, in that order. They were to provide the bread and wine, vegetables and fruit, and fish and eggs for special occasions, which Benedict prescribed as the diet for his monks. Benedictine monasteries farmed land for grain; they dug fishponds to supply them with fish, which quickly became a major item of the monastic diet; they kept bees and they grew fruits and vegetables, vines, flavouring and healing herbs and plants yielding dyes, inks and incense.

The first monasteries were built along the lines of Roman villas, which were self-contained farmhouses, like mini villages, enclosing vegetable gardens near the outbuildings, neat little flowerbeds, shady walks and trees around the front of the house, and a colonnaded, fountained courtyard, called the atrium, at the heart of the complex. It was a design conducive to the keeping of gardens. The most striking thing about the ground plan of the perfect Benedictine monastery, which was drawn up at St Gall, near Lake Constance, Switzerland, in the ninth century, is the number and variety of its gardens (see Fig. 1). It is a diagram of an ideal, not of an actual foundation, and it amounts to an extended Christianized edition of a Roman villa estate with a wealth of gardens.

At the centre is the cloister garth, divided into four squares, with a savina (holy water stoup) in the middle, fringed with grass and flowers. The cloisters were the main arteries of community life, and the garden they enclosed was one of peace and repose, often planted with flowers, and sometimes containing statues of saints or of the Holy Family. At other parts of the complex a school, hospital and guest-house also have cloisters, descendants of Roman peristyles, around their courtyards, but there is no indication of what was planted in them.

There is a hospital or 'physic' garden next to the doctor's house and the drug store. It is quadrangular in shape and planted with roses and lilies which the plan calls 'herbs both beautiful and health-giving', with sage, rosemary and other 'kitchen herbs' in sixteen little parallel beds. On the other side of the hospital, to the south, is the cemetery, planted with rows of fruit and blossom trees, between which are the monks' graves, with a cross in their midst. It is an almost architecturally planned garden and has the 'ordered regularity' beloved of classical designers and poets.

Next to this garden, in the south-east corner of the plan, is an oblong, simply marked 'Garden'. It is bigger than the physic garden, but laid out in the same style with eighteen parallel beds, planted with vegetables ranging from the medieval favourites – onions, garlic, leeks and shallots, in the first four beds – to parsley, chervil, coriander, dill and poppies, which we would distinguish as herbs or flowers.

At both the east and the west end of the church there is a semi-circular space, open to the air, labelled 'Paradise'. The word 'paradise' comes from the old Persian *Pairidaeza*, meaning enclosure. There had been parks or paradises, with pools of water and shady trees, in Persia and all over the Middle East from time immemorial, and the word entered Christian Church history as the name for the porticoes adjoining the oldest Byzantine basilicas, planted as gardens. The Moslems took paradises with them to Sicily, whence they were taken to northern and western Europe by the Normans.

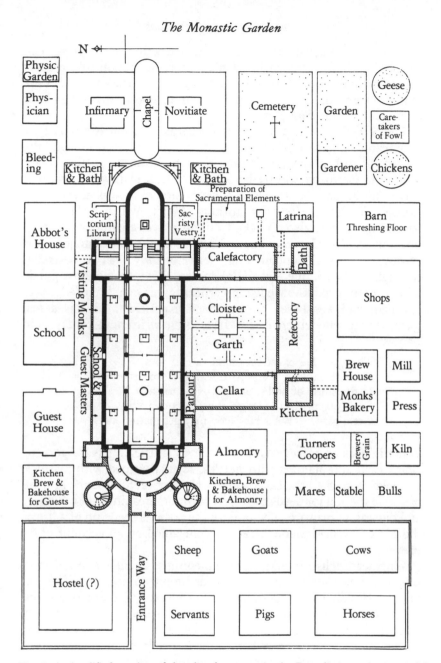

Fig. 1: A simplified version of the plan drawn up in the Benedictine monastery of St Gall in the ninth century, showing an ideal monastery and its gardens.

A lot of medieval churches, particularly in monasteries, had paradises, which were enclosed places for meditation and prayer, planted with flowers. They were nearly always at the east end of the church behind the high altar; it was rare to find a paradise at both ends, as in the St Gall plan.

The St Gall plan is a blueprint for perfection, but it shows how vital gardens were considered to be to that perfection, and the records of real monasteries bear this out. A ninth century poem, written in Germany shortly before the St Gall plan was drawn up, leaves us in no doubt that monastic gardening was thriving in Europe at this period. Its author, Abbot Walafrid Strabo of Reichenau Abbey, also on Lake Constance, was a gardener, and his poem is called *Hortulus* (The Little Garden). The subject was obviously a very popular one, for *Hortulus* was a bestseller throughout the Middle Ages. Walafrid wrote it for a monastic public with a pretty good knowledge of gardening; his own knowledge was excellent and was based on first-hand experience. This is a real gardener's poem which might have been written yesterday, and begins:

> Though a life of retreat offers various joys,
> None, I think, will compare with the time one employs
> In the study of herbs, or in striving to gain
> Some practical knowledge of nature's domain.
> Get a garden! What kind you may get matters not.

Walafrid goes on to say that his kind was a little courtyard garden, facing east, and plagued with nettles, so that 'armed with mattock and rake, I attacked the caked earth.' He goes on to describe how he prepared the soil for seed-sowing by turning, breaking and raking it, and digging in manure. The bulk of the poem is made up of a list of the herbs Walafrid planted, each accompanied by an account of its uses.

Whether English monks were gardening as keenly as Walafrid at this period we cannot tell. The records simply do not exist. There is just one British gardening tradition that we can trace, and that is the Celtic one. Strictly speaking, it does not belong in the story of English gardening, since it is above all an Irish tradition, but for nearly three hundred years before the Benedictine St Augustine of Canterbury brought Roman Christianity to Britain in AD 597, Celtic monasticism was unchallenged there.

Celtic Christianity was inebriate with love of nature. The remote huts to which its saints retired were not in the wastelands, like those of the Egyptians, but 'facing the south for warmth, a little stream across its enclosure, a choice ground with abundant bounties which would be good for every plant', as the seventh century Manchán of Liath, or one of his ninth-century disciples, described his ideal retreat. God was experienced through nature, which was the garden he had given man for that purpose, and which the Celtic anchorites lived off and celebrated in rhapsodically sensual poetry.

Even so, the monks still enclosed little garths round their huts. They made clearings with wells and pools and added one or two homegrown vegetables to their supplies. So there were some sort of rudimentary vegetable gardens among these Celtic cenobites, and probably in the big Celtic monasteries too, and in the Anglo-Saxon monasteries that began to reappear after the ninth century Viking invasions.

The other patron saint of gardening, besides St Phocas, was a Celtic hermit. His name is St Fiacre, and he was an Irish or possibly a Scottish prince in the seventh century who went to join a monastery near Meaux. Wishing to cut himself off from his roots still more, Fiacre got the abbot's permission to live in a solitary dwelling in the forest, where no one would know him. The abbot offered him as much land as he could turn up in a day, to surround his hut. Fiacre wasn't Irish for nothing, and he managed to enclose a large area by turning up an outline with the point of his staff, instead of driving his farrow with a plough over all the ground. He then cleared the ground, built an oratory in honour of the Blessed Virgin Mary and a cell for himself, and made the ground into a garden. He spent his time cultivating it and praying.

For the history of monastic gardening, St Fiacre's emigration to Gaul – one of many such moves that brought Ireland into contact with the Continent – is important, for it was an Irish nobleman, who had joined a monastery in County Down and then gone with St Columban to evangelize the Franks, who founded the monastery of St Gall in the sixth century, where three hundred years later the plan of the ideal monastery was drawn up.

How much the Benedictine and Celtic gardening practised on the Continent influenced Anglo-Saxon England it is impossible to say. England's contacts with the Continent were mainly through English monks who went there as missionaries. Boniface in the eighth century received letters from home asking for more books on simples (medicines) and complaining that it was hard to get foreign herbs, so there was enough horticultural contact to make the monks in England feel they wanted more. Any such hopes were dashed by the Viking invasions, which extinguished monastic life in England until its revival under the Abbot-Bishop Dunstan and King Edgar in the middle of the tenth century.

We have only two hints of monastic gardening in the tenth century: a grant of a vineyard at Pathensburgh in Somerset to Glastonbury Abbey by King Edwy, and mention of the first identifiable gardening abbot: the Anglo-Saxon Brithnod, Abbot of Ely in 970. According to the Ely chronicler, Brithnod was 'skilled in planting gardens and orchards around the church, considering this to be a fit and venerable place for the shade of trees.'

He was making a kind of wooded paradise. One of his two monks, Leo, helped him to lay out these 'gardens and orchards elegantly, and he planted choice fruit trees there in regular and beautiful order', and he also planted shrubs. There was something of the landscape gardener about Brithnod. He laid out his gardens thoughtfully, and with some technical skill, for the chronicler says: 'In a few years the trees which he planted and ingrafted appeared at a distance like a wood, loaded with most excellent fruits in great abundance, and they added much to the commodiousness and beauty of the place.'

Benedictine Gardens:
The English Beginnings

It was the Norman Conquest that brought English monastic gardens to full bloom, and to our notice, for it brought about a Norman takeover in the English Church. Normandy was a land of abbeys. England became one in the century after the Conquest.

All Benedictine abbeys were built according to a basic pattern, which was designed to accommodate the three basic constituents of Benedictine life: liturgical prayer, private prayer and spiritual reading, and manual work. To appreciate fully how gardens fitted into that pattern, and how numerous and varied they were, it is necessary to envisage it.

At the heart of the monastery was the church, built east to west, with the nave forming the north side of the cloister garth, which it sheltered from wind and cold. The cloister garth was the meditative kernel of the cloisters, which were the centre of community activity. The north cloister walk was a sort of living-room, with bookcases and writing desks in the window recesses overlooking the garth. The south cloister walk backed on to the refectory (frater). The west cloister range, adjoining the west front of the church, was virtually the entrance front of the abbey, and was usually two, sometimes three, storeys high with a guest hall, kitchen, buttery and undercroft of cellars. The east cloister range was also two storeys high, the top storey being the monks' dormitory (dorter), with a toilet (reredorter) at its south end, and the ground floor taken up with the north transept of the cruciform church, the chapter house, parlour (locutorium) and calefactory, or warming-room, where the fires were lit for the winter on All Saints' day.

East of the church and cloister block, sometimes quite far to the east so that it would be in a quiet position, was the infirmary for old and sick monks and those who had just given blood. It consisted of a hall, chapel, kitchen and toilet, and sometimes a small refectory. These buildings were usually arranged around a courtyard, and were known as 'the little cloister'. In this courtyard, or in a garden next to it, was the infirmarer's garden, planted with medicinal herbs.

Beyond the cloister and the little cloister there was occasionally a kitchen court, and beyond that there was a large area containing the rest of the abbey's buildings and gardens, orchards and vineyards, a lay and a monastic cemetery, a forecourt and, as time passed and the abbot became increasingly powerful and independent of the community, the abbot's lodgings and gardens. The forecourt was a collection of domestic accessories, which were attached to every big medieval house. There was no stereotyped plan to their arrangement, or to that of the gardens, fishponds, orchards and other plantations within the outer wall. In monastic forecourts there was often a guest-house as well, projecting as a wing from the cellarer's range, or standing just apart from it. If the abbot lodged separately from the community, his quarters were usually by the gate-house, and they often included his private garden, and a private guest-house and garden for his friends. Most monasteries used the land north of the church as a lay cemetery, and there was also a cemetery for the monks, often depressingly near the infirmary.

The most isolated block in the monastery was the almonry, which gave food, alms, education and shelter to the local poor. It therefore belonged in part to the town or village outside, and was built along the other wall, facing outwards. It was a self-contained unit, with a chapel, living quarters and administrative office of its own, sometimes a kitchen too, and sometimes a garden.

The first visual record we have of this basic pattern is a ground-plan of the monastery of Christchurch, Canterbury, drawn up in 1165 to show the new drainage and water supply system that Abbot Gervase planned to install (See illustration p. 65). Christchurch was exceptional in that its buildings were on the north, instead of the usual south side of the church, for reasons of space. But its basic pattern was the standard Benedictine one, and it is especially interesting to us because its plan contains the first visual record of a Norman monastic garden in England. North of the church nave there are two courtyards, and in the one at the east end, which looks as if it is divided in two by a fence, the artist has put the label 'herbarium'. This word was used in the twelfth and thirteenth centuries to mean virtually any kind of garden: herb, kitchen, lawn, pleasure or simply general. The Canterbury herbarium, however, can be identified as a herb garden because it lay in the little cloister, just west of the infirmary, bordered by a *'via quae ducit ad domus infirmorum'* (passage leading to the infirmary). Like the little cloister, it almost certainly belonged to the infirmarer, and was planted with medicinal herbs. The artist drew coloured, flowering plants in it, like the medicinal roses and lilies in the St Gall plan.

The rest of the cloister courtyard seems to have been a plain lawn like the main cloister garth. On the other side of the church, to the south, is the lay cemetery, with a fountain in the middle of it. This not only graced the cemetery, but also supplied water to the water tank, or possibly fishpond, in the south-east corner of the enceinte, in the area now known as 'The Oaks'. South of this pond, along the eastern end of the south wall, are some large plants which look like flowering trees. They could be fruit or nut trees, or trees put there to make a shady, blossomed walk. This last seems to be the most likely explanation, as they are not labelled as any particular variety of tree, and are drawn in rather impressionistically. On the other hand, they may have been more specifically functional; we know from the chronicles of the monastery that there were vines grown along the west wall of the kitchen in the twelfth century, but there is no sign of them in the plan. The artist was chiefly interested in the water system, at the expense of representative accuracy, hence his elaborate drawing of every fountain and washing-place, and in particular of the enormous necessarium, or reredorter. The herbarium was the only garden he thought worth a mention, but it may not have been the only one in the monastery. There were probably quite a few more gardens or orchards than the plan shows. The chronicler reported that in 1170 the knights sent to the monastery to murder Thomas à Becket laid their cloaks under a wide-branched sycamore, and Becket, in fleeing from them, ran a different way from 'the usual passage through the orchard to the west end of the church'.

There are no flower gardens marked on the plan, though the new hall in the north-west corner looks grand enough to have merited one, and there may also have been a paradise east of the church. Outside the north wall, east of the main enceinte, the artist has marked in an apple orchard (*pomarium*), a vineyard (*vinea*) and a single small field (*campus*), which was not one of the abbey's big crop fields. It was probably a flax or hemp patch, since this was often placed in the no-man's-land between the fields and the estate gardens because it exhausted the soil but yielded useful supplies of linen, canvas, rope and twine. At Canterbury it was part of a stretch of cultivated land belonging to the central enceinte rather than the fields, though outside the walls: a sort of exterior garden belt that closes off the Christchurch gardens.

Benedictine Gardens:
The Different Kinds

Having looked at the basic pattern of monastic gardens geographically, one must now do so administratively, because the fact that Benedictine monasteries were run by specialized administrators explains the extraordinary number of specialized gardens they contained.

The Rule of St Benedict originally committed the administration of the monastery to the cellarer, under the abbot. But as the original, single unit of the monastic estate was added to parcel by parcel, with some of the added properties lying far from the monastery and from each other, stewards were appointed to run the estates and collect their produce and rents for the monks. These estates were often devoted to specialized production of vegetables, corn or fruit, and by the tenth and eleventh centuries, the produce was being assigned to specific purposes at the monastery: wine for the altar, wax for lamps, candles and tapers, corn for distributions of bread by the almonry, all kinds of foodstuffs for the kitchen. The departmental officials who received these products were known as obedientaries, because of the obedience they owed to their abbot and community, though each one ran a department of his own, and in big houses there could be as many as two dozen. Since they were in charge of the everyday organization of monastic life, they were in charge of its gardens, and the best way to understand the distinguishing characteristics of these gardens is, as it were, obedientarily.

The most important obedientary was the cellarer, the original 'mother' and joint administrative head of the community, together with the 'father' abbot. He was the chief provider, and had to supply the entire house, including its servants and stables, with food, drink, and fuel. The west cloister range belonged to the cellarer, and sometimes there was a little garden attached to it, growing fruit and vegetables.

At Battle Abbey in Sussex the cellarer was in sole charge of providing for the monks and their guests, the abbot and his household and guests, and the convent kitchens and servants. To help him feed this multitude he kept a garden where he grew oats, barley, peas and beans (an unusual case of growing field cereals in a garden) and onions and leeks. He also grew fruit trees, and hired villagers to pick the apples and make them into cider, any surplus apples being sold. Occasionally he sold a little hemp or grass from the garden.

The cellarer at St Peter's, Westminster, had a large garden some way off from the main buildings, and is referred to in the accounts as 'the cellarer and gardener'. So important was his garden that it was called 'The Convent', in Norman French 'Le Couvent', and gave its name to the site now known as Covent Garden.

Cellarers often grew bitter herbs, which they used to make beer. Ale, made of malted barley, and beer, made of herbs, were the staple drinks of English monasteries all through the medieval period and their cellarers became master brewers. Every monastery had its brewery, run by the cellarer, and sometimes as many as four brewery assistants.

The monks took to marking their barrels of ale with three, two or one crosses, signifying that they swore on the Holy Cross that the brew was very good, sound or fair; later these marks became trade marks signifying treble, double or single strength. Weak ale was improved by the addition of bitter herbs, known as gruit herbs; by the thirteenth century gruits were being added to all kinds of ale, which is how beer came into existence.

Monastic houses had recipes for their own patent gruits, often based on a mixture of sweet gale (bog myrtle), bog rosemary, milfoil (yarrow), tansy and other herbs chosen by the cellarer. One of the wild herbs used was ground ivy, hence its nickname 'ale-hoof'; another was ling; gale twigs were so commonly used that 'gale beer' continued to be drunk for centuries after the medieval period. Beer made with 'groot' was still being made in the south Hams of Devon in the early years of this century, and Celtic poets from the sixth to the sixteenth centuries celebrated 'beer with herbs' as one of their favourite drinks. Most of the gruit herbs recorded by cellarers grew wild, but the cellarers did not record their secret recipes, and we can only speculate about the herbs grown in brewery gardens like the one at Norwich Cathedral Priory, where the gardener made this entry in his accounts in 1451: 'To the cellarer, when his herbs failed for the beer, ¾d.' Beer gained steadily in popularity and, until licences began to be granted to professional brewers in new towns in the early fourteenth century, the monks were beer monopolists.

The first corporation of lay brewers to rival the monks was the Guild of Our Lady and St Thomas à Becket, established in the good beer country of Kent. It was with the lay intrusion into beer-making that hops, introduced from France, began to take the place of gruit herbs. Their astringent flavour meant that they went further than the herbs and worked out cheaper; they were in use in all the big London breweries by 1464. In the end, as the monks couldn't beat the new beer they began reluctantly to make it, but for most of the Middle Ages the monasteries were the homes of mead, cider, ale and true gruit beer, and many a monastic cellarer cultivated little corners of herbs, to add to the ones he collected from the wilds to make his gruits.

He also grew apples to make cider and, to a much lesser extent, pears to make perry. A lot of cellarers had orchards outside the monastery walls, as well as fruit gardens inside them, and fruit became something of a monastic speciality. St Teilo, the sixth century Bishop of Llandaff, crossed to Brittany to stay with Bishop Samson of Dol, who had been a student with him, and planted not just an orchard but 'a whole forest of fruit trees', said to have extended over three miles. Five centuries later it was still there, known as the *'arboretum Teliavi et Samsonia'*.

Monks were natural importers and exporters, constantly improving their knowledge and resources by exchanging plants, personal and horticultural gossip with members of other monastic families.

Monastic commerce was at once more personal and more international than any other in the Middle Ages. A good cellarer could at least keep up the standard of fruit production if not initiate a new strain of it. The Ely cellarer had an extensive terraced orchard and a garden attached to it adjoining the outer courtyard called 'The Pondyard'. This was where horses entering the monastery were watered, while their riders were given something stronger from the cellars.

In big monasteries there were a number of officials running departments under the cellarer's overall supervision: the grainkeeper (granatarius), the refectorian or refectorer, and sometimes a sub-refectorer, who was in charge of serving and clearing away meals, providing washing facilities and looking after the frater. About five times a year the refectorer had to renew the rushes and sprigs of rue that were strewn on the hall floor to keep it fresh. On Holy Saturday it was customary to welcome spring by scattering bay leaves in the air; at the Augustinian priory of Barnwell in Cambridgeshire, the refectorer had to sweeten the air with flowers, mint and fennel, and in summer he had to make fans, probably of rushes. He needed a garden.

Another cellarer's official was the kitchener, who was in charge of the cooking, fuel and staff in the kitchens. As kitcheners were not usually responsible for producing the food they dealt with, they did not usually have gardens, though where the kitchener was a very important official, having some of the responsibilities normally assigned to the cellarer, he often had a kitchen garden. This was the case at St Mary's, Abingdon, where the kitchener was recorded in 1219 as having a garden by the Thames, where he may have had a house of his own, though none of his accounts for the garden survive. The best surviving kitchen garden accounts are the thirteenth-century ones from the Abbey of Beaulieu, in Hampshire. Though a Cistercian house, the obedientary system was so closely modelled on the Benedictine that their kitchen garden will serve as a Benedictine model.

The first duty of the kitchen gardener was to provide new beans for the daily pottage, which was a thick, starchy soup made of peas and beans that supplied the liquid part of the starch diet everybody lived on. He sent leeks and onions to the lay and monastic infirmaries each day, so that pottage could be made for the sick at the ninth hour (lunch-time), and again after Vespers. He provided new beans for the community pottage, and pot-herbs for the monks' infirmary and guest-house. It is hard to over-emphasize the overpowering role of starch in the medieval diet, and the ancillary role of vegetables to it. Monastic kitchens used more vegetables than most because, until about the mid-fourteenth century, they supplied a meatless diet. Thereafter, as meat was eaten more frequently, they moved over to some extent from vegetables to herbs, which had always been extensively grown and were now grown with particular regard to meaty compatability.

Beside peas and beans, the most popular vegetables were those that tasted strongest: leeks, onions and garlic. The 'seasoning vegetables' grown at Worcester Priory also included saffron, from the saffron crocus, and cumin, which the cook there seems to have used in prodigious quantities.

At Beaulieu there were a lot of kitchen gardens, supplying various of the obedientaries, under the overall control of the keeper of the curtilagium. This was a kind of back yard, often planted with herbs and vegetables. In 1269 it was Brother John who had overall charge of the Beaulieu kitchen gardens and, in order that the main one should keep up the supply of beans and other vegetables required of it, he paid 3s.6d. to workmen to plant beans and leeks in it. The year before must have been a good one because it had left him with 20d. worth of surplus leek seeds to sell, 28s. 6d. worth of leeks, 22d. worth of onion seeds and 5 quarters 5 bushels of beans which he sold for 18s.9d.[1] He sowed over 5 quarters of cereals and beans in the garden, which must have been very big, and may have covered several acres.

He also grew some hemp and cider apples and had enough beehives to produce a surplus of 5 gallons of honey and 2 lbs. of wax, which he sold in 1270. This must have been a good area for bee-keeping; most of the kitchen gardens at Beaulieu and on its Hampshire manors had beehives, some of them yielding as much as 8 gallons of honey and 22 lbs. of wax a year. Most of the gardens also had fruit trees, which produced a total of 18 barrels of cider in 1269. All the gardens were hedged or walled.

Among the gardening expenses the obedientaries entered in their accounts were sums spent on the usual leek, onion and herb seeds, on the mending of manure carts and on horse irons, on harrows, spades, forks, buckets, gloves, sieves and on hired help to do the cultivation with these tools. Brother John bought one load of gravel for the main kitchen garden, presumably for making paths. These

(1)   A quarter was approximately 512 lbs., and a bushel 64 lbs.

were typical monastic kitchen gardens, big and basic, producing the standard medieval fruits and vegetables. Wherever monastic kitcheners kept gardens, they would have been much like these.

The opposite is true of infirmary gardens, which were small and highly specialized. Every monastery had an infirmarer, and every infirmarer had a garden from which he made salves, medicines and tonics for those in his care. 'Before all things and above all things special care must be taken of the sick', says the Rule of St Benedict, 'so that they may be served in every deed, as Christ himself, for he saith: "I was sick, and ye visited me", and "What ye did to one of these My least brethren, ye did to me." ' Such was the infirmarer's commission, which made him outstandingly important. He was not a doctor as we understand that term today; he was a nurse, comforter, expert at careful and sympathetic custody, and herbalist.

Infirmarers were the first specialist gardeners, growing the herbs needed to keep the community healthy, and self-sufficiently so if possible. They also cared for the neighbourhood sick, and Benedictine nuns earned themselves widespread acclaim for their teaching and dispensing of medicine to all who needed it.

Sometimes infirmarers had their gardens outside the 'little cloister', as at Canterbury and Westminster, where it was attached to Edward the Confessor's buildings at one end and to the 'grete garden' at the other. More often, infirmary gardens were just walled or hedged round in a sunny position next to the infirmary. St Peter's, Gloucester, had a small infirmary garden tucked in between the infirmary, its chapel and the outer wall. The little twelfth-century infirmary garden at the Augustinian priory of St Edburg, Bicester, was called 'the Trimles', a name derived from the old English 'trimble' or 'trumble', meaning to walk unsteadily. It may have been given this name because it grew plants for the sick who could not walk well, but it is more likely to have been because its patients actually exercised in it. Infirmary gardens were usually small, sheltered and neatly laid out in beds, and the shakier brethren could trimble a few steps in them, enjoying the scented air.

They certainly did at Westminster Abbey, where the infirmary garden was an acre in extent, with plenty of room left for walking. In the fifteenth century, archery butts were set up in it; the standard of infirmity must have declined in the later Middle Ages. At Ely there was a hall next to the infirmary, to accommodate those who had let blood, and there was a garden attached to it where the convalescents could trimble together.

Usually infirmary gardens were easy to maintain; the only help needed was in carting manure to them, and making and mending walls and beds. In the big cathedral priory at Norwich, the only help the infirmarer hired was a boy, whom he paid 7d. or 9d. a year. Maybe he got his patients to help him when they began to feel better. The tools he used were the same as those in almost all infirmary gardens: sieves, trowels and hoes, for working the fine soil that suited herbs. Some infirmarers built little aqueducts to keep their gardens watered. Hardly any sold produce from their gardens; anything that was not used at once was dried and stored. Our word 'drug' comes from the Anglo-Saxon 'driggen' – to dry, and the infirmary shelves were lined with drugs made from herbs grown in the garden or bought at markets and fairs.

Like cellarers, infirmarers were great exchange and import men. By experiment, specialization or just careful cultivation, they supplied their patients with medicines, purgatives, skin ointments, eye drops, cordials and infusions, sedatives, stimulants, cough medicines, air and floor fresheners, tasty tit-bits for convalescents and pot-herbs for the meat meals they were allowed to cook for those recovering their strength after letting blood. Traditionally, the first meal given to a monk after blood-letting was sage and parsley, washed in salt and water, and a dish of soft eggs. After that he moved to meatier stuff. Amongst their other accomplishments, infirmarers were dieticians.

If a monk was ill enough to receive the Last Sacraments, he was not left on his own, day or night, but attended by two of his brethren who prayed the hours of the monastic office with him if he was well enough, and prayed them for him if he was not. They saw to it that any wishes he expressed were fulfilled if possible, and they comforted him and watched with him constantly. The infirmarer kept a candle by the bedside of the dying monk at night, and gave him a fresh bed to lie on and a clean habit to wear. Though it is not the sort of thing that gets entered in infirmary accounts, there seems no reason to doubt that flowers would have been put by the bed of the dying monk if he wished for them, and around the crucifix that hung over the door. These could be picked in the infirmary garden, where the infirmarer grew them for their medicinal properties; he was an omnivorous survival gardener.

The survival of the parish poor depended on the monastic almoner, who handed them old clothes from time to time and leftovers from the monastic tables every day. Black rye bread was the lowest form of sustenance, and the almoner's chief task was finding enough of it to feed the poor, the refugees of war, and the almonry school boys. The grain for making bread was grown in the fields. Gardens only grew accessories to it, and when an almoner had a garden it was usually a crude one, with fruit trees and a fishpond producing extra bits of food to add to the almonry distribution. Where the almonry was a very big one, a number of gardens might be assigned to it. At Evesham the almoner's income was made up of the usual rents and tithes, and he also received a tenth of all bread baked or bought by the Abbey, and charge of the monks' garden 'to provide vegetables for the poor'. In general, the almoner was too busy organizing the hand-out of these provisions to spend much time gardening.

Equally busy was the keeper of the works, an official found only in the biggest monasteries, whose job was to maintain the fabric. But of course there was nothing to stop him having a garden if he wanted one. The keeper of the works at Abingdon had one, and so did the one at St Swithun's, Winchester, where his garden was called 'Le Joye' because it was a pleasance, or pleasure garden. Pleasure is as good a reason as necessity for keeping a garden, if one can afford the time, and 'Le Joye' is one of the earliest proofs of the fact that the religious life went in for beautiful flower gardens long before the secular world felt secure enough to do so. In a successfully integrated religious life devotion and aesthetic pleasure complement each other, and monastic flower gardens were places for meditation and enjoyment as well as places for growing altar, shrine and church decorations.

Monastic houses sometimes had pleasure gardens that belonged to the whole community, like Brithnod's garden at Ely. It is worth singling out just one community pleasure garden from the great number that existed in the Middle Ages, because it is so delightfully described by its chronicler and because it shows how long women have had a gift for making shrub and flower gardens, as they still do today. The woman in this case is Euphemia, Abbess of Wherwell Benedictine nunnery from 1226 to 1257. Her garden speaks for itself in this description and needs no further comment. 'She built a place set apart for the refreshment of the soul, namely a chapel of the Blessed Virgin, which she adorned on the north side with pleasant vines and trees. On the other side, by the river bank, she built offices for various uses, a space being left in the centre where the nuns were able from time to time to enjoy the pure air . . . She surrounded the court with a wall and the necessary buildings, and round it she made gardens and vineyards and shrubberies in places that were formerly useless and barren, and which now became both serviceable and pleasant.'

The monks at Durham in the fifteenth century had a more sporty approach. 'There was a garden and a bowling alley belonging to the Common House, on the back side of the said house, towards the waste, for the novices sometimes to re-create themselves'.

Besides these community gardens, there were the central cloister garths, which had been planted with flowers, trees and herbs in some parts of Europe ever since the eighth century. As far as England is concerned, there is the famous story of King William Rufus (crowned 1092) going to the nunnery at Romsey where the twelve-year-old Matilda, future wife of his brother Henry, was staying. The abbess was fearful for Matilda's safety and dressed her in a nun's habit. The King went into the cloisters as if, says the chronicler, 'he only wanted to admire the roses and other flowering plants', while Matilda went past safe and unmolested, walking with the nuns.

Quieter even than the cloister garth was the paradise. The fifteenth-century doorway into the one at Winchester is still standing though its garden has long since gone. It was looked after, as all paradises were, by the sacrist, who was the obedientiary in charge of the church, and therefore of these church gardens. Paradise flowers were used to decorate the altars, statues, shrines, and the whole church on feast days. Members of the community could meditate and pray in the paradise, which was enclosed, and often circular in shape. The oldest meaning of rosary is that of a rose-garden, and the enclosed rosary was the perfect garden of Marian devotion. The bigger houses had Lady Chapels and chapels dedicated to their patron and neighbourhood saints, looked after by a chapel-keeper, whose little garden was a miniature paradise.

Roses and lilies were the greatest devotional flowers of the Middle Ages, and can be assumed to have grown in most monastic paradises. In 1872, when T. A. Dorrien-Smith took over the Tresco Abbey estates in the Scilly Isles and began cultivating daffodils on a commercial scale, he chose two kinds that he found naturalized in the Abbey ruins. They became popular under the names Scilly White and Soleil d'Or. Their origin is unknown, though the former is probably partly north African, brought to the Islands along monastic trade routes. Maybe the Tresco paradise was a daffodil one; there was no monopoly on floral prayer, and the Scilly daffodils were the obvious choice for that locality.

The monasteries that had paradises usually sited them next to the monks' cemetery, which was north of the church. The cemetery, like the paradise, was looked after by the sacrist, who had to keep it neat and tidy and free from weeds and, at Winchester, to stop horses and sheep from feeding there, so that the departed could have the most tranquil and beautiful repose until the Last Day. To this end, cemeteries were often embellished with trees, flowers and fountains, and of course a central crucifix or cross.

As for the church, the sacrist supplied it with flowers as well as light, and he had all the flowers that grew wild outside the monastery to supplement the ones he cultivated. Occasionally the records hint at the growing of fumitories, also called fume-terres: the 'smoke-of-the-earth plants' mentioned by Chaucer in his *Nun's Priest's Tale*. Incense could be made from this, and from centaury and wormwood, all of which were sometimes cultivated as well as gathered from the wilds.

The monastic gardens most likely to elude the accountants altogether were the abbot's private gardens, because they were under the care of his steward, or of the community's overall gardener. They were accounted as one item of the abbot's household expenses, and the wide variety of plants growing in them escaped close scrutiny. The abbot might choose to have a pleasance with flowers for himself and his guests, like the 'recreation' garden at Haughmond in Shropshire. He might also wish for a herb, fruit, vegetable or fish garden to supply his private kitchens. The heads of late medieval monasteries had become so independent that they lived apart from their communities, in their own block of buildings, complete with chapel, guest-houses, kitchens and, more often than not, gardens. As early as 1160 Abbot Adam of Evesham made himself private lodgings at Offenham, with houses, a park, a fishpond and a chamber fitted with glass windows. By the thirteenth century gardening was the fastest spreading high-society cult and was taken up by nobles, including churchmen, in a big way. Men like William of Colerne, Abbot of Malmesbury 1260-92, made parks and gardens that were really little estates within their monasteries. The chronicler wrote of Malmesbury:

> Next to the abbots garden William built a great and noble hall and another, lesser hall at its gable end, roofed with stone tile; and had the building which had formerly been the hall con-

verted into a chamber . . . beside the abbots garden he had a
vineyard planted and surrounded with a stone wall on all sides.
He also made an erber next to that vineyard alongside the Kings
wall, and caused vines and fruit trees to be planted all over the
abbots garden.

There is one charming example of a prior's garden being used as a
country house garden, though it was within the monastery. In 1277
the Queen Mother, Eleanor of Provence, went to stay at Gloucester
Castle, which had no room for an adequate garden. So the prior of
the adjacent Abbey of Llanthony had a bridge made from the castle
to his garden, so that Eleanor and her ladies could exercise there – a
reversal of the usual association between an abbot or prior's garden
and members of the royal family, for usually it was royalty who gave
gardens from their manors as gifts to nearby religious houses.

The gardens of abbots and priors differed from one another more
than most monastic gardens, for they were made to suit individual
tastes. All we know of the one at Canterbury is that it was big. At
Ely the prior had 'a little garden and a poultry yard and ponds'; by
the late Middle Ages there was a dovecot in it too. At St Edburg's,
Bicester, the prior's garden was a little one, shaded by ash trees. At
Westminster it was an apple orchard. Quite a lot of abbots' gardens
were orchards, where the abbots walked with their guests in spring
and summer.

There was a medieval tradition of fruit-keeping and gardening
heads of religious communities in Britain, where gardening has
always been reckoned a noble way to spend one's time. There was
Brithnod, the grafter and tree planter at Ely; Thomas Crystall, the
gardening Abbot of Kinloss; Abbess Euphemia of Wherwell;
Prior Philip of the military order of St John of Jerusalem, who
planted a garden at Clerkenwell that was still there 150 years after
his death; Alexander Neckham, Abbot of Cirencester in 1213,
who wrote a description of his garden, which was rather overgrown
with plants from classical horticultural treatises, and from the
gardens he had seen when he lived in France; Henry of Eye, the
tenth prior of Barnwell, Cambridgeshire, who held the office of
gardener (hortolenus) there for many years, even after he became
prior, because there was nothing he liked doing better than gardening.

Being head of a religious community, especially a big one, involved a lot of entertaining and accommodating of visitors. John of
Crawden, the fourteenth-century Prior of Ely, was a friend of Queen

Philippa, and built a long chamber, its windows opening into a garden, for the Queen when she came to stay at short notice. Gardening, like building, was perfectly congruent with the headship of a monastery.

The monk who hardly ever had time to garden was the financial head: the treasurer or bursar. He spent his days between the counting-house and the chapel, with no time for gardens. At Worcester all the gardens were under the financial control of the bursar, but the only bursar recorded as taking horticultural decisions and having a garden of his own was the one at Durham, who occasionally bought leek and onion seeds 'for his garden'. By 1413 this had obviously grown into a wilderness, for he spent 16s.6d. that year on 'five pigs for the garden'.

As a rule, the treasurers left gardening to officials with more trifling duties than their own. The pittancer, for instance. He was a minor official, but he must have been a popular one, because his job was to provide treats and tit-bits for the community on feast-days. The pittancer did not often have a garden, for he was the official of the exotic and could not be expected to grow the things he dealt with. But as his duties did not occupy him every day he sometimes undertook a second job. At Abingdon, for example, Brother Will More, the pittancer in 1369, was also the community gardener. His garden was a pretty rough affair, most of its income being from the sale of faggots, twigs, straw and grass, and apples, Warden pears and nuts. Among the expenses necessary for its upkeep were payments to fruit gatherers, and also 'the repairing of houses in the garden', both of which entries give the impression that the garden was what we would call an orchard, and a scrubby one at that. There was also a fishpond, large enough to be fished with several draw-nets, though it is not clear whether this was in the garden or not, a patch of malt barley 'for making good ale', and vines, probably trained along the garden walls.

Pittancers quite often kept vines. By adding mulberry or currant juice to their grape juice, it was possible to make a sweetish table wine. But pittancers didn't try to specialize in gardens producing sweet fruits and drinks; it wouldn't have been practicable under English conditions. In the few cases where they gardened, they grew what they could in that line, but bought most of their sweets, spices and wines with money from the combined income of their property rents and their gardens.

It is hard to tell whether the precentors too bought the specialist materials they needed for their job, or whether they grew them. Most probably they did both. The precentor was the choir master, archivist and librarian. He had charge of the community's books, which he usually kept in big chests in the north cloister walk, where the monks sat at carrels (desks) in the window recesses facing south. They worked at their own book production both here and in the scriptorium, which in some houses was the only room with all year round heating, because the monks could not be expected to produce good work with stiff fingers.

The most skilful and demanding form of manuscript work was illumination, the perfection of which was one of the most dazzling achievements of medieval England. To produce illuminated psalters, devotional books and bibles, paints and inks were needed, and some of them could be made on the spot. The top medieval colour was blue, and one of the best blues for painting and writing was the vegetable blue, turnsole, made from the juice of elderberries, mulberries, bilberries and centaury plants. Another good blue was folium, made from the seeds of morella (heliotrope).

Purple dye, archil, was made from the lichen *Vocella tinctoria*, sap green from buckthorn berries mixed with alum, and iris green, very popular with fourteenth and fifteenth-century manuscript painters, from the juice of iris flowers, also mixed with alum. This was a good substitute for the expensive verdigris. Celandine petals mixed with mercury and egg yolk gave a weak gold effect, and buckthorn and weld (a relative of mignonette) both yielded a yellow dye that was sometimes used in book painting. The best vegetable yellow, however, came from the saffron crocus.

The best manuscript colouring agents, like gold leaf, vermilion, and cobalt, had to be bought, but the precentor could grow and make his own substitutes if he was short of them, or of the money to buy them. At Christchurch, Canterbury, in the late Middle Ages, the precentor had a little ink factory in the tailor's shop. Ink was needed for all the clerical work, notices, accounts and records of the monastery as well as its literary and artistic manuscripts, and its manufacture was therefore an important part of the precentor's job. But the precentor was essentially an indoor obedientiary, without a vested interest in gardening.

Likewise the chamberlain, who had to provide the community with its clothes and bedding, and also its laundry, shaving and bathing services, was a major obedientiary, and had enough to do without attempting to grow any of the required materials in his garden. Some nunneries made their wimples out of linen from home-grown flax, and every monastery used straw and rushes to fill the palliasses on which the monks or nuns slept. But the chamberlain was a buyer, not a cultivator, and when he gardened he did so to add to his income, or for his personal pleasure. At Canterbury and at Ely the chamberlain had a small garden, with fruit trees and vines, and at Ely he had a pond.

The Ely hosteller (also called the guest master, hospitarius or hostellarius) also had a pond in his garden, as did most of the hostellers who kept gardens. These probably fulfilled a decorative as well as a functional purpose, as places for guests to walk by and refresh themselves. Abbot William of St Albans (1214-35), according to his chronicler, 'protected the three-sided cloister which extends from the kitchen to the door towards the tailory by surrounding it with a wall of wattle-work, so that there should be free access for all persons to the space in the middle, namely the little garden. And that garden he arranged should belong to the guest-master'. The fact that medieval gardening was part of the medieval fight for survival doesn't mean it had to forgo its natural aesthetic appeal. A good guest-master extended his housekeeping to his garden. St Benedict laid down in his Rule that every guest was to be treated as if he were Christ himself. This was a counsel of perfection, and many guest-masters must have fallen far short of it, but hospitality was always one of a monastery's top priorities. Where there was room for guest-house gardens to exist, as at Christchurch, Canterbury, for instance, they were often kitchen gardens, small orchards or touched-up amalgams of both. If the guest-house was a large, busy one, its garden was probably looked after by the gardener obedientiary, appointed to look after some or all of the monastery gardens.

The Monk Gardener

In some monasteries each obedientiary looked after his own garden, but in others there was a monk gardener (a hortulanus, hortarius or gardinarius) responsible for the gardens. In either case, casual labour from outside was hired to help if the monastery was a big one with a lot of gardens. Helpers did the digging, weeding, planting, felling and trimming of trees, fruit picking, grass cutting, the making and repairing of walls and hedges, ponds and ditches, and all the unskilled jobs that should not take up too much of the monks' time. As well as casual help, some monasteries had one or two resident lay gardeners, who lived and ate with the other monastic servants, such as smiths and cooks, in the lay dormitory and refectory, and were given a salary and their keep. It was customary for monasteries, like all employers, to give their most important lay employees a robe or livery of office every year, and gardeners were usually given a pair of boots or a pair of gloves, or both, as their livery, partly to honour their status and partly for practical reasons. At Norwich the two gardeners also got a pair of thick protective leggings each, as they cut down and sold a lot of branches, roots, faggots and thistles in the course of their work every year; all their helpers were issued with thick gloves.

The helpers were hired each year to help the Norwich gardeners hoe in summer, plant and weed the beans, mow hay, collect the bean straw and catch moles. As a mole-catcher was also hired every year, he was either not much good or else the Norwich moles were particularly resilient; there is no mention in the accounts of their skins being used or sold. There was even a rat-catcher hired once or twice, a rarity in medieval garden accounts, and one which may have been due to the fact that chickens were sometimes kept in one of the gardens. Every few years a gang of hired men cleaned out the ditches round the gardens, and most years there were minor repairs to be done to the 'garden house', which must have been the tool-shed where they kept the big collection of tools they used. There were axes, hatchets and saws for making the faggots, trimmings, osiers, small timbers and firewood from fallen branches and trees which brought in a third of the garden's income every year. The garden accounts mention white poplars, oaks, crab-trees and a few ashes and elms sold regularly as timber and fencing, probably from the garden referred to in the later accounts as 'the great meadow'.

Other tools were ladders, sieves, spades, shovels, forks and dung-forks, some bound with iron, some unbound. The heavy, bound shovels would have been the more suitable for cleaning out the ditches that surrounded some of the gardens. Other gardens were sur-rounded by fences – it depended on the state of the drainage and the position of the garden. Medieval gardens, more than modern ones, used all kinds of hedges and palings, walls, ditches and banks to enclose the land, and in 1340 the gardener, Brother Peter of Dunwich, smartened up the ones at Norwich by having the gates and palings whitewashed. Among his tools were spare locks and keys to the garden gates and doors, and hooks, nails and lathe nails for mending them. Brother Peter was in overall charge of the gardens at Norwich and made all the planning decisions, hired and fed the staff, kept the accounts and answered for them to the auditors, but it is impossible to tell whether he or his successors at the top ever actually got their hands dirty.

Among the small items in his tool-shed were knives for cutting vegetables, lengths of string and rope, linen bags, skeps (big trugs), cloths for covering apples until they were sold, tallow candles and parchment for the drawing up of the annual accounts which the monk gardeners at Norwich kept so faithfully that we are able to put together this detailed picture of the gardens under their care. There were scythes for cutting the long grass, reeds, sedge, bean straw, hemp and thistles (for use as teasels), which were all sold each year from the big meadow gardens and the orchards, of which there were at least two. One of these was a cherry garden or cherry yard; another produced apples, pears, walnuts and filberts, some of which were sold and some sent to the cellarer and infirmarer.

Other tools were hoes, rakes, buckets and pails; one year there was an eight-gallon brass pot bound with iron, and barrows and carts, one of these a muck-cart with iron wheels. A lot of tools were needed, for there were several gardens adjoining each other, east of the monks' cemetery and the prior's house, and they were all under the gardener's care. It is not clear from his accounts how specialized his planting of these gardens was. Besides the wood, fruit, hemp and grasses already mentioned, they produced vegetables, herbs and occasionally a few flowers for sale. These were lilies, only sold two or three times, and only ½d. worth each time. They were probably grown for the church, and the ones that were sold were ones that had been picked and then found to be superfluous, and sold because they would quickly go past their best. It is impossible to tell whether they were grown in with the vegetables, in the orchard, by the pond (there was a fishpond somewhere in the gardens), or in a corner by themselves – perhaps the 'little garden between the garden gates'.

Occasionally madder was sold too. Its roots yield a yellow dye that was much used in England and France in the Middle Ages, and their juice can be used instead of rennet to turn milk into curds. In 1387 the gardener sold 8s.2d. worth of madder, a big load, but again it is impossible to tell where he had planted it.

The surplus vegetables sold each year were exactly those which one would expect, and they serve to underline the extent to which the leek family dominated medieval kitchen gardens. Leeks always headed the list, then porrets (pot-leeks), vegetables, onions and garlic. Herbs and herb seeds were also planted, and herbs were bought and sold each year. The varieties were not specified, except for mustard and parsley, and these were listed along with 'all the other herbs' after the vegetables on the account sheets. There seems to have been only a tiny infirmary garden at Norwich, and some of the herbs in the main gardens may have been sent to the infirmary as well as the kitchen. The chances are that the herbs and vegetables were grown together. The inevitable beans also appear among the vegetables, and were usually sent to the refectory, only the bean straw from their foliage being sold. The kitchen garden was carefully weeded and its soil manured and broken up; among the gardener's expenses there was always the cost of cider, beer, and bread, given to the hired helpers as tips and payment in kind.

In the uncultivated orchards and wooded meadows there was a fishpond and also a hermit's hut; there were chickens and ducklings, once or twice even a cow and calf, and sometimes there was a patch of hemp. As well as looking after all these, the gardener had to keep the cloister garth mown, and he once paid some workmen 6d. to 'extract the moss from the cloister green', which must therefore have been a lawn, with all its attendant problems. Despite all the help he had, the Norwich gardener was a busy man, yet the gardens constituted only a very small item of the monastic income. They brought in between £7 and £14 out of a total income from the obedientaries of about £1,500 each year, and they cost roughly £7 to £14 to maintain, so their value was in the fruit, vegetables, herbs, flowers and pleasure they provided. By the early fifteenth century they were being leased out for annual rents, and the accounts were just short lists of lessees and rents and any extra expenses incurred by the monastery as landlord. The gardener had an accounting house, 'the gardener's great checker', where he worked out his finances.

The Norwich gardener was typical of monastic obedientary gardeners, who were often also responsible for cider and mead-making, bee-keeping, the cultivation of cereal crops, fishing in the ditches as well as the ponds, and the keeping of vines. The gardener was never a major obedientary as far as finance was concerned, though he might have as many as ten gardens under his care, as at fifteenth-century Ely. But, as anyone who has a garden will understand, he was a major contributor to the happiness of the community.

At Westminster the gardener was a minor official but mentioned in affectionate detail in the thirteenth-century customary of that house, which outlined the duties of all its obedientaries. The gardener was allowed two companions and not more, unless by special licence, to help him in the garden. His garden brought the Abbey only £6 a year in cash, and 30s. and a pile of beans on two Pittance days. Its main supply was of food. On St James's day (July 25th) the gardener gave the community apples, cherries, plums, big pears, nuts and medlars, if he had them in the garden, to celebrate high summer. In Advent and Lent he supplied apples to the brethren in the misericord (infirmary refectory).

His duties did not excuse him from attending all the monastic offices, and he had to make sure that he took off his cape and boots before coming into church for them. The under-gardener's dog shared his master's bread allowance. Like obedientary gardeners everywhere, the gardener had one day each year which was completely his own, celebrated by the community under his leadership, and paid for by all the other obedientaries.

Somewhere in every obedientary account is the entry: 'To the gardener, for his O – 26s.8d.', or whatever the standard contribution was in that house. Sometimes the entry refers to the gardener's 'O et Olla', sometimes just his 'Olla'. Whatever the form of the 'O', it signified the gardener's special day, and there were six other obedientaries who also had 'O' days. The origin of the 'O's is a mosaic of excerpts from the Prophetic and Sapential books of the Old Testament, all beginning with the invocation 'O'. Each of the seven 'O' antiphons was awarded to the obedientary whose job most closely corresponded to its opening words. For instance, the one beginning 'O Clavis David' (O Key of David) belonged to the cellarer because he had charge of all the keys of the house. The 'O's were sung at Vespers on successive nights from December 16 – 23, making a festive preparation for Christmas, and on the day of his 'O' the obedientary led the singing of it in choir, had a day off work and had a feast laid on for him by the other obedientaries.

The 'O's were big occasions, and the third of them 'O Radix Jesse' (O Tree of Jesse), belonged to the gardener, which made him a more important obedientary than his small budget, indeed his non-existence in some houses, would imply.

In continental monasteries other 'O' antiphons were added to the Advent seven, until as many as eighteen were sung in some houses. But English monasteries kept to seven 'O's and kept their

celebratory pittances comparatively restrained, if only so that digestions lasted through the week. At Durham on the day of the prior's
'O', 'O Sapentia', the Master of the Common House provided 'a
solemn banquet of figs and raisins, ale and cakes, and thereof no
superfluity or excess, but a scholastical and moderate congratulation
amongst themselves'. Obedientary status entailed more than enough
work and responsibility to merit some ale and cakes and moderate
congratulation once a year.

Monastic Gardens other than Benedictine

From the twelfth century onwards, monastic life proliferated into
abundant individuality, with the foundation of new orders and the
establishment of variations on the Benedictine Rule. The Cistercians, for instance, were an offshoot of the Benedictines and had a
very similar obedientary, and therefore gardening, system. Work
was the partner of prayer for them even more than it was for the
Benedictines, for the Cistercians did not allot the time to intellectual
work and spiritual reading that the Benedictines did.

The most famous medieval Cistercian, St Bernard, constantly
stressed the importance of manual labour for the monks and
encouraged them to garden. Cistercian monasteries were often by
rivers and had riverside orchards and gardens, like the pear orchard
at Warden, and the big garden at Melrose Abbey which ran down to
the Tweed. Cistercians, Templars and Knights of St John of
Jerusalem were exempted from the payment of garden tithes, which
the King took from the monasteries of all the other orders. The
Cistercians deserved this exemption, and depended heavily on their
gardens, for they excluded even fish and eggs from their diet, though
they relaxed this in the later Middle Ages.

Their main foods were bread and vegetables. Cistercian dinners
consisted of 1 lb. of coarse bread, of which a third was kept for
supper, and two dishes of vegetables, boiled without grease. Their
drink was diluted wine, thin beer or a decoction of herbs called Sapa,
which was more like thin vegetable soup than anything else.

The gardens of the Augustinian canons also belong with those of
the Benedictines, since this order too was administered on the
obedientary system. The canons followed the Rule of St Augustine,
a basic Rule of prayer, poverty, chastity and work, which was
adapted and taken as their Rule by a number of orders. The first

really important step for the Augustinians in England was the establishment of St Botolph's Priory, Aldgate, by Queen Matilda in 1108. In 1125 there was a church (Holy Trinity) there, a large garden and a canon appointed to supervise the property and to administer the sacraments to the parishioners. There is evidence from a little later of a vineyard too. The Aldgate records mention a great, a small, and a number of unspecified gardens, and a prior's garden in the fourteenth century, which fits the priory's obedientary scheme of administration.

The Gilbertines were a double order, and had granges (farms) worked by lay sisters as well as brothers. Their churches were split down the middle by a wall, the monks worshipping on one side and the nuns on the other. The monks had their buildings east of the church; the nuns had theirs north of it,

> and these should be more beautiful and honourable than those
> of the men. Their parlour is to be set apart, in the garden, and
> only occasional entry is to be made to it, and confessions are to
> be heard there,

said Gilbert of Sempringham, the Englishman who founded the order in 1131.

The Gilbertines were a real amalgam: the Rule of their canons was Augustinian, but that of their nuns was Benedictine. Both groups had the usual basic monastic buildings: cloisters, dorter, frater, common-room, a guest-hostel, in a corner of the garden, apart from the paths and view of the nuns, an oratory, and workshops for the lay brethren 'within a walled garden, so that no danger of souls might arise', and stables, and sheds outside the walls if necessary. Gilbertine houses were small, administered by a few obedientaries, and they had the usual obedientary gardens. The brother in charge of the hostelry sent the nuns honey and fruit from his garden. But this was not enough to make a success of the Gilbertines, and there were never many double houses of any kind in England after the Norman Conquest, though before it there had been plenty, and double monasteries were often ruled by abbesses.

There were fewer nunneries too after the Conquest, and they were all priories, subject to the ultimate control of an abbot, head of the fatherhouse. Medieval nuns were almost exclusively aristocratic women. Unlike women of low birth, they did not have to labour all day for their living; unlike bourgeoise wives, they did not engage in business or trade. They either went on the marriage market or entered a convent, and sometimes their experience of the first drove them to the second as soon as widowhood permitted. Abbesses and prioresses were important figures in the countryside. Their houses used the same obedientary system as that of the monks, and had the same variety of gardens, though naturally they needed to hire more servants than the monks, and were run with a good deal of outside help.

But the sisters could economize on domestic servants by doing their own laundry, washing, cleaning, making of clothes, vestments and church furnishings, cooking and housekeeping. They could also garden, but had to hire help for heavy digging and for lopping trees, for cutting up firewood, pruning and tying up vines, and making garden beds and walls. There are no records of any obedientary gardeners in medieval nunneries; they were not big enough to need them. The nuns and their helpers managed the gardens between them. These gardens are often mentioned but seldom described in the few records left to us of medieval nunneries. They would have been similar to those of the monks but perhaps one may think of them as being a little more decorative, more flowery, less strictly utilitarian, and laid out with a feminine touch.

When the bishop visited the Cistercian nunnery of Nuncotton, Lincolnshire, in 1440, he was told that the nuns there kept little private gardens and that some of them did not come to Compline because they preferred to spend their evenings wandering about in their gardens, gathering herbs. The Cistercian nuns at the little convent of Sinningthwaite, Yorkshire, were ordered to get themselves a competent gardener for their curtilage, so that they would always have enough fresh vegetables for their kitchen. Evidently they had let it run to sweet-smelling seed. Visitors to nunneries in England and on the Continent often mentioned the pretty gardens, and the bishops who visited them to check on their discipline and way of life ruled that the nuns should stay within their convent walls, resisting the temptation to come out and socialize, and content themselves with treading the 'small grass' of the cloister, or at least of their own little gardens.

Hospital and Hospitaller Gardens

Medieval hospitals were religious institutions, and religious women often did outstanding work in them. They were run by priests, and staffed by 'brothers' and 'sisters', who usually wore monastic habits, though they might be either lay or religious, and whose aim was caring for the patients rather than curing them, and strengthening their souls in the face of death, for their patients were lepers, poor, destitute sick, and pilgrims in need of a resting-place. Because they were corporate religious institutions and because gardens sometimes had a place in them, albeit a small one, they have a small place in this chapter on monastic gardens.

At first, leper hospitals had common dormitories for all their inmates, but by the thirteenth century these had given way to separate dwelling places. There was a hospital chapel, a frater, domestic quarters and a house of residence for the staff. Sometimes these buildings were arranged around a quadrangle, with a 'lepers' well' in the centre. Most were probably grass quadrangles with flowers, so that it was a pretty garden as well as an exercise yard, as was the case in monasteries. The St Giles leper-house in Canterbury had several lawns, a pond, an orchard and a garden in the later Middle Ages.

The same buildings were common to all medieval hospitals but they were not laid out according to a set pattern. Some had a single infirmary hall with the chapel either built on to the end or detached. Some had a group of separated buildings, built round a narrow courtyard, or in a row or a cluster. Some had little pleasances and garden walks, others little more than the courtyard. Ospringe hospital in Kent had a flax and hemp garden somewhere in its grounds. The Master's accounts for 1293-4 have this little set of garden entries:

> For one spade, iron-bound, 2d. For one hoe, 2½d. Wages of
> women picking flax 1½d., and picking hemp 4½d. To a man
> hired to dig the gardens at 1½d. per day, 3d.

So there was more than one patch of garden, but only two days' worth of hired digging. Maybe women patients made linen and rope out of the flax and hemp. At Ewelme, Oxfordshire, the hospital did without outside help. The inmates were to pray and read when they were indoors, and to 'keep clean the cloister and the quadrangle about the well free from weeds and all other uncleanness'.

Before leaving the subject of hospitals, consideration should be given to the Hospitallers or, to give them their full title, the Knights of the Order of St John of Jerusalem, for they began as both a monastic and a hospital order, and are therefore doubly qualified for inclusion in this chapter. Their origin goes back to the year AD 600 when a hospice, with a hospital attached, was established in Jerusalem for Latin pilgrims. When the crusades began, the Hospitallers quickly developed from a group providing hospitality for pilgrims and crusaders into a military order.

In 1118, at about the time this development was being completed, two Frankish knights, crusading in the east, took vows of poverty, chastity and obedience, and so founded the Order of the Templars, also with the original purpose of helping and protecting pilgrims and also militarized almost immediately. These two orders acted as a corporate police force in the Middle East, and they made enough appeal to the crusading spirit in England to be endowed with quite a bit of property there. Both military orders housed their communities in priories, to which these estates had to account each year. The Hospitallers' headquarters was just outside the walls of medieval London, in Clerkenwell, where there were three priory gardens, an orchard and a fishpond, besides the private gardens of the prior and sub-prior, and little courtyards and a yard around the church, with its famous bell-tower. We don't know what grew in the gardens, but the prior's garden was probably very attractive, for it was planted by Prior Philip of Thame in 1338, and was still there, just as he had made it, in the reign of Henry VII, a century and a half later.

Being the garden of a religious and military order, it would not have contained any of the novelties these orders brought back with them from the Middle East, where gardens were luxuriant, ornate and dominated by the ultimate prestige symbols of a desert climate: pools and fountains. It was the gardens of aristocratic English society that went in for these novelties. Both military orders had close contacts with that society, the Templars in particular being closely connected with the Royal Court. For a short while, probably until the English climate overcame the desire for prestige, bathing pools became all the rage in English society gardens; most of them were small fonts in which ladies dangled their hands and feet. Tents made of rich tapestries were a garden accessory for the socially competitive, and iron trees, usually maypoles around which people danced, became popular when stories of the gold, silver and jewelled trees of the eastern palaces were brought to England; the golden tree in Titurel castle, in the story of the Holy Grail, is based on one of these legendary trees.

As regards the introduction of plants, it is hard to say much about the influence of the military orders, except that it must have been very small, for climatic reasons. Tradition has it that returning crusaders brought back with them a species of oriental mallow (probably *Althaea cutica*, which grows profusely in the Holy Land) which was called holy-hock, and the Turks Cap Lily (*Lilium martagon*) became naturalized on one or two sites belonging to the military orders in Kent, Devon and Scotland.

Tradition also gives a crusading connection to *Anemone coronaria*, the garden anemone native to the Holy Land and to Mediterranean countries, where it grows so profusely that it is thought by some to be the New Testament 'lily of the field'. The oriental plane tree was probably brought to England by the Templars, who planted the first one at their priory of Ribstone, in Yorkshire. The saffron crocus, an important spice plant, was brought to England by pilgrims returning from the east, and it still grows in abundance around the remote sites of Hospitaller houses in Yorkshire, especially their priory at Halifax. But their imports were random, individual and varied. The Military Orders were small, and the arrangement of their houses, unlike that of monks' and nuns' houses, was not particularly conducive to gardening.

Their headquarters were their showpieces, and the Templars' headquarters had a very famous garden. The first 'Temple' was erected in St Andrew's, in the London parish of Holborn, in 1128, complete with a round church in imitation of the church of the Holy Sepulchre in Jerusalem, and a garden. A new Temple was subsequently built on a better site on the north bank of the Thames, where the Inner and Middle Temples are today. It was practically open country then and the Temple gardens went right down to the Thames, and were planted with trees along the river's edge, for it was a wide, shallow river without an embankment.

When the Inner and Middle Temples were separated into distinct institutions, the fifteenth-century Inner Temple was divided into several enclosures, including 'a great garden', 'the Nutgarden', and 'Nuttrey Court', so it looks as if the orchard had a lot of nut trees. It was probably a decorative as well as functional orchard, carefully laid out as a showpiece, for in the seventeenth century there were plum, nectarine and cherry trees in the Temple gardens, 'ancient and set out in rows'.

Shakespeare chose the Temple gardens as the setting for the scene in Henry VI where a red rose and a white rose are plucked and taken as the symbols of the houses of Lancaster and York. Was he writing about a rose garden that really existed, or did the roses grow only in his imagination? Either way, Shakespeare obviously thought of the Temple gardens as somewhere that one would expect to find roses. These gardens were widely admired for their beauty in the Middle Ages.

The Order of Gardening Monks

Like the Templars and Hospitallers, the Carthusians came to England in the twelfth century, and like them they were always a small minority in its religious life. But how different they were in every other way! The Carthusians were the most self-contained, secluded, contemplative monks in England, and every single one of them was a gardener.

The order was founded by St Bruno, a canon of Rheims Cathedral, who decided to withdraw from the world and live a life apart from all its corruptions. Taking six friends with him, he fled to the mountains, where they built an oratory and seven small cells, and called their foundation La Chartreuse, in English 'The Charterhouse'. They followed the Rule of St Benedict, but in far more austere fashion than anyone else had attempted. They allowed themselves no bodily comforts, such as furs or skins, beyond their hair shirts, habits, girdles and sandals. Each monk slept in his own cell, on a blanket-covered board, with a bolster made of coarse skins stuffed with rags. He also ate his strictly vegetarian meals in his cell; they were pushed through a hatchway in the wall, and in that cell the monk ate, meditated, prayed, read and worked. He said the office there on his own, silently, and the only times he met the other monks were at church services, in the refectory on feast-days when the community ate together, and at one of the few recreation periods when they were allowed to exercise together, which also had to be in complete silence.

The challenge of Chartreuse attracted new members and one of them, called Hugh, was to become a bishop, a saint and the head of the first English Charterhouse, at Witham in Somerset. Henry II gave the land for this foundation in 1173. It had cells for thirteen monks, the standard Carthusian contingent, in imitation of Jesus and his twelve apostles. There were quarters and a church for sixteen lay brothers, who did the work required to keep the place going, and farmed the outlying property. The cells were built around a cloister garth, in the centre of which was a water conduit from which water was supplied to each cell by lead pipes, and this cloister was the heart of the monastery. Along one side of it was the church, and beyond that another cloister court, with chapels, a guest-house, and sometimes a stable attached to it, quarters for the lay brothers, domestic buildings and stone houses, all built around it. There was no infirmary needed in a Carthusian monastery because if a monk fell sick he was nursed in his cell.

The second courtyard was the cemetery, where the monks were buried side by side, without coffins, and with only wooden crosses, bare of any inscription, to mark their graves. No one but the prior and the procurator, who was in charge of all the temporal business of the house, ever went to the monastery gates, and this cemetery garth was the last earthly destination of the brethren. It was the nearest thing they had to a community garden. For their gardens, like their cells, belonged to them individually. Behind each cell, on the side facing outwards from the cloister, was 'a little garden which the recluse cultivates and trims according to his taste', in the words of one of these recluses.

In his garden the monk cultivated, meditated and exercised. In one of the gardens in the 'Locus Dei' priory at Hinton, Somerset, there was a paved walk along the south side of the wall separating this garden from the next one. One of the stones that had edged this little pavement was still in its upright position when excavations were done there earlier this century. The owner of the garden must have put down this tiny path as an exercise strip. And it was tiny too: the gardens there were only about seventy three feet square. At Mount Grace Priory, Yorkshire, the prior and sacrist had slightly bigger cells and gardens, as was quite often the case, but none of them was big (see Fig. 2). Their gardens were little individual patches and paradises. Their owners could do as they liked with them: they could plant flowers, trees, fruits, vegetables or shrubs, or just leave them as grass. No one else ever came into them.

There is a somewhat less than academic story that can be told here because it illustrates the secret, individual nature of the Carthusian vocation and of its gardens. Only a few years ago, during an oppressively hot summer, one of the monks in an Irish Charterhouse decided to dam the stream in his garden, and as it was such a small garden he managed without much difficulty to flood it and make a swimming pool. All perfectly in accord with the Carthusian ideal of looking after one's own life. But of course the monks in the cells

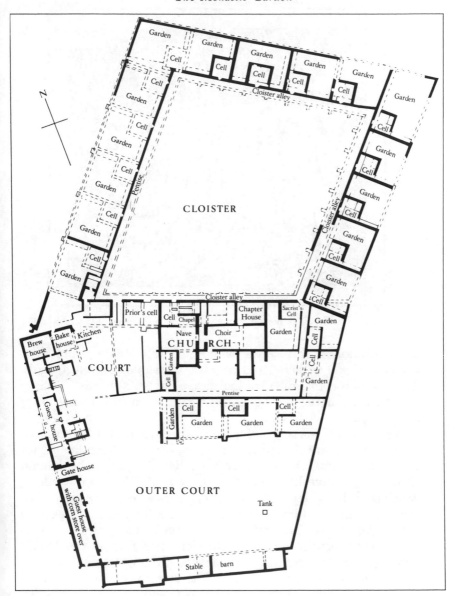

Fig. 2: The Charterhouse at Mount Grace, Yorkshire, with its individual cells and gardens.

Fig. 3: A hermit in the garden outside his cell.

below his found themselves without a water supply and their gardens quickly withered and died and their toilet ceased to flush. The upshot was that rarest of Carthusian events: a chapter meeting, which voted that the dam be removed. Even a cenobitic monastery is a community.

We have no such insights into any medieval Charterhouse gardens, which are as hidden from us as they were from the monks on the other side of the garden wall. Excavations of the Hinton Charterhouse revealed a door in the wall dividing two gardens, which is a baffling discovery. Sharing gardens would have been a fundamental contravention of the Carthusian Rule, and no other connecting doors have ever been found on any of their sites.

A wooden pentise ran along the cloister wall of all the Mount Grace gardens, and another one along the dividing walls to the outer wall, to give cover in wet weather. The seventh cell had one with a tiled roof, running right round the garden, and it also had a wooden seat, in front of which was a two feet deep pit, the access point to the sunken stream. The occupant of this cell had made himself a throne of a toilet, and a covered walk that was, by Carthusian standards, lavish and flamboyant. One of the cells had a tank in the garden.

These are the only hints we have of how the monks arranged their gardens. There is no way for us to find out more.

At Witham the cloister garth was known as 'the enclosed garden', and at Hinton the cloister along the side of it as 'Monk's Walk'. Characteristically, it was only four feet six inches wide, surrounding a cloister garth just thirty eight and a half feet square, by contrast with the magnificent cloisters of Benedictine abbeys. There was, however, some decoration at Hinton. In the fourteenth century it was floored with encaustic tiles, patterned with diamonds along the south side and with diagonal stripes along the east side, with a dark blue border two feet wide all the way round. Once a week in the early years of the order, more often later, each monk could walk in these cloisters, which may seem an unbearably meagre outlet to us, but has been described by a Carthusian as 'a long and spacious corridor where he may walk up and down in the hour for recreation'. The real room for movement in Carthusian life lies within. At its heart are the long hours of solitary prayer in cell and garden.

Medieval cells were usually about twenty-seven or thirty feet square; those of the prior and sacrist a bit bigger, but some much smaller. One at Mount Grace was only sixteen feet by five feet.

They were two storeys high. The top storey, all one room, was the workshop, and it had a little window opening on to the garden. The ground floor was divided by wooden partitions into a lobby on the cloister side, with stairs at one end and a door on to the garden at the other; a living-room, with a fireplace and door and a window on to the garden, and a tiny bedroom, also with a garden window. In such a small house one always overlooked the garden. The monks had nothing in their cells except what they needed to work, eat and sleep, but they may have brightened them up with flowers in summer. St Hugh used to tame little birds and squirrels at La Grande Chartreuse, to keep him company in his endless tussles with the Devil, but his prior was an iron man and forbade this. Birds, animals, perhaps a few fish occasionally, garden plants and an invisible God – these were the monks' companions, while the mechanics of life were carried on by the lay brothers and servants in the outer court and on the monastery estates. At the London Charterhouse they ran a kitchen garden and an orchard, north of the monastic buildings, which yielded apples, hay, three hundred carp, fruit trees, and assorted shrubs and herbs each year.

It doesn't need much imagination to realize how important his garden must have been to the Carthusian monk. Presumably the prior gave him the tools he needed to cultivate it, for a 1259 customary from Mount Grace only assigns to each monk 'For works – one axe.' However minimal their tools, the London Charterhouse at Spitalcroft managed to make some fine gardens.

When the King's Commissioners descended on these gardens at the Suppression in 1538, this is what they took away with them:

> For the gardeners from Hampton Court [sent specially to take the famous Charterhouse evergreens] – cypresses, bays and yews. For the King's Gardener – all such bays, rosemary, grafts and other such like things as was mete for his Grace in the said garden [this came to three loads of grafts and three of bay trees] . . . For the caterer of the Lord's Privy Seal – three baskets of herbs. For the King's Gardener, out of the orchard at the Charterhouse, three trees, and grafts of all sorts as doth offer a pear by the pits where they were taken. Sum: 91 [fruit] trees. For Master Leyton: a bundle of roses.

It is the perfect epitaph for the English Carthusians.

Hermit Gardens

The Carthusians never really appealed to the English in a big way. Hermits and anchorites (stricter hermits) did. The country was dotted with cells whose inmates spent their solitary lives in prayer, and often in cultivation as well. A hermitage might be a cave, a little shack or a barn; it might be absolutely bare or it might have a few fittings. But it nearly always had a garden, and often a patch of farm land as well.

The early hermits followed the Celtic example, tilling the soil to grow grain, and eating wild herbs, roots and fruit. But before long they were all gardeners (see Fig. 3). This was something the English understood. They respected their hermits, provided they were not 'cell-breakers', and supported them generously.

At Warkworth, Northumberland, the hermit had an orchard and a garden adjoining the chapel, the garden reached by winding steps cut into the rock. Emma Scherman lived for many years in a cell in Pontefract 'with a little garden contiguous thereto, for the sake of taking fresh air', and when she got permission in 1401 to move to another cell because the first one was plagued by too much noise and too many people, she was granted 'another cell with a like garden'. It was most unusual for a hermit to move in this way. He could leave his cell for a short while if there was a particular reason for doing so; some hermits, for example, went out and preached, but essentially he had rooted himself there. He was a one-man monastery.

The author of *The Quest of the Holy Grail*, who wrote in about 1220, gave this description of one such remote hermitage, which some travellers came upon in the middle of a forest:

> It consisted of a poor dwelling and a tiny chapel. When they approached, they saw in a small yard beside the chapel an old, old man plucking worts[1] for his table, like one who had tasted of no other food for many a day.

Godfric of Finchale did more ambitious things with his garden, namely, planting and grafting and keeping cows, so successfully that he was able to refuse all the offers of food made to him by nearby villagers. Right in the centre of Pontefract, near the house of the Friars Preachers, there was a garden, ninety feet by thirty feet, belonging to a hermitage, and just east of it was another cell, in the chambers in Black Lane, where one Adam of Pontefract was living in 1368.

Friary Gardens

Friaries commonly had anchorites and hermits living in cells within their precincts, usually belonging to the community and therefore without their own gardens. Indeed, two of the smaller orders of Friars began as communities of hermits and only organized themselves as orders under the influence of the great preaching friars, the Dominicans.

All the orders of friars had their most important houses in towns. The Dominicans were preachers, teachers, scholars and controversialists, whose aim was to defend the Church against heretics and establish its dominance in the new centres of learning, the universities. Towns were their natural homes. They and the Franciscans were the intellectual shock troops of thirteenth-century Christianity, filling the gap left unfilled by the sedentary, agricultural religious orders. They were spiritual freelances, without the lands of the established orders, dependent on alms for their survival. They took

1 A general medieval term for plants. One medieval manuscript version of this story has worts translated from the original old French as nettles.

Europe by storm, and within fifty years of their foundation in the early thirteenth century they had houses in most major European cities.

The friars aimed at building their houses near the main urban thoroughfares, and found that the outskirts of towns offered them the ideal combination of room to expand and proximity to the town's population. From outdoor pulpits and preaching crosses in their big enclosures the friars preached to packed congregations. Sometimes there was also an 'anker-house' within the cemetery precinct, where an anchorite lived, and prayed for the friars. At the Dominican priories in Salisbury, Dartford and Newcastle the anker-house was a 'pyler', or round tower.

Most friaries also had gardens. Obviously they didn't go in for the variety and specialization that distinguished the obedientiary monks: they never aimed at self-sufficiency in the same way. But they had gardens to supply them with fruit, fish and wood, of which the most important was wood. Water, timber and firewood were the friars' most urgent needs because of the urban situation of their houses, and not surprisingly they became expert water engineers and nursery tree-gardeners. They built long water conduits, often under city streets, to bring spring water to their houses. In this way the Dominican priory in Holborn got its water from a spring at Clerkenwell, so named because it was the site of 'the clerks' well', and the same spring supplied their priory at Ludgate with its drinking water.

The big kitchen garden at Ludgate was bordered on one side by Water Lane. There was a priory community garden too, about one acre big, east of the complex of buildings across Friar Street from the prior's lodging, and the chances are that this was an orchard. Fruit trees were the main inhabitants of friary gardens. The surveys made by the King's Commissioners at the Dissolution show that most priories had an orchard and a garden (they frequently use the words 'garden' and 'orchard' interchangeably) and a close of trees on the out-of-town side of the precinct. Fruit trees and timber trees were friary specialities. The Dominican priory at Ilchester had eight orchards and a small grove in the later Middle Ages. In the grove were 220 ash trees and 'a great number of elms'. Groves and closes like this one were common friary appurtenances.

It is an interesting and curious fact that quite a number of friary gardens and orchards later became important nurseries. The big garden of the Dominican friary in York, for example, became one of the most important provincial nurseries in England for the three centuries after the Dissolution.

The friars' gardens may have become commercial and nursery gardening centres because they tended to lease them off to expert laymen, leaving themselves free of the labour of cultivating them, so that after the Dissolution some of these gardens remained in the hands of the lessees. Often the gardens and orchards were outside the friary walls, only a small infirmary and pleasure garden being allowed to take up precious space within them, so some of them escaped destruction when the friary buildings and precincts were pulled down.

The End of Monastic Gardens: Survivals and Specialities

When the monasteries were destroyed by Henry VIII's commissioners, all their gardens were destroyed with them. There is one exception to this which made such a gallant bid to survive that it should not be passed over without mention. Westminster Abbey was dissolved in 1540 but, most unusually, the Benedictines returned to it in Mary's reign, under Abbot Feckenham. After Mary's death they lost it for good, and what else should Abbot Feckenham have been doing at the moment when the abbey was taken from him but gardening? In the words of the old Tudor historian:

> Queen Elizabeth, coming to the throne, sent for Abbot Feckenham to come to her, whom the messenger found setting of elms in the orchard of Westminster Abbey. But he would not follow the messenger, till first he had finished his plantation.

This was Feckenham's last activity as a free man and a monk, for his refusal to conform to Elizabeth's laws caused him to be thrown in prison, where he remained until his death. His abbey was made into a college, but his elms survived as a row of trees until 1779, when they were cut down.

The survivors of the Dissolution were the monastic cathedrals, which continued as the cathedrals of Anglican dioceses. Some monastic churches were saved by their parishioners, who found enough money between them to buy them for their own parish use, a few were converted into houses by their new owners, but most were destroyed along with all the monastic buildings and gardens around them. There was no point in saving the gardens for, unlike the cathedrals, they had no part to play in the life of the new Church, no purpose without the monasteries to which they belonged.

Part of the old monastic cloister survives at Ashridge, in Hertfordshire, and encloses a modern garden. Near it a thick yew hedge surrounds a small garden. The Hospitallers' garden at Hampton is now the Hampton Court garden, and the garden the Templars planted by the Thames in the twelfth century is now the garden of the Inner and Middle Temples. Newstead Abbey, in Nottinghamshire, was one of the very few monasteries taken over intact, except for its church, and incorporated into the home built there by its new owners. The claustral complex has survived, but its old gardens have been cultivated out of medieval recognition by generations of gardeners.

What has been left virtually untouched at Newstead is the fishpond, or 'stew', as such ponds were called. It is a big one, overshadowed by ancient yew trees, and in its depths a brass lectern in the shape of an eagle was found some years ago. It was full of monastic deeds, and must have been hidden there at the Dissolution. At Hatton Grange, in Shropshire, the four original fish-stews of Buildwas Abbey remain, with their old names: Abbots, Purgatory, Hell and Bath. Deeply dug and steeply banked, they form a sequence separated by earthen dams, which was the standard arrangement. The fish ended up in the lowest pool, where they were caught.

The science of irrigation was a monastic strongpoint. It supplied water to the fish-stews, horse-ponds and gardens, fountains and waste disposal systems. The last had running water, in streams or conduits, to make a sort of naturally flushing sanitation system, sometimes ingeniously extended to feed the monastic compost heaps. All through the Middle Ages monks were outstanding engineers of water conduits and pipes, wells, fountains, dams and artificial pools. At Leeds, in Kent, they dammed a spring high up on the hillside to make fish-stews, whence the water was channelled under the buildings for drainage, and then emerged to work the mill. This is part of an early twelfth-century description of a Cistercian Abbey:

> Where the orchards leave off, the garden begins, divided into several beds, or cut up by little canals which, although standing water, do flow more or less . . . this water fulfils the double purpose of nourishing the fish and watering the vegetables.

Fish were part of every monastery's survival kit. In the early Middle Ages the Benedictines and Augustinians, and all through the period the Cistercians, Orders of Friars, and most of the other Orders, kept to a meatless diet, and fish was their mainstay. There were moving water and still water monastic fish-stews. The latter were the easiest to maintain, and were the home of that paragon of medieval protein food: carp.

Carp need neither food nor running water. They feed off the murky depths of still ponds, living too far below the surface to be eaten by herons and other predators. They are prolific breeders, and their flesh is richly nutritious, albeit of a sinewy texture, as one would expect of such a low, slow, ugly fish. They and their relations are free food for the taking. In eastern Europe and rural France and Germany carp are still eaten today as a delicacy, cooked in medieval style: for a long time with lots of herbs. The whole of Europe ate carp as a major protein food in the Middle Ages. Every estate had its fish-stews, and at least one of these was usually stocked with carp. Monastic fish-stews were heavy-cropping water gardens, and they were indispensable.

Much less common were 'coney garths', or rabbit gardens, where rabbits could breed in safety. Not only rabbits but all kinds of game were kept in these enclosures, which were usually down at the end of the gardens, or in a nearby patch of meadow. Like fish-stews, they yielded a welcome addition to the monastic diet. Some orders did not count game as meat, and allowed it into their diet by the late thirteenth century. From then on, it was common to find game eaten in Benedictine houses.

It was also common to find woods outside the precincts if the monastery needed timber or wanted a wooden grove of extra-mural delight. The chronicler of Dunstable Priory wrote in 1287 that 'the little wood to the north, which Brother Henry of Newton had planted there a little time before, with ash trees and other trees of divers kinds, was high by this time and very delightful to look at.' Measured against eternity, the time it took for a wood to grow was indeed only 'a little time', and woods were planted to be memorials to their founders and as investments in the indefinite future, when future generations would enjoy their slow-growing beauty. When Edmund, Earl of Cornwall, gave sixteen acres at Rewley, in Oxfordshire, for the foundation of an abbey there in 1281, tradition has it that twenty-one elms were planted in rows between the inner and outer abbey gates, and a solitary elm at the upper end, representing the monks and their abbot.

Like orchards, woods were planted both for aesthetic and functional reasons, often with great skill and ingenuity. King David I of Scotland founded an Augustinian priory on Inchmahona, in Monteith Lake, Perthshire, and the monks made a plantation of Spanish chestnuts that still survives in some measure today. The Cistercian abbey of Cupar, also in Scotland, founded in 1164, had both woods and orchards on its granges. Most abbeys adorned 'God's Acre', the monastic cemetery, with beautiful, shady trees. There were as many monastic uses for woods as there were woods planted to fulfil them.

It is appropriate to end this chapter as it began, with an echo of the wood garden of Eden. This short excerpt is from an excavation report on a small Oxfordshire priory, and it reveals the obedientary system working at its considerate, expert, paradisical best:

> Within the little wood was a neat little place, walled with brick
> and paved with six-inch square tiles, ornamented with plain
> circles and flowers of various kinds.

'For the Enjoyment of Rest and Quiet':

Gardens
in Cities and Towns

Medieval England was an agricultural country full of forests, fields and flowers. It had already been cultivated for centuries when William the Conqueror seized power in 1066. All over Norman England vast stretches of wood, marsh, moorland and hills were broken by settlements where villagers ploughed and sowed the land, grazed their sheep and cattle on the heathland and waste, and cleared the woods of undergrowth by turning their pigs out to feed on acorns and beech-mast. The Domesday survey revealed to England's new Norman King a country with settlements in all but the most densely wooded and flooded areas, and all but a very few of these settlements were villages. The very few were towns, but so small that today we would consider them no more than overgrown villages. They were ports, through which England's trade with the Continent passed, and market centres for the countryside which lay immediately outside their surrounding walls, wooden palings, banks and ditches.

None of them was independent of the countryside in any way; nobody in medieval England was. The very word 'town' comes from the Old English 'tun', of which the two oldest meanings are: a fortified place or camp, and an enclosed place, field, garden, yard or court. Such an enclosure was usually attached to a dwelling-place: a farmhouse, manor or village, the land and buildings of which came to be called a 'tun'. After the Norman Conquest, a village or hamlet was often called a tun; the Norman and French word 'ville', like the English 'village', is an expansion of the latin word 'villa', meaning a farm or country-house. From being a village the tun moved easily to being a town, in our modern sense of a larger group of buildings than a village, with a more complete and independent local government system.

But the roots of the town, like the word itself, have always been in the soil, and many modern towns continue to bear witness to this fact. They not only contain the word 'tun' in their names, but also specific allusions to the kind of tuns or garths they originally were. For example, Mosstown means moss town; Walton means wood farm; Pirton, in all its various spellings, means pear-tree farm; Plumpton means plum farm; Appleton means apple farm; Leighton or Latton means leek patch. Countless English towns have agricultural and horticultural names, as do their streets, squares, parks, gardens, markets and neighbourhoods. It is only natural that they should.

Many properties in medieval English boroughs (the word 'borough' comes from the Old English and Old Norse root 'burh', which could mean either fortress or town, and often meant both), were annexed to manors in the open country nearby. In Leicester, for instance, 134 houses were attached, singly and in groups, to 27 different manors. The lord of the manor could stay in his town house in time of trouble or when he came to town to buy and sell, and it formed a profitable outpost of his estates. There were about a hundred English boroughs in William the Conqueror's time, of which only sixteen, such as Lincoln and Norwich, were big enough to be accounted district centres, equivalent to the French *cités*, and therefore classed as cities in Domesday. Less than one in ten Englishmen lived in boroughs, and most of these lived like peasants, in houses set in a bit of land, and held land in the open fields. They were farmers as well as merchants, and by virtue of being householders they were often gardeners too.

Medieval towns were far more spacious than we tend to imagine, with wide market streets, a lot of ponds, wells and streams, orchards and stretches of grassland, and gardens of all sizes (see map of Winchester, Fig. 5). Among the officers of medieval boroughs were pound-keepers, to look after the animals brought in on market days; pinders, to deal with stray household pigs, sheep and fowl that wandered about the streets; haywards; brookwardens; grassmen; warreners; hedge-lookers; mole-catchers; field-drivers; swineherds; pasture masters; moss-grieves; (a grieve was a bailiff or overseer) woodwards; moor and moss men in Lancaster; a field-grieve in Newcastle-on-Tyne, and a keeper of the Greenyard in London. Boroughs were farm produce centres, and their inhabitants were countrymen living together in bigger settlements than the usual villages and hamlets. Their courts were area courts, not specifically

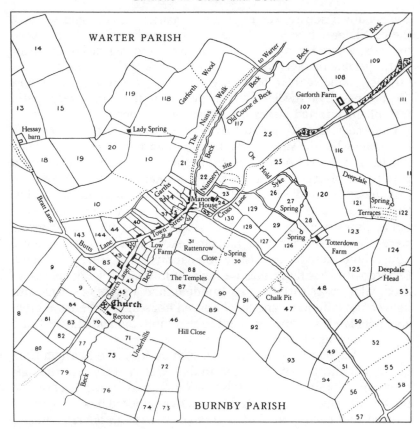

Fig. 4: A field plan of Nunburnholme, Yorkshire, in the Middle Ages, showing garths behind the houses in the main street.

urban ones, except in London, and they were assessed for royal taxation in the standard way: according to carucates (plough-team areas). They held land in return for landgable rent and the performance of works, just like peasants, but the works were specially adapted to suit merchants, for townsmen were first of all agricultural merchants and only secondarily, and later on in the period, craftsmen, administrators and financiers.

They dealt mainly in wool, cloth, corn and stock, all of which townsmen as well as villagers produced from their holdings in the fields. The oldest surviving street names of English towns, such as Cornmarket Street, Oxford, and The Corn Exchange, Milk Street and Bread Street, London, recall their marketing past. Almost every ancient town square was originally a market square, and some of them still are. Besides corn and stock markets there were herb markets, where herbwives sold their herbs and vegetables, and fruit and vegetable markets where successful gardeners sold their surplus produce, some of them becoming professional market gardeners in the process. The medieval urban picture is the same everywhere: few inhabitants and plenty of animals and gardens.

Domesday Oxford had just over seven hundred taxable houses, including what the survey described as 'a lot of houses and gardens' (horti). It was one of only about twenty Domesday towns with a population of over a thousand out of a total English population of just under one and a half million. Most towns were much smaller than Oxford, and all, as far as one can tell from the records, contained 'houses and gardens' of all sizes. Among the biggest towns were York, Norwich and Lincoln, each with over a thousand houses, and therefore a probable population of six to seven thousand; Oxford with slightly less, as we have seen; Ipswich with eight hundred; Gloucester with over six hundred, and a score of towns with between two hundred and five hundred houses, and therefore probable populations of one thousand to two thousand five hundred, and a good number of gardens.

Many English towns suffered very badly from the Norman Conquest, but most revived by the mid-twelfth century. At strategic sites, castle-building led to town-building, and in the twelfth and thirteenth centuries between four and five hundred new towns were created, and even more rural settlements raised to burgal status.

The loss of Normandy in the late twelfth century meant that those Normans who chose to stay in England became very loyal to it, and it was in their interests that towns inside their territories should prosper. New, commercially sited towns began to outnumber militarily strategic ones, and the market-place to displace the castle as the dominant urban feature. By far the biggest and most important town in Norman England was both a military and commercial centre: the capital of the kingdom.

The Gardens of Medieval London

London was in a class of its own, and was not included in the Domesday survey. But it is going to be a major part of this survey because of its exceptional importance and its exceptionally full and informative gardening records. It had every kind of urban building and garden, and provides the perfect model for finding out about them.

For centuries before Domesday, London had been by far the biggest and most important town in England. Though it only amounted to what we would consider a small county town, it was 'the queen of the whole kingdom'. William Rufus built the first palace of Westminster, and held his first court there in 1099, but London only gradually reached its position as the permanent seat of the court and government, the earliest reasons for its importance being commercial.

A measure of independence already distinguished London from the other English towns at the time of the Conquest. Unlike many of them, it submitted to the Conqueror at just the right moment, and so escaped devastation. English towns were the first victims of the Conquest, but London prospered, and emerged from it more dominant than ever. It was guarded by three fortress castles and surrounded by its Roman walls, through which seven sets of entrance gates led inside. Like all English towns, its buildings were mostly wooden, with thatched roofs, and a wooden bridge joined the north to the south bank of the Thames at Southwark. Six hundred of its buildings were blown down by a fierce gale in 1091, and St Paul's and many of the eastern suburbs destroyed by a fire in 1135, after which its wealthiest citizens rebuilt their homes in stone, and twelfth-century London began to look like a capital city.

We have a charming description of London in 1178, written by Alexander Neckham, then a young clerk teaching in Dunstable. He set out from there on a journey to London, en route to Paris, where he was going to study. His first sight of London was the tower of St Peter's Abbey, standing out above Westminster. He and his companion headed towards it, along the banks of the Old Bourn, which gave its name to the surrounding district of Holborn, and began to pass through the affluent suburbs which extended far along the Thames to the west and to the east. This was where wealthy merchants and bankers, landowners, Church dignitaries and courtiers had their town houses; where they stabled the horses they used for hunting in the countryside beyond the city walls, and cultivated their gardens and vineyards. The chronicler FitzStephen said that in this part of London the houses had gardens attached to them, in which there were trees 'both spacious and pleasing to the sight'. Holborn was the most magnificent of London's garden suburbs, and Neckham described it as full of houses and pretty gardens.

These houses were enormous, two-storeyed, set well back from the street, planned like manor houses, with hall, kitchen, chamber, chapel and other apartments around a courtyard, and huge gardens reaching down to the riverside, where there were rows of trees and mud flats.

Beyond the beautiful gardens of Holborn and the Embankment, Neckham came into central London, where there were rows of wooden houses, some faced with tiles, others with wattle and daub (mud stuck over wattles and lathes), almost all of them elaborately decorated with carvings and smeared with a preservative and insulating mixture of pitch and linseed, coloured red, blue or black. There was the odd stone house, made of quartz or flint, also painted, and probably adorned with a fashionable Norman chimney stack, rising from an ornamented cornice to a conical chimney-cap pierced with smoke holes. Shopkeepers made goods in their houses and sold them over counters across the front, which had openings for going in and out, or in stalls tucked in between the house fronts.

These frontages were sometimes very narrow, like the plots of garden behind them, which were approached by a passageway or back entrance at one side of the building, and were known as 'back-sides'. Medieval London was packed with little back-sides, where householders grew a few fruits and vegetables, separated from the back-sides on either side by walls, banks or fences. Only in the late Middle Ages, when overcrowding grew desperate, were one or two properties built without gardens attached; they were for workmen and poor tradesmen whose shops, warehouses or wharfs were elsewhere. They were called 'chambers', and were self-contained flats, built in four- or five-story blocks, and usually sold, not rented, to the occupants. A block of chambers, each chamber labelled with a letter from A to S, was built in the churchyard of St Michael's, Cornhill in the late fifteenth century and, unusually, they were let out for annual rents. But this was an exception, a presage of a later age. Medieval Londoners lived in houses and gardens.

Every parish church had its churchyard. There were one hundred and twenty six of them in Neckham's time, and thirteen religious houses, with their own enclosed lands and gardens; later there were many more. There were gardens inside the walls of London's fortresses; the Tower had not only a garden but also a vineyard between it and the town wall, and a mill just beyond, on the river-bank. Neckham was much impressed by the royal manor of Bermondsey, which ran along the Thames from London Bridge to Rotherhithe,

A large, late medieval town garden, with a cistern at the back, and a gate on to the street through its side wall.

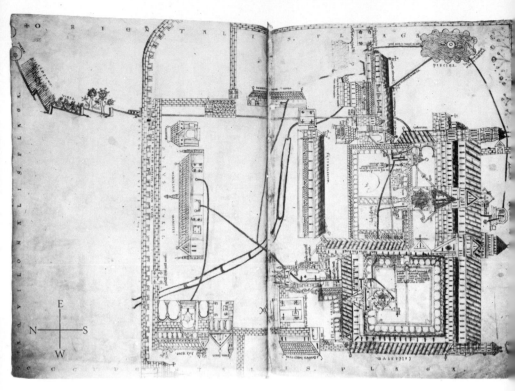

The earliest surviving visual record of an English monastic garden: the
ground-plan of Christchurch, Canterbury, in 1165.

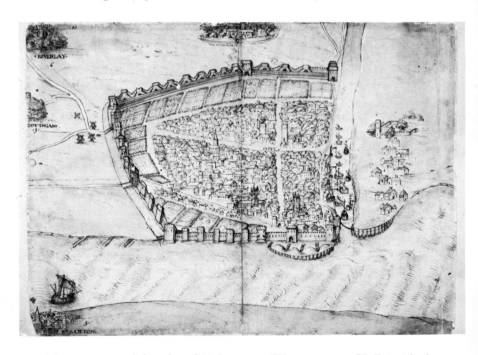

Allotments round the edge of 15th-century Kingston-upon-Hull, inside the
town walls.

with tilled fields and all the usual manorial buildings and gardens.

This was only one of several big expanses of land, free of any urban building, that were to be found both inside and outside the City walls. Neckham approached London from too far north to see the forty- to fifty-acre estate of Fulham Palace. It was the country residence of the Bishops of London, and had not yet been made into the farm, great garden, vine garden and wood that it had become by the fifteenth century. It was still basically a stretch of wild marsh, covered with birds; the name Fulham is a shortened form of *Volucrium Domus*, which means 'home of the birds'.

In 1415 a gateway on to the moors east of Smithfield moors was erected, hence the name Moorgate, and public gardens were laid out there, and remained there until the end of the eighteenth-century.

The two things that struck Neckham most about the City were its open spaces and its medley of sounds. He heard the canonical hours rung from the Church of St Martin le Grand, amid the bells of countless other parish and monastic churches, for he was there on a holyday, when no one worked and everyone went to church. The other sounds he heard were the cries of street-sellers, who sold their hot pies and homemade medicines, soaps, needles, perfumes, apples, pears, plums, nuts, quinces, herbs and onions on holy days and working days alike. Many of the fruits and vegetables came from private gardens, the great number of which Neckham remarked upon with approval. But he didn't get a chance to go into any of them, so he did not give any details in his account, and in order to obtain some we must leave his description and look at some of the City's medieval records: wills, deeds of conveyance, building plans and inventories.

Most of the surviving records are from the fourteenth and fifteenth centuries, by which time London had greatly expanded. Its population in Chaucer's day was about thirty five thousand, which exceeded the combined populations of York, Plymouth, Bristol and Coventry, and it had become the centre of government, finance and the law. More and more magnates, lay and ecclesiastical, kept permanent houses in London. The royal wardrobe found a permanent home near Baynard's Castle, on the east bank of the River Fleet. London's craftsmen formed themselves into gild companies, and set up company halls alongside the monasteries, shops and houses that filled the City. For all this, London was still a country town in the way that all medieval towns were. It's citizens lived only a walk away from the fields upon which they depended for survival, and when the bells of Bow Church sounded the curfew, it was a warning not only to the City workers but also to those working out in the fields of the onset of darkness.

City workers lived where they worked and most of them, whatever their jobs and social standing, had gardens. In 1331 the Barbican, then called Le Bas Court by Crepylgate, was granted, 'with all its houses, gardens and appurtenances', to Robert Offord, the first Earl of Stafford. In the fifteenth century it was described as 'the chief messuage of Basecourt, together with fourteen other tenements and gardens in the same parish', which is a lot more gardens than one can find in the Barbican nowadays.

There were gardens all along the City wall in Aldgate ward, most of them belonging to the London houses of magnates like the Abbot of Bury St Edmunds, who had a palatial house and gardens at Bevis (Bovies i.e. oxen) Markes, in Aldgate. Big gardens in the City were usually square or rectangular, not narrow like most of the City gardens, through lack of space, and they were enclosed by clay, brick, or stone walls, or thick thorn hedges. Fashionable gardeners built banks of earth against the walls, faced them with stone or brick, and planted the top of them with sweet-smelling herbs. They put turf seats in recesses cut into the walls, where the women, for whom these gardens were a refuge and a delight, could sit in peace, doing needlework or playing with their pets, talking with friends or making flower garlands. In the later Middle Ages these town gardens were laid out in rectangular beds of herbs and flowers, bordered with stone or woodwork and raised a few inches above the plots of thyme and camomile, which made fragrant ground covers. If the garden was big enough, it might be criss-crossed with gravelled or sanded paths, and it might have a cistern or fountain at the centre, and an arbour in one corner (see illustration p. 64). Most City gardeners kept one or two fruit trees, for their shade and their fruit, the latter being picked and used in the kitchen, and sold if there was a big surplus. In less fashionable and more practical gardens there might also be some vegetables grown.

Some City gardeners made pleasure gardens; others made gardens like the ones near Grass Street, which was so named because of the grass and herbs grown in them and sold there. Others again were little shopkeeper craftsmen, and grew just a few herbs and vegetables, and perhaps a fruit tree or two. There was no archetypal City garden or gardener, because there were so many different kinds of people living there. Within a few hundred yards of each other in

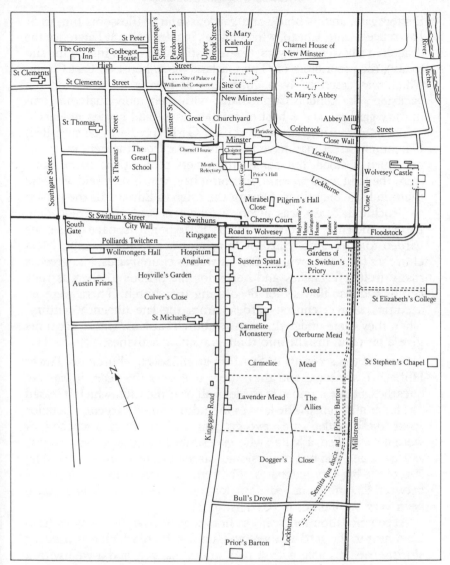

Fig. 5: A plan of Winchester in the late fourteenth century, showing the large number of gardens and open spaces typical of most medieval towns.

the fourteenth century lived John Carpenter, the Town Clerk, who had a hostel and garden in St Peter's, Cornhill; the cottagers and shopkeepers living on the Scrope family's property, known as 'the Erber'; the Neville family, proprietors of the Dolphin Inn, Without

Bishopsgate, and its house and gardens, and of Blossoms Inn, in St Lawrence's Lane, Cheap, which had a sign depicting St Lawrence the deacon in a bower of flowers; (there is still a Blossoms Inn on the site today); the proprietors of 'The Garland' brew-house in East Cheap, which was described by a chronicler as having 'a garden on the backside'; the London Carthusians, with their individual and community gardens, and a host of smaller house and garden holders.

There were gardeners who caused Garlic Hythe to be so called. Fenchurch Street may have taken its name from the Fen, or moor, on which it stood, but some chroniclers thought the name came from the latin word *faenum*, meaning hay, which they said was sold there in large quantities. During the reign of Edward III the parson of Fenchurch Street was given 'a tenement with its curtilage and garden, and entry thereto . . . the house to be a parsonage house; the garden to be a churchyard or burying place for the parish'. Most churches had their own gardens as well as churchyards, and grew as many fruits, vegetables and herbs for the priest's kitchen as they could, and also flowers for decorating the church. There were no accounts kept of church gardens until the late fifteenth century, when they came under the care of churchwardens, whose accounts give a bit of an insight into their gardening activities.

Some of the accounts of St Mary-at-Hill, a big church on Tower Hill, have survived, and they show that over the years it was bequeathed a large number of gardens all over the City, which it leased out for annual rents. The lessees included a fuller, carpenter, a tailor 'next to the garden gate', two grocers, a couple of men whose jobs were not specified, a 'wife', who is described in some of the accounts as a gardener, and two professional gardeners, no doubt employed by two of the big City magnates. The rent for most of the gardens was between 2s. and 4s. a year, but for one of them, which must have been very big indeed, it was 13s.4d.

Accommodation for visitors' horses at St Mary's seems to have been next to the garden; there was a house there which was used for storing oats, a stable with a rack and a manger, and a well with a bucket and an iron chain. The garden itself was on the river side of Tower Hill, and was enclosed by a thorn hedge. There is no mention of what was grown in it but, like a lot of urban churches, St Mary's could not grow as many flowers for decoration, or find as many round about, as country churches could, and there are purchases of flowers and foliage in the accounts most years. This church decorating was usually known as 'garnishing', and the main garnishes were birch for Midsummer Day (still used in some places on the Continent); yew, the emblem of immortality, for Easter (this was mainly used in country districts, and was used in West Somerset, Worcester and Herefordshire until the nineteenth century); box or willow for Palm Sunday, the catkin-bearing willow being the English palm; holly and ivy for Christmas; red roses and white sweet woodruff for making garlands for processional feast-days like Corpus Christi; lilies, used on all the feasts of Our Lady, and in Lent, since the colour for the Lenten season was white, and other unspecified flowers, which were usually St John's wort, gillyflowers and orpine.

The first mention of garnishing expenses at St Mary-at-Hill is in 1479, when 4s.7d. was paid 'for flags, garlands and torches for Corpus Christi, St Barnabas and other days. And for six men to bear the same torches'. On occasions such as these garlands, which the churchwardens at St Mary's seem to have bought ready made, were hung on processional crosses, and worn by the clergy as crowns, and then hung on the rood-screen and the choir after the procession. In 1487 two and a half dozen rose garlands were bought for St Barnabas Day, at a cost of 8½d.; some birch boughs for Midsummer, at a cost of 3d., and box, palm, flowers and obleyes for Palm Sunday, at a cost of 8d.

'Obley' means offering, and it usually referred to the Communion wafers offered and consecrated at Mass, but as this entry is for Palm Sunday, it may be meant in its other sense, which is that of a cake or a biscuit: cakes and flowers were often showered down on to the congregation from the roof of the church porch, or from the tower, when the Blessed Sacrament procession had returned to the church by the south door, after processing round the churchyard. In 1490 and 1492 the garnishing expenses were much the same as in preceding years, but included some woodruff garlands for Corpus Christi, and in 1492 20d. for feast-day wine and ale for the priests and clerks. The next year the churchwardens bought 3d. worth of rushes 'for the new pews'. Most churches were unpaved, and rushes, green ones in summer and dried ones in winter, were strewn on the floor, and in this case on the pews as well, to keep them relatively warm and clean.

It was also common to strew sweet-smelling herbs in churches, but only fennel and rosemary ever appear in churchwardens' accounts, the rest coming from the church gardens. No herbs are mentioned in the St Mary's accounts. The biggest set of garnishing expenses there was in 1519-20, when the wardens bought three dozen garlands for the Corpus Christi procession, at a cost of 15d., two dozen green garlands for the same at a cost of 2d., three garlands at 2d. each, for the three crosses, a branch of three flowers 'that standeth before the Trinity, weighing 15½ H,[1] at 5d. per H – cost 6s.5½d., and a branch of 'laton' (hawthorn) before the tabernacle of Our Lady of the Assumption, weighing 32 H, at 5d. per H – cost 13s.4d. Not only in the cultivation of their properties, but also in their liturgical celebrations, the City churches were resplendently horticultural, and all from local garden resources.

The same horticultural resourcefulness is characteristic of just about every property holder in the City, however unlikely this seems to us today. Right next to St Mary's, for instance, the Tower of London was a garden centre as well as a royal residence. In 1261 King Henry III wrote to his chief gardener, Edward, commanding him 'to buy perrie (pear) plants, and set them in the place without the Tower of London, within the wall of the said City, which of late he had caused to be enclosed within a mud wall'. Two years later the Constable of the Tower was directed to buy no less than £10 worth of 'plants and other necessities for the King's garden next to the tower,' which may have been the tower known today as 'Bloody Tower', and in the Middle Ages as 'garden tower'. Most of these plants seem to have been fruit trees. In 1275 Edward I bought some peach trees, which required very careful expert attention, for the Tower garden. The slopes of Tower Hill were terraced with vines and fruit trees, and were one of the King's favourite gardens.

Tower Hill was also the site of some of the earliest English market gardens, many of them on Corporation property. The sale of garden produce, especially fruit, was so profitable that people rented gardens and orchards that were not attached to their houses, and grew produce for the London market. A lot of the St Mary's gardens were rented in this way. In 1372 the City Corporation took action against the Tower Hill gardeners over the refuse they had allowed to pile up there. All down Tower Hill, and along the City wall and riverbank nearby, were gardens, some of them remunerative enough to be leased for 10s. a year.

There were gardens of this sort, not attached to households, at Billings-gate, East Cheap, Lothbury, Coleman Street, Lombard Street and Bow Lane in the fourteenth century. Most of them were fruit gardens, since fruit sold best in the markets. The church of St

1 H probably stands for Havoirdupois, i.e. a lb.

Martin Pomery in Ironmonger Lane, Cheapside, is said to have been named after an apple orchard that was there in medieval times. In 1348 a tenement near the church of All Hallows, London Wall, was let for 24s. a year and half the fruit in the garden. This was probably the same tenement as the one next to All Hallows church that belonged to one John the Long, a fruiterer, in 1215; judging by the rent, it was a sizeable orchard. John was one of a substantial number of fruiterers in London who brought from gardens and sold in the streets, individually and in markets, of which the main one was at St Augustine's Gate, at the west end of Watling Street. Gardeners and servants of the big London property owners had stalls in this market, and were often given part of the produce as payment. This was the famous market that was so noisy and popular that it made the celebration of mass in St Paul's impossible, and had to be moved to a new site near Blackfriars, south of the cathedral.

Like the City gardeners, the fruiterers effectively existed as a company as early as the start of the fifteenth century, though they were never incorporated as one, and the gardeners were not incorporated until 1605.

The history of the City companies really begins in the fourteenth century, when the craftsmen and tradesmen of London began to receive royal charters to organize themselves into gilds.

The companies had their own liveries, and they built themselves halls where their members met to administer, dine, socialize and display their companies' wealth. It was only natural that these halls should have beautiful gardens attached to them.

There is not a single one surviving today. The Grocers' Hall gardens, which were made in 1431 'with the fair erber (arbour) and all the new vines with all the new rails', flourished bravely through four and a half centuries and three rebuildings of the Hall, only to be buried under the Bank of England when it was expanded on its present site in 1802. The Bank is also the graveyard of another big and fine livery company garden, that of the Drapers. Drapers Hall Gardens is now a street name, but until 1802 it was part of the patchwork of pleasure gardens that filled the livery area of the City in the fifteenth century. The original mulberry tree, planted in the Drapers Gardens when the hall was built in 1364, lived to a fruitful old age, until a storm finally brought it down in 1969. Cuttings taken from it are bearing fruit today in the little plot of garden that remains next to the Drapers Hall, off Throgmorton Street.

Only a few of the City companies had gardens as big as those of the Grocers and the Drapers, but they were all concerned to make them beautiful. The Tylers and Brickmakers put a garden and forecourt in front of their hall, so that it made a frontage on to the street. The Merchant Taylors had a little courtyard enclosed within the central quadrangle of their hall, and it is still a garden today, but of the paved patio variety. It is still the beadle who looks after it, as it was in the Middle Ages. Most of the small companies left the care of their gardens to the beadle, and only hired outside help to prune fruit trees and vines. It was absolutely *de rigueur* to have a vine, and to provide members with a bunch of grapes from it each year. The Poulterers' garden, in Lime Street, had a vine trained over a wooden frame which carpenters repaired and added to now and again, and most years it rewarded them with a barrel of sour verjuice (grape vinegar). By the late fifteenth century the Poulterers had also planted beds of herbs, which they trained up 'rods and poles', and the whole garden was enclosed by railings. Even the tiny Cutlers' garden had a vine, pruned each year by a gardener who pruned their fruit trees at the same time. These were probably mulberry trees, the favourites of the livery companies.

The little Girdlers' Hall Garden, in Basinghall Street, survived much as it was in the Middle Ages, with its vine, mulberry tree and cistern, right up until 1940. The Barbers were exceptional because they had a physic garden, full of herbs, which was appropriate to their quasi-medical role as blood-letters. Doubtless some of the herbs were sweet-smelling and pretty, and were laid out decoratively, for livery company gardens were primarily intended to delight.

It must have required a lot of paid help, hired from the gardens of London's big houses, to keep the gardens belonging to the biggest company halls up to top standard. But most of the company gardens were quite small, and it was small gardens that were most popular with the wealthy landowners in the City and its eastern suburbs. Sir Hugh Clopton, the merchant, bought the great house at the corner of Chapel Street and Chapel Lane, opposite the chapel of the Holy Cross gild, and its garden, which was just ¼ acre big, and was probably an orchard.

By contrast, the gardens at the west end of the City, in Holborn, were huge. This was the garden showpiece of London, home of the foremost earls, Church dignitaries, and in time, legal institutions of the kingdom. Everyone passing through Holborn, walking along Saffron Hill or through Pear Tree Court, was struck by the houses and gardens there. They were urban manor houses, with courtyards, outbuildings and gardens that were bigger and more ambitious than any attached to manors in the country. The Earl of Lincoln's house and garden will serve as an example.

It was on a site that had originally belonged to the Dominicans, but had been granted to the Earl by Edward I in 1286, after the friars had got themselves a new site just outside the City wall, on the site to which they gave their name: Blackfriars. The Earl had manors and gardens all over England, but none of his gardens was as successful as this one at Holborn. Maybe its years of monastic cultivation gave it a head start. It stretched down to the river, surrounded by wooden palings and divided into flower, fruit and vegetable gardens. It had a coney garth, stocked with all kinds of game, not just rabbits, and a fish-stew and vineyard left by the friars. This last was more than just a status symbol: it was one of the most productive vineyards in London, yielding forty nine gallons of verjuice one year – enough to stock the Earl's ample kitchens and give him a saleable surplus. He also sold vine cuttings, presumably to other London viticulturists. Like most English vineyards, its grapes were not used for making wine, and the Earl looked to this orchard for home made alcohol.

He grew apples, pears, large nuts and cherries in it, and took a personal interest in their welfare. He was one of the first 'improving' estate gardeners, and sent to the Continent for slips of new apple and pear trees, employing an expert gardener to graft and look after them. The Costard apple arrived in England at about this time, as did the Pearmain, used for making cider, and they were probably both among the new breeds of apple the Earl imported. We know for certain that he got two cuttings of the Costard. Also pear trees: two Martins, five Caillous and three Pesse-pucelles in one year, thus providing his kitchens with eating, stewing and perry-making pears, and putting himself in the vanguard of English fruit growers. He sold a big surplus of fruit every year, and his orchard in springtime must have been a mass of blossom, full of fragrance and fruity promise.

The Earl grew the statutory leeks, onions, garlic and beans in his vegetable patch, and also hemp, all of which were produced in big enough quantities to yield a sizeable surplus for the market. The sale of produce from the Earl's garden brought in as much as £8 or £9 most years, which was as much as most of the big monastic gardens brought in. Besides fruit and vegetables, he sold 'little plants', which suggests that he was running a commerical nursery garden. It is even possible that he had a nursery rose garden, for he sometimes sold roses, which was most unusual for a private garden. One year he sold 3s.2d. worth, which means either thousands of roses or a smaller number of rose plants.

The fish-stew, like everything else in the Earl's garden, was the last word in professional horticulture. It is referred to in the garden accounts as 'the Greater Ditch', but ditch is hardly the word for a pond that was surrounded by a ditch and paling, and contained pike that were fed on small fish, frogs and eels, bought specially for them by the bailiff. He was one of a whole gang of assistant gardeners who were paid £5 a year between them for maintaining the pond, dressing the vines, manuring the ground, etc. The head gardener received the princely salary of 52s.2d. a year, and a livery or robe of office. Presumably his jobs demanded more skill than those of his assistants, as well as responsibility, and he had only one rival for the title of top London gardener: his opposite number at the Bishop of Ely's town house in Ely Place, Holborn.

The gardens attached to this house, like the house itself, were immense. There was a kitchen garden, probably the one referred to in the accounts as 'the Big Garden', surrounded by 666 yards of thorn hedging in 1372. North of the mansion there was an orchard, and a vineyard enclosed by a thorn hedge with locked wooden gates in it. There were some inner gardens for the Bishop's private use, and a meadow, usually called 'the Grassyard', from which hay was sold each year, a tithe of the proceeds going to the Rector of St Andrew's, Holborn. It was separated by a fence and locked doors from the vineyard, which was four acres big, and faced on to the street called after it: Vine Street. Not to be outdone by the Earl of Lincoln the Bishop hired gangs of labourers to work in it: men to do the digging; women and a boy to dress and weed the vines. In 1372 the vineyard produced thirty gallons of verjuice, a very big crop, but not as big as the Earl's, and the Bishop seems to have found his vines more bother than they were worth a lot of the time, and leased them out. In 1378 the garden, vineyard and pasture next to it were leased to Adam the vineyard-keeper for 62s., a really enormous annual rent.

The Bishop did not run his gardens as commercially as the Earl, only occasionally selling some of his fruit. His palace, chapel and private garden were part of an exquisitely designed whole, which several of the Bishops altered and improved to suit their taste. They spent a lot of time at Ely Place, and it was more of a home to them than the Earl's palace was to him. The episcopal gardens were very big and very fashionable, like all the big Holborn gardens, but they were more personal than the Earl's gardens; they were the Bishop's very own London conceits.

The episcopal rose garden was an exhibition piece, and it must have been a deliciously fragrant one too, surrounded as it was by high walls which kept in the perfume. But like all good medieval gardeners, the Bishops had the most practical of vegetable patches, growing enough onions, garlic, leeks and beans-in-the-husk for some to be sold each year, and also hyssop, savory and parsley. One peck of parsley seeds, and one quarter each of hyssop, savory and leek seeds were in store in 1372. There was also a lot of grass from an uncultivated corner, which was cut and sold. One year workers and women (the two are distinguished in the accounts) were paid the vast sum of 69s.1½d. for digging over the courtyard and inner yard and pulling weeds out of the courtyard; these were big gardens indeed. There is not so much as a weed in a corner left of these gardens today, and St Etheldreda's Chapel, all that survives of the buildings, is surrounded by acres of stone and concrete.

The Earl of Lincoln contrived to guarantee his gardens a longer life. In 1310 he began to take law students into his house, and by 1312 their society was renting buildings known as Lyncolnesynne from Thomas of Lincoln, the King's serjeant of Holborn. In 1412-22 the lawyers moved to a site close to the present Old Hall, and the present Lincoln's Inn Gardens are on part of the Earl's famous garden. His crest of a Lion Rampant and Fifteen Mill Irons is the crest of Lincoln's Inn, and guards the gateway from it into Chancery Lane. The Inn acquired Coterell's Garden, on the site of Stone Buildings, and a coney garth, which formed the lower part of the garden and was walled off from the upper part. Students who used their bows and arrows on the rabbits in the garth were penalized.

The only remnants of the game that once lived there are the wild duck on the lily pond in New Square, which is on the site of the old garth. The Inn also acquired land, including 'a place and a garden', on the west side of Chancery Lane, covering the site of Old Square and Old Buildings, from the Bishop of Chichester, whose landlordship is commemorated today in the names 'Bishop's Court' and 'Chichester Rents'.

Lincoln's Inn Gardens are the private property of the Inn, but are opened by courtesy of the Master of the Benchers 'for the enjoyment of rest and quiet', which distinguishes the Master as an upholder of the best medieval tradition of City gardening. Nearby Gray's Inn also began as a private estate. In 1280 it was rented from St Paul's by Lord Grey of Wilton for 42s.2d. a year. It consisted of 'a messuage with gardens, thirty acres of land, one dove-house and a windmill and a chantry'. The thirty acres made up Gray's Inn Fields, and were used as open air sports and archery grounds. With its big stretches of grassland, Gray's Inn was typical of the legal Inn Gardens.

To men like Lord Grey, property in the city was only worth having if it had a garden. Landlords were for ever getting involved in property disputes with their neighbours, and the source of the trouble was usually either the garden wall or the garden. In 1311 a protracted dispute between the proprietors of the Guildhall and their neighbours on the west side, over the size of the Guildhall garden, was finally settled by Mr Dode, the neighbour in question, building a wall between his garden and the Guildhall garden.

In 1356 a college for five priests was founded on another part of the property, with a messuage and garden south of the chapel. This time they were leaving no room for dispute: they recorded the measurement of their messuage and garden as being exactly 71 ft. 3 ins. by 66 ft. 2 ins. The College estate therefore included a vicar's garden and the Guildhall garden, both of them within private courtyards. In some years the Guildhall garden was leased out. Proprietors who wanted their gardens kept in good shape but hadn't the staff and time to see to it themselves often leased them out.

Having a well kept garden was such a social imperative that landlords who were not suing their neighbours for horticultural trespass sued their lessees for sub-standard gardening. The canons of Holy Trinity Church in Aldgate leased a large patch of their garden to one John of Canterbury. It was twelve by ten perches[1] and lay between a 'great garden in the east' and a new garden, which they must have made in the meantime, in the west, and it was leased out for the high rent of 9s.3d. a year. John was to put up and maintain a fence round the patch, and was not to build against the Priory garden wall. Another Priory garden in the east was also leased, with the stipulation that the canons could take it back if the lessees let it decay, or tried to sell all or part of it.

There was no shortage of gardeners capable of taking over and

---

1   A perch was usually 16½ ft., though subject to much local variation.

looking after such plots. Besides the lessees of their Priory garden, two of the canons' tenants were professional gardeners. Almost every householder was an amateur one. The Tudor City surveyors complained that the ditch by the City wall, originally made for the defence of the City, had long since been 'neglected into a filthy channel, or altogether stopped up for the gardens planted, and houses builded thereon, even to the very wall.'

The most innovative London gardens were those that belonged to the King, who could afford to experiment, and London's two best sets of royal gardens were the ones at the Tower and the ones at Westminster Palace. They were not the most exotic of the royal gardens, but they were the most fruity.

The gardens at the Tower, which were stocked with plants on a lavish scale, were ultimately the Constable's responsibility, but they were looked after by a full-time gardener. In 1267 he was a man called William, whose name we know because the King's accountant made a special note that his salary was a year in arrears. When there were walls to be built and repaired, and big loads of plants to be put in, gangs of helpers were hired.

Henry III sent writs to one of his gardeners, telling him to plant Caillou pears, the most popular English variety, in his gardens at the Tower and at Westminster, and in 1292 Edward I's fruiterer listed Martins (very exclusive: 8d. per hundred), Dreyes (2d. per hundred), Sorells (3d. per hundred), Gold-Knopes (2d. per hundred) and Cheysills (3d. per hundred) among the pear trees he was planting there. All the thirteenth- and fourteenth-century kings, Henry III in particular, seem to have taken a personal interest in their palace gardens, and to have specialized in growing fruit in their London ones.

Royal fruiterers supplied nuts, quinces, peaches, cherries and gooseberries, to be planted in the Westminster gardens, and all kinds of pears for the Tower gardens. In 1186 Henry III paid his chief clerk 6s.8d. to make him raspberry and strawberry drinks, probably from his garden fruit. While they were staying in London the kings enjoyed the fruits of their gardens. The King's clerk and surveyor of works in the fourteenth century had a dwelling-house with 'a long garden' on the west side of Westminster Hall. The top men at Westminster all had gardens.

The King had a vineyard at Westminster, which was repaired every few years, at a cost of one mark (13s.4d.).

There was also a rose garden at Westminster, where the gardens were obviously something of a pleasance. In 1259 the gardener there, William of the Garden, supplied several loads of lime to the Court, and in the same year twelve workers were paid 1s.3d. each to carry rubbish for a week to level the surface of 'the garden by the cistern'. It sounds as if there were beds, paths and a fountain in the garden. Its upkeep involved a lot of heavy work, and several men, including William the Gardener, worked on the Palace and Abbey buildings and also on the Palace gardens, according to the weather and work conditions. William was helped in the garden by carpenters and builders. But other Westminster gardeners were specialists, not just labourers, and were hired to look after the pleasances there. One such was Roger the Herberer, who was paid 2½d. a day by Henry III for work on the herbery at Westminster.

The English kings enjoyed gardening. As time passed and they built themselves more palaces and comfortable weekend homes, they designed parks and gardens to go with them. These were some of the first architecturally sensitive gardens, designed as part of the palace buildings. The striking thing about royal gardens in London is that they were made and enterprisingly maintained at such an early date. When Richard II (ruled 1377-99) appointed the first royal Professor of Botany, John Bray, he was making an academic institution of royal gardening, which his predecessors had been sponsoring for over a century. From the early thirteenth century on, the royal court was a hothouse of experimental gardening. One can see the same horticultural pattern in most medieval towns, on a much smaller scale. Palaces had the most artistic and experimental gardens; next after them were wealthy suburban houses, and then the majority of houses, which were very small, with gardens which were a mixture of kitchen and herb garden, orchard and grass.

More pleasure gardens were made by more people towards the end of the Middle Ages. In 1469 William Syndys, a Norwich mason, left his widow Katherine 'my twin tenantries hanging on the same messuage, with the drawing of water at the well and her pleasure in the garden at all times'. There is no need to repeat the descriptive details of all the kinds of gardens people made, and anyway no town has records that reveal them as fully as London's records do.

A brief look at the horticultural records of four medieval English towns will suffice to confirm that they all had plenty of gardens and that the character of these varied with the character of the town and its inhabitants. The four sets of records give us a panoramic view of urban gardens in medieval England, for they record the gardens of an important city, an important university town, a provincial market and cloth town, and a planned royal foundation. The gardens of a few other types of town are mentioned in passing, to complete the panorama.

Some Northern City Gardens

After London, York was one of the biggest towns in medieval England. It was the commercial capital of the north, and its biggest gardens belonged to its most prominent citizens: merchants and monks. Most of the great York merchants lived at St Saviourgate in houses overlooking the marshes, which were drained and made into solid ground in the thirteenth and early fourteenth centuries. Then they were made into gardens, sheltered by the city wall at their northern end, and stretching away to the King's fishpond and the house of the chantry priests at their other end. By the fifteenth century the merchants in St Saviourgate had made themselves a garden suburb, which they could admire through the south-facing windows of their houses.

There were also a lot of smaller property deals in the marsh area east of St Saviour's church in the twelfth century, and in nearby 'Little Belgate', which had been a group of closes and gardens at the start of that century and was a housing estate by the end of it, with new churches built near by to serve it. The twelfth and thirteenth centuries saw extensive housing developments in York, as its population rose and people encroached on open space inside and outside the walls. In 1252 a new field, gardens and orchards were made outside Walmgate Bar, and similar building developments were made all round the peripheral areas and suburbs.

The biggest gardens were all in the wealthy southern suburbs, where there was plenty of space and sunshine. John Isabell of Micklegate was a prosperous cook who ran an eating house on the main street of York, and had a garden and two vineyards in the southern suburb of Clementhorpe. When he died in 1390 they were in good condition, and the vines may have provided him with ver-juice for his cooking. Two of the biggest York gardens were bequeathed by the merchants who owned them to the poor. One was in Blossomgate suburb, and was left to the poor of John Bedford's Maison-drew (Maison Dieu, i.e. almshouse) in Little St Andrewgate; the other was in Whitefriar Lane, and was left by Richard Kuketon to his executors on condition that all the poor in John Haine's Maison Dieu had part of the garden assigned to them, with free entry and exit to it.

The King did not treat his gardens at York Palace so philanthropically. Inside the palace walls, they were sealed off from the outside world, and from our enquiry, except for the odd reference to them in the palace works accounts, such as the one in 1306 to 2s.6d. spent on '1000 turves to repair the King's herbaria there'.

The King and his courtiers and the prosperous merchants of York had enough gardens between them to provide work for a number of full-time professional gardeners. Several men who described themselves as gardeners were doing well enough to be subject to the 1381 poll tax taken in York. The register of York freemen listed 'Gilbert of Ilkeley, gardener' in 1334 among its craftsmen and tradesmen, and in 1351 it listed another gardener, Robert of Hornburgton, and a herberer, Robert of Godesburgh. As gardener and herberer were listed as separate occupations, the latter probably meant a specialist in pleasure gardens and arbours, like Roger the Herberer, whom we saw earlier working for Henry III at Westminister. Gardening was one of the 'miscellaneous' crafts, like malting, bookbinding, mouldmaking and scrivening, that could be pursued by a freelance operator who did not belong to a gild or company. By the mid-fourteenth century gardeners of this kind were making a good living in towns like London and York. In Oxford and Cambridge they couldn't go wrong.

A Group of Academic Gardens

Like London and York, and indeed most medieval towns, Oxford had a lot of well-to-do families who lived in houses with big gardens: the Segrims, Kepeharms, Halegoods, Padys, to name but a few from the thirteenth century. Sometimes the early colleges bought or rented properties of this kind; sometimes they were bequeathed them; sometimes they bought up small properties.

Thirteenth-century Balliol was a collection of small tenement houses and gardens. In the late Middle Ages these were made into private chambers, and their occupants were allotted one garden each, which was to be planted with herbs and vegetables. University College and Exeter College also had sets of small halls and gardens in the early days of the college system, which began in the thirteenth

Playing chess on the front lawn of a manor house. House and gardens are enclosed, and the garden subdivided, by wooden palisades.

A late medieval castle garden, with ornamental beds and railings.

The Virgin and child
seated on a grassy bench
in an enclosed garden,
in a Garden of Eden
setting.

Lovers in an enclosed
love-garden, leaning
on a rose trellis.

century. The colleges inherited monastic gardens that had been expertly cultivated for generations by the monks and nuns, and were therefore perfect institutional delights.

Some of these had their own special traditions that the colleges took pride in keeping up. For instance, there had been a swannery at Magdalen since the earliest times, and there was still one there in Tudor times. One of the medieval college servants was a swan keeper, who received a generous allowance to spend on the care and feeding of his charges. Most of the colleges had a variety of different kinds of monastic gardens, and the ones which serve as model Oxford gardens, being the best documented, are those of Queen's College. They give us just one hint of a monastic association in the shape of 'The Nuns' Garden', the origins of which are unknown, but the rest of the gardens are recorded in detail.

They were extensive. The account rolls mention a higher and a lower garden, a cook's garden, two church gardens, a little garden, a garden known as 'the disportum' (strictly translated, disportum means grounds), a little disportum, a vineyard, and in the fifteenth century 'a garden against the new college'. The earliest account is for 1341, and records that the sale of parsley, onions, garlic, leeks, chibolles (small onions), vegetables, fennel seeds and fennel stalks that year brought in 6s.0½d. plus 8d. for tree trimmings: 4s.11d. of this 6s.8½d. total was spent on garlic, onion and leek seeds, and 7d. tithe given to the Vicar of St Peter's. It sounds like a pretty big kitchen garden, and in 1350-1 it needed as much as 9s.1¼d. worth of hired labour to keep it going.

The 1351-2 account is uniquely informative. It records the payment of 1d. to the gardener, and of 4d. to one woman for planting beans (bean gardening seems to have been a female speciality) and removing stones, and a further 1½d. to the same woman for planting vegetables. Then it records that hemp, onions, leeks and beans were planted, and some parsley 'and other small seeds'. It then goes on to detail the small seeds: cauliflowers, which were much smaller in the Middle Ages than they are today, hyssop, ox-tongue, savory, thyme and borage. In 1359 the gardener, John Godspeed, added more borage to this list. This is rare inside information on a medieval herb-garden, though we don't know whereabouts in Queen's it was or how it was laid out.

The vegetable patch, of which it may well have been part, since there are no references to a separate herb garden or herbarium, was dug, weeded and manured each year by workmen whom the gardener hired to help him. The cook often worked in 'The Cook's garden', also called simply 'The Garden', which was probably this main vegetable patch. Whether it was the same garden in which faggots were sometimes gathered and branches, timber and trees cut down, is hard to tell. It probably was, as the timber receipts are entered next to the vegetable receipts under the heading 'From the Garden'. In the fifteenth century more trees were allowed to grow there, and it was less extensively cultivated. Part of it was made into a chicken run, payments to workers decreased, and only onions, leeks, parsley and peas were planted, though there was one addition: after 1415 crocuses were planted and sold in large quantities.

The hemp and flax patch was enlarged, and the linen obtained from it used to make napkins and tablecloths for the College High Table.

The development of college life led not only to more linen gardening but also to more attention being paid to the disportum and the little disportum, which were planted with garlic and 'seeds', and cultivated like the other vegetable patch. Walls were built all over the college grounds, subdividing a couple of the gardens and enclosing them all, so that entrance to them was through locked doors and gates. The first mention of a wall is in 1399, and it was made of wood and straw, and roofed with tiles, like most good medieval walls. Four years later there is a solitary entry: 'Received for the graves in the garden, from those who wish to remember, 13s.4d.' One of the two church gardens must have been a graveyard, walled in like the other gardens. It was probably made in 1354, when some money was given for a garden next to the church by someone with the suggestively sepulchral name of Nicholas Letusbury.

In about 1405 the college decided to clear part of its main garden and make it into a little pleasance. Men were hired to make a fountain and to supply it with water by building an aqueduct from it to the street, a distance of six leagues,[1] at the street end of which there must have been a water source. Two years later a new fountain was built, which lasted for fifty years. Then it was cleaned of a lot of muck, and surrounded by tiles 'to make a common place', and by slates, moss and young trees. So, by the end of the Middle Ages Queen's had a college quadrangle garden something like the ones we know today, with a central fountain-pleasance.

---

1 A league was usually three miles, but is more likely in this case to have been three yards.

It also had a little vineyard, like the ones in the London livery company gardens, only this one was enclosed as a garden by itself. Like most of the company vineyards, the Queen's vineyard was very small and only produced verjuice. It was never much good, and failed altogether by 1448. From then on the gardener had to buy verjuice, and in 1469 bought some crab apples and tried making it out of them. His helpers were not experts on viticulture, or indeed on any sort of horticulture, except in so far as everyone in medieval England knew how to garden well. They were casual labourers, paid by the day, and kept going with bread and beer. They often included boys and women, since these could be paid less than men, and on one occasion the boys brought their brothers and sisters along to help. The only professionals working in the gardens, apart from the head gardener, were carpenters, hired now and again to make doors and gates into the gardens.

But the gardens were kept in cultivation all through the period, and were constantly being adapted, brought up to date and experimented with. Trinity Hall, Cambridge, made itself a vineyard, herbaria and a fashionable pleasure garden within a few years of its foundation. Gardens like these were among the heralds of Oxford and Cambridge's horticultural excellence, which got its versatility and high standards in the first place from the monastic tradition to which the colleges were heir. In this way Oxford, Cambridge and Winchester, with William Wykeham's foundation of a college there in the late fourteenth century, were privileged above the other English towns, which all had gardens, but not institutional ones of this class.

Monastic gardens, except for some which were attached to friaries, belonged to their monasteries, not to the towns in which the monasteries stood, but the gardens of public Church dignitaries belonged to the towns to a much greater extent. Many bishops and archdeacons were also abbots and obedientiaries, but it was by putting their monastic gardening skills to diocesan use that they encouraged and influenced urban gardening. When Hubert Walter and his successors rebuilt the archiepiscopal palace at Canterbury in the twelfth century, they kept to the original Lanfrancian layout, with a courtyard to the north and a garden to the south, opposite Turnagain Lane.

It was a Bishop of Worcester who founded Stratford-on-Avon, and he did so in the grand, spacious, monastic manner. He laid out streets fifty feet wide; the main market street was ninety feet across.

Tenement plots were each ¼ acre big, which meant they included a back-side behind each house, and were leased out for 1s. a year.

Depending on the town site, tenement plots were sometimes much smaller, as at Salisbury, where the average size was 115 ft. by 50 ft., let for 1s. annual rent, and sometimes much bigger, as at Thame, where 1s. plots were one acre big, some of them with frontages 60 ft. wide and gardens 650 ft. to 700 ft. long. Some of its burgage tenements were built over open field land; almost every medieval town had great stretches of land near by into which it could expand. Towns which were planted with castles, like Lincoln, expanded beyond the old city walls, and a medieval town's suburbs were often as extensive as its gardens, yards and orchards inside the walls were numerous. Most townsmen had some land attached to their houses, where they kept animals and planted gardens. Some had only a house, and depended completely on trade for their living. In that case they usually owned some land outside the city walls. At Leek, in Staffordshire, each burgess had a half-acre tenement inside the walls and half an acre of land outside the walls. It was so general for a house to stand in a plot of land that at York detached bits of land outside the walls were known as 'strays'. Sometimes the whole commonalty of the town owned its strays. Medieval Lincoln had a lot, and so did individual townsmen in York, Colchester, Exeter and Cambridge.

Most townsmen had their gardens outside their back doors (see Fig. 5, which shows the small medieval town of Nunburnholme, in the East Riding of Yorkshire.)

But one must look at a bigger medieval town, with which more people today will be familiar, to see what the medieval gardens of a provincial town were like. Leicester, being a middle-sized medieval market and cloth town, will suit the purpose.

Provincial Gardens in the Midlands

We have seen how much fruit and vegetable gardening went on in London, and doubtless in every medieval town. The same is true of stock-keeping.

Pigs about town were a common medieval nuisance, and town councils were always trying to keep them off the streets.

Edward II's tax rolls for Shrewsbury show that in 1313 most of the townsmen there kept livestock, and that husbandry, not commerce, was their chief interest, and of course they gardened.

The taxation and Guildhall lists of freemen in thirteenth-century Leicester mention Richard the Gardener and Alan, his son; William the Gardener and Alan, his helper; two gardeners called Alan, though these may be the two already mentioned in conjunction with Richard and William, and Philip the Gardener. These are only the men whose profession was gardening. Plenty of others had their own gardens. In 1352 William, the son of John Black, signed over to his brother Ralph all his rights to 'an orchard in the city and four plots in the suburbs'. Lots of gardens were bequeathed in wills, and lots were bought and sold. There was one law case in 1394 which gives us an idea, in its incidental description, of the number of gardens there must have been, most of them not appearing in the records. The case was to settle a dispute over two tenements and 'a garden at Torchmere, lying between the garden of Thomas at the Hall and the garden of William Andrew in the east, and the garden of Roger Locke in the west, and stretching from the garden of Simon of Sheford to the garden of William Turner'.

One large garden in Soapers Lane, Leicester, in the parish of St Peter's, was divided among the members of a family in 1481 because all of them wanted a bit of garden. Subdivisions of garden plots of all sizes were common in English towns until about 1350, when plague and economic decline depleted the population enough to leave vacant plots inside the walls. There were half and quarter burgage plots as early as the thirteenth century, in which people still managed to keep a pig or a sheep, and some poultry, and to grow some herbs.

The Town Cross, surrounded by public gardens, was the focal point of medieval Leicester. It was the site of the important Wednesday market, and near it were the Town Hall, Guildhall, castle and the most prosperous of Leicester's churches: St Martin's. Inns, houses and gardens lined the streets leading to it. This whole area comprised St Michael's croft, which was the most rural part of the town, and had a lot of big gardens, like Walkerscroft and the Soar Lane area adjacent to it in the north and west.

The church of St Martin's was burnt down in 1173, and the streets near it became green lanes and the sites of houses were converted into orchards, and remained as such until redevelopment began in the later Middle Ages.

Almost all the property deals in St Michael's croft concerned gardens, orchards, dovecots, plots of ground and crofts; there were hardly any house deals. The gardens were often very big. One garden in St Michael's parish was hedged by 88 ash trees and two aspens. This north side of Leicester was its garden side, St Michael's parish most of all. But there were also crofts and gardens all along Parchment Lane; there was a galtre (either a cultura, i.e. cultivated plot, or a gallows tree) above Gallowtreegate; gardens attached to the houses of the wealthy citizens living on the west side of the town; a garden attached to St John's Hospital, and monastic and nearby memorial gardens which do not count as town gardens but as big, self-contained extras. Most medieval towns were more like Leicester than London in that they had only a few magnificent gardens, and many small and humble ones. The most luxurious garden in medieval Leicester was probably the one that belonged to the Corpus Christi gild, in Soapers Lane.

Medieval towns were full of orchards, inside and outside the walls. Pope Alexander III's 1175 bull confiscated the property of the monks of Winchenley, Glos. with 'the town of Swiring and all its orchards'. Scottish towns as far north as Lothian and beyond had orchards.

Planned Town Gardens

It now only remains to look at one group of towns that were designed and built from scratch in the Norman period, and included gardens and orchards in their design. They are the medieval planned towns, and their plans were always partly horticultural.

There were only a few of them. Medieval English government was never strong or secure enough to take the initiative in civic settlement on any scale. In the few cases where it did, it was usually in order to increase the defensive security of the realm. King Henry III built eight new towns along the Welsh border, each one presided over by a castle with a permanent garrison, Conway and Carnarvon being the most strikingly dominated by their castles. But it was Edward I who was the keenest town planner. One of his titles was Duke of Aquitaine, and it was in Languedoc that he found the blueprint for the towns he built there and in England, which were known as bastides.

The word *bastide* (*bastille* in northern France) means fortress. All bastides were laid out according to the same plan. A square or rectangular site was procured, sometimes protected by a castle, as was the case in the English Marches; sometimes just by a wall or ditch, as was often the case elsewhere in England and in France. The town was laid out in squares or rectangles, with straight, narrow streets crossing each other at right angles, the main ones leading straight from the gates to the Town Hall. This was the centre of the town, and stood in a big square, which was often edged by arcaded streets. Next to the main square was a smaller square, which contained the parish church.

Settlers were given a block of land each, with ample room for a garden behind the house, which was built by each settler for himself. He was often given timber for this building, and always some arable or pastoral land, and sometimes an orchard or vineyard near the town; the medieval townsman, whatever his craft or trade, was always a cultivator, and had to have a patch of land. The most famous of these house-and-garden planned towns in Britain are Berwick-on-Tweed, Winchelsea, Salisbury and Hull.

Originally Hull was a tiny hamlet called Myton, which grew into a small town called Wyke ('Wick' means town or hamlet), at the confluence of the Hull and Humber. Edward's plans for its growth and prosperity were only slowly realized. Plots of waste ground were leased out to encourage settlement. By the mid-fourteenth century trade, and with it population, had increased enough for a lot of property to be bought, sold and developed. Houses were built on old and subdivided plots, and extended into their gardens. By the late fourteenth century the smaller streets were densely populated and built up, and almost all the open ground was in the west, away from the main streets. The biggest house there was the one known as the Court Hall, which the Poles bought from Edward's Keeper in the early fourteenth century. In 1347 it had a hall, chapel and garden, and an outhouse in the grounds.

By the late fifteenth century population had risen so far that there was not room for everyone to have a garth behind his house, and the garden plots were all round the edge of the town (see illustration p. 65). Allotments would appear to have a medieval pedigree, and to have been much bigger then than they are today.

But on the whole it is true to say that there is an unchanging English ideal of a town as a combination of house and garden: English towns always expand, and always have expanded, into suburbs.

FitzStephen's description of London's twelfth-century suburbs, with their 'rows of houses and gardens . . . containing large trees both spacious and pleasing to the sight' could have been written today, when gardens are as fundamental a part of suburbs, and suburbs as inevitable an extension of towns, as they were in the twelfth century. People make excellent gardens out of tiny patches which back on to roads and railway lines, just as they did in the Middle Ages out of the little curtilages that backed on to the fields and woods. Urban gardening is as keen now as it was then, despite the odds that are now stacked against it, or perhaps because of them. Town councils build ever more widely and densely, but at the same time maintain parks and gardens of better quality and in greater numbers than town councils anywhere on the Continent. Town and garden are no more incompatible today than they were in the Middle Ages.

3

Castle, Palace and Manor House Gardens

The great tower, that was so thick and strong,
Which of the castle was the chief dongeon,
Thereas the knights were in prison,
Of which I told you, and tell shall,
Was even joined to the garden wall.

In this one sentence from *The Knight's Tale* Chaucer gives us the
main argument of this chapter: castles, those strongholds of
medieval masculinity and militarism, contained gardens. This
chapter is an account of the different kinds of castle gardens, and also
of the different kinds of palace and manor house gardens in the
medieval period. By the end of that period the distinction between
these three types of residence, and with it the distinction between
their types of garden, had blurred to such an extent that it was no
longer tenable. Early Norman castles were purely military institutions; they were defensive centres in an age of siege warfare. As that
age passed, and conquest developed into government, castles
developed into homes as well as military headquarters. Always
defensive, they became increasingly residential and domestic until,
by the late fourteenth century, many of them were no more than fortified palaces or manor houses.

All the palaces considered in this chapter were royal ones. There
were none of these until the twelfth century, when the Crown felt
itself secure enough to build a few hunting lodges and weekend
homes for itself and its household. For over a century after the Conquest the royal household was endlessly peripatetic, touring its
newly acquired dominions to keep them securely under its control.
The building of residential palaces, with provision for leisure
activities and female members of the household, at favourite resting-

places on the royal itinerary, reflects the increased security of Norman rule in the same way that the domestication of the castle does.

While castles developed domestically, palaces developed both domestically and numerically, until by the late fourteenth century there were palaces all over the kingdom, built by barons as well as members of the royal household.

Those who could not afford to build palaces built large manor houses, fortified, extensive and ubiquitous, like palaces and castles. The only things that distinguished them from these two types of building were that they were smaller and that they retained many features of their humbler, agricultural origins. Medieval manor houses were basically farm houses, but as time went by they developed into more comfortable residences, like castles, and became more numerous, like palaces.

By the late fourteenth century there was often little to chose between a castle, a palace and a well-to-do manor house, and the gardens of the three of them are considered together in the last section of this chapter. However, they are considered separately in the early sections, which deal with castle, palace and manor house gardens until the late fourteenth century.

Castle Gardens in the period from the Norman Conquest to the late fourteenth century

The account begins with the Norman Conquest, after which King William's regents, Bishop Odo of Bayeux and Earl William Fitz Osbern 'wrought castles widely throughout the nation and oppressed poor folk', in the words of the chronicler. Doubtless there had been castles of some kind in England long before this: Roman camps, the fortified towns or 'burhs' and the individual fortresses of the Anglo-Saxons, but, to quote the chronicler again, 'the fortresses which the French call castles have been very few in the English provinces'. These castles, which the Normans built to guard the towns and strategic routes of their new province, were something new. They were nearly all of the motte and bailey type. Motte is the French word for a mound, from which we derive the English word 'mote', meaning hill, and 'moat'. A bailey is a fortified courtyard.

Almost all motte and bailey castles were hastily erected and therefore made of timber. Their buildings and courtyards must have been rough affairs, the nearest they got to garden accessories being wells, ponds, mills, ditches, fish-stews and fowl pens. Norman castles were bare bastions of survival.

They continued to be so all through the troubled reigns of William Rufus and Henry I, and the anarchy under Matilda and Stephen, when 'every lord built himself a castle so that the land was filled with castles', as one chronicler wrote. It was not until the accession of Henry II in 1153 that castles began to be built in stone, and even then wood went on being used for palisades, outbuildings and sometimes for the whole castle in the reigns of Henry III and Edward I. In one sense stone castles imply insecurity; stone was used because it resisted the onslaughts of battering rams and slings better than wood, and because it did not burn. It was a stronger defence in an age when defence was crucial to a feudal lord's survival. But in another sense stone castles bear witness to the greater security that England enjoyed after the mid-twelfth century. They took more time and skill to build than wooden ones, and were built by men who felt they could afford both these indulgences. They were built on a grand scale, not only to accommodate the increasing number of armed followers that these barons commanded, but also to accommodate the increasing number of domestic servants that made up their households. For by the late twelfth century the military aristocracy did not just fight in their castles; they lived in them.

By this time baileys were beginning to be enclosed with stone walls or 'curtains', protected by a gate-tower and sometimes, as at Ludlow, by angle towers. The wooden palisade on the mound was replaced by a high stone wall which formed what is known as a shell keep, like the ones at Lincoln and Berkeley. But most twelfth-century castles were new buildings, not conversions, and their central feature was a massive rectangular keep.

The keep was generally three storeys high. The basement was used as a storehouse, the ground floor as living quarters for the men-at-arms, the first floor as quarters for the lord and his retinue, and the second floor as quarters for the women and as bedroom apartments. The keep in which all these quarters were contained was known as the dungeon, a word derived, via the French word *donjon*, from the latin *dominium*, meaning lordship. As the years passed, baronial lordship developed domestically as well as militarily. The first sign of the castle's domestic development was the existence of stone dungeons and a growing number of domestic apartments and outbuildings, kitchens in particular; the second sign was the appearance of gardens, and of gardeners on the castle staff.

At first they were mostly orchard-keepers, men like Henricus Arborarii, hired by the King in 1158 to look after his orchard at Windsor. The earliest castle gardens were orchards outside the castle walls, like the ones in the stretch of ground eighty yards wide, still visible but now gravelled in, between the Roman ditch and the south curtain ditch at Carlisle, which were destroyed when the castle was besieged in 1173-4. Ranulf III, the sixth Earl of Chester (1181-1231), granted to William, the keeper of his castle orchard and garden in 1191, 'his restingre[1] and the residue of the Earl's apples after the shaking down of trees of the existing garden and those of the garden to be made in the castle ditch'. The existence of this orchard all through the medieval period is confirmed by later account rolls. In 1353 Philip Raby, the castle gardener, was 'entitled to the refting tree and the residue of the apples by ancient custom'. Either the central stock tree was over a hundred years old, which is quite possible, or it was replaced by a new one from time to time. The garden in which it stood continued to exist until 1745, and was an integral part of the castle, as castle orchards often were.

When Gerald of Wales (1147-1220) described his home castle of Manorbier, near Pembroke, the things he considered most important about it were its strong defensive position, 'on the summit of a hill extending on the west side towards the sea port', then its horticultural amenities: 'on the north and south side a fine fishpond under the walls, as conspicuous for its grand appearance as for the depth of its water, and a beautiful orchard on the same side enclosed on one part by a vineyard, and on the other by a wood, remarkable for the projection of its rocks and the height of its hazel trees'. Besides the fact that the castle had an orchard, this description reveals the interesting fact that it had a vineyard. Vineyards are the products of settled, confident domestic life; a castle with a vineyard was much more than an austere fortress.

One of the earliest mentions of castle gardens in England is in connection with a vineyard. In 1156-7 the accountant at Windsor Castle paid one of the castle staff '11s. for the work in the vineyard and garden'. Windsor began as a motte and two large baileys, and came into favour as a royal residence under Henry II, who established the vineyard. There are yearly accounts during his reign of the planting of vines in the Little Park there, and of wine-making

1   refting tree; – from 'reaving', meaning taking away/splitting off: a stock tree for grafts.

from their grapes. Twelfth-century Windsor is evidence of that transition from temporary fortress to permanent home that is typical of English castles at that period. The transition is particularly noticeable in royal castles, for the simple reason that the King had more resources to effect it than anyone else in England: he had the most castles, the largest household and, therefore, the highest aspirations towards comfort and luxury, and the most money. There was more domestic comfort than one imagines in many twelfth-century castles; there certainly was in royal ones like Windsor.

Henry II spent a lot of money on the 'houses' of his favourite residential castles, which were Windsor, Winchester and Nottingham. He had his chambers at Winchester elaborately decorated soon after he had established the vineyard there, and in 1181-2 he spent 70s. on having them painted. He had mews, dovecots and a park made at Nottingham, a chase at Bristol, fishponds at Rye, Sawrey and Newcastle-under-Lyme. Parks, chases and fishponds are in the same category as orchards: that of the most primitive approach to castle gardens; Henry II's royal gardens and vineyards were precociously sophisticated. But others like these were appearing, as we can gather from Gerald's description of Manorbier. The fishponds, orchard, vineyard and woods there were all outside the walls, which was the case with all the earliest castle gardens. The vineyard garden at Windsor was described as being 'nigh on to our said castle', not inside it. Such gardens were usually entered from the castle by a door concealed in the fortifications. Walking in the garden was a perilous pleasure, not to be indulged in too frequently. The only safe place for ladies to walk in disturbed times was the castle terrace, known as the 'allure', a walk on top of the ramparts. The castle walls were at least six feet to eight feet thick, often much more, so the allure was wide enough for easy walking, and it was protected in front by an embattled parapet, and in the rear by lower and lighter walls. There was an allure at Carlisle Castle, which was always in the thick of Anglo-Scottish fighting, called 'Ladies' Walk'.

But with the development of curtained castles, walks and gardens were laid out inside the walls. Henry III let his wooden castles decay, and concentrated on strengthening his stone ones and improving the comfort of those which he favoured as residences, particularly after his marriage to Eleanor of Provence in 1236. Eleanor's mother was a daughter of the Count of Savoy, and the marriage inspired Henry to provide good accommodation and gardens for his wife and her sophisticated Savoyard and Provençal entourage, just as Henry II's marriage had inspired him to accommodate Eleanor of Aquitaine as luxuriously as he could.

Henry III's building accounts are full of orders for new oriels to keep out draughts, new wardrobes, gardrobes (privies), alley-ways, chambers, glazed windows and also garden walks, gardens and arbours. Developments of this kind were undertaken at Windsor in the first half of the thirteenth century, and the royal accounts from that period show the considerable, but still cautious, extent to which gardening had prospered there since the reign of Henry II. His accounts have just the one garden and vineyard entry for 1156, but forty years later there was a large expenditure of £30, for works on 'the King's garden'.

He had glass windows put in the Queen's chamber, an extravagantly generous gesture, distinguished still further by the fact that they were made so as to open and close, and the fact that a stained glass window depicting the Tree of Jesse was added into the gable end of the chamber. But the interesting thing about these windows, as far as this book is concerned, is that they are described in the accounts as 'facing on to the King's herb garden', which was a new garden, specially laid out next to the Queen's chamber, so that she could look at it through her windows.

Henry had a large new chapel seventy feet by twenty eight feet, built opposite the royal chambers, on the other side of the plot of grass which was overlooked by the Queen's chamber, and was now partially enclosed as a garth by the construction of a hall and some new apartments along a third side of it. This cloistered garden, like another one in the lower bailey which the accounts describe as a 'herbarium', was obviously a lawn. There was a salaried gardener at Windsor from 1237 onwards, and in 1319 and 1320 Adam the gardener dug up 3,300 turves to lay on it, and repaired the gate that led into it and the wooden palings that surrounded it. The other herbarium was also relaid with turves, and both of them were carefully maintained, and their turf continually replaced and treated, except for a hiatus after a fire in 1295. The fact that they were turf lawns does not mean that they were bare of flowers. They may have been planted with small flowers – violets, daisies and periwinkles, to make the 'flowery meads' so beloved of the Middle Ages. In 1310 a stone bench was made in a recess in the castle's north wall so that the King and Queen, Edward II and Isabella, could sit next to the cloistered garden if they were tired of walking in it: it was their private pleasance.

The King's garden mentioned in the 1156-7 and 1165-6 accounts was outside the castle walls, and the work done on it in the 1230s programme was repair work on 'two breaches in the wall of our castle towards our garden', so that it was solidly backed. in 1239 the bailiffs surrounded it with a ditch, and in 1240 they gave one John Fitz Andrew bushes, probably of thorn, and paling, and orders to enclose it 'with a quick hedge (i.e. a live one, as opposed to one made of uprooted, dead branches) and paling, and to cause the garden gate to be new made of oak'. The garden was reached by a bridge across the ditch which led from the castle to the gate; otherwise it was completely enclosed. The hedge around it was repaired in 1246, and in that year the first hint of garden plants at Windsor appears in the records. There were two gardeners, earning the high wage of 2½d. a day, and they were instructed 'to make in the same garden a fair shrubbery'. However, a large part of the garden remained as a vineyard: in 1253 thorns were brought from Windsor forest to enclose the King's garden and 'great switches of alder to support the vines therein'. And at least some of its shrubs were fruit trees: in 1322 the accountant recorded a receipt of '6s.6d. for fruits and herbage from the King's garden outside the castle'. So by the mid-thirteenth century Windsor Castle had several kinds of gardens, inside and outside its walls, and Henry III, who spent a lot of time there, maintained them through all but the most bankrupt stages of his reign. In 1256 he had a freestone well sunk in his garden, and in October 1260 had the gardener's house moved from its position next to the garden gate 'to a more suitable spot towards the east, and covered with tile'. In fact it was completely rebuilt the next January, and the hedge around the garden replaced with an earthen wall. In 1261-3 a freestone fountain was made in the garden, and over the next five years Henry's final efforts were realized in the shape of another well, returfed lawns, and drains and conduits under the gardens.

These gardens were similar to many others belonging to baronial castles in the thirteenth century; they were not exceptional. Eleanor, Countess of Leicester, wife of Simon de Montfort, had several castles in her charge, for which she kept accounts. A glance at two sets of these accounts reveals the differences between the two castles to which they belong, and therefore between their gardens.

Until 1265 Simon de Montfort was head of the baronial party which confronted King Henry III, then defeated him at Lewes in 1258. From 1258 until 1265 he effectively ruled England, and by

far his most important castle was the royal castle of Dover, nicknamed 'The Key to the Realm'. With its commanding position, its
massive twelfth-century keep, and its walls, averaging twenty one
feet thick, it was a dogmatically military fortress. It had to accommodate a large household and retinue, and vast numbers of visitors,
also with retinues, but it was never a family home. There were no
gardens in Dover Castle.

Odiham, by contrast, was a small, homely castle in Hampshire, to
which a manor, park and hunting facilities were attached by King
Henry when he gave it to Eleanor in 1236. The castle had been built
by King John on a twenty-acre site, primarily as a resting-place and
a hunting-lodge on the way from Windsor to Winchester. It was on
low, marshy land, and the ditch around it became a natural moat:
castle ditches were usually dry; this one was sufficiently full of fresh
water for the custodian of the castle to seek the King's permission to
stock it with bream. The castle walls were only half as thick as the
walls at Dover; Odiham was not a military castle. An enclosed
garden was made in the castle park, surrounded by a boarded fence
with five doors. Inside this garden there were seats protected by turf
roofs and a garderobe discreetly screened by a hedge: it was a
feminine retreat far removed from the unrelieved stone of
Dover.

Women like Countess Eleanor were at once fighting and feminine.
They ran the castles, and led their defences against sieges while their
husbands were away, often for long periods, and they ran the castle's
domestic life and enhanced its homeliness while their husbands were
there. If a castle had gardens, they were often herb gardens and
pleasances next to the Lady's chamber. Apart from the orchards and
vineyards which were outside the walls of many castles, it was usual
for there to be either no gardens at all in a castle or else just pleasure
gardens: utilitarian compromises such as vegetable patches were
rare. It would have been hopeless to try and feed all the inhabitants
of a castle from the produce of its gardens. Monasteries were hardly
ever able to feed their inhabitants in that way, and they devoted
much of their time and manpower to gardening. Castles, with their
huge, shifting populations and with very few gardeners, never
dreamt of attempting it. As they grew to their thirteenth- and
fourteenth-century rôle of homes as well as fortresses, they made
more room for gardens, but these were for pleasure, not for supply.
Pleasure, like survival, could be fitted inside a castle; supply required
the ample acreage of a peaceful home. So most castle gardens were

accessories to a lady's bower.

Winchester castle, like Windsor, was fitted with two little pleasure gardens in the late twelfth century, and a herb garden for the Queen and a house for the King's birds. In 1252 the lawn between the new chapel and the chapel of St Thomas, and the lawn outside the hall door, were repaired, and they were both maintained as carefully as the buildings until Edward I completed the domestication in 1306 by having a garden laid out for his Queen – a small turfed enclosure with a stream of water running through the middle of it.

But the castle which best demonstrates the simultaneously spartan and gracious amenities of a medieval military stronghold is Nottingham. It was founded by William the Conqueror on his way to York in 1068, on a sandstone rock high above the Trent, and for five hundred years it was the chief fortress of the Midlands. Enlarged and further fortified by King John, Nottingham was the head-quarters of royal government north of the Trent during the 1216-7 French invasion. For the next twenty years repairs to the castle were routine but, significantly, they included for the first time repairs to 'the King's garden'. The King's garden was between the Great Gate and the Queen's chapel, and it was surrounded with pal-ing. Concessions to comfort at Nottingham were always minimal, but they did stretch to one enclosed garden. After a hiatus during the mid-thirteenth century period of baronial reform and rebellion, domestic works were again undertaken in the fourteenth century, and the gardens, including one 'at the end of the great hall', were repaired. In 1476-80 £3,000 was spent on new buildings and repairs, but we are not told which gardens, if any, were included in these. The wonder is not that there were so few gardens at Not-tingham, but that there were any at all, in view of its remorselessly military rôle.

Palace gardens in the period from the Norman Conquest to the late fourteenth century

A large number of palaces were built by kings and noblemen as hunting-lodges and country houses. Hunting was the consuming passion of the Middle Ages. Both men and women hunted with hounds, hawks and falcons, and a park to hunt in was the pre-requisite of every palace and, if the defensive site allowed, of every castle too. It was rare for a castle to be without a park, if not surrounding it, at least near by. Nottingham had a huge one. The perfect example of a medieval country palace, complete with parks and gardens, is Clarendon Palace in Wiltshire, now no longer in existence. It stood right in the centre of a forest, on a hill overlooking the site of New Salisbury. Perhaps because it was in such excellent hunting country, it became the favourite residence of Henry II, and included a large wine cellar to lubricate the frequent royal visits. There was no formal building plan for palaces such as there was for castles, because there was no strategic reason for one, though palaces, like castles, were usually moated or walled, with fortified gateways.

Clarendon, like most medieval palaces, was a collection of irregularly shaped buildings with irregularly shaped courtyards between them, which were often laid out as lawns and gardens. In 1247 a herb garden was made for the Queen, near her chamber, which was 'suitably' paved and fitted with a window overlooking her herb garden. In the same year the King's great garden beside the wall was fitted with a bench all round the wall, and the wall above the bench was whitewashed. This walled, painted, furnished garden was an integral part of the buildings, and was almost as much of an architectural as a horticultural achievement. The King completed his designs by having a garden made beneath his chamber in the north, and paling put round the burial garden where the body of his brother, Geoffrey de Leizignan, lay. Not to be outdone, the Queen had her garden remade, smartened up and enclosed with a fence in 1252.

These were the central palace gardens. Less protected ones lay near the outer buildings, next to the park. In 1254 the bailiffs of Salisbury castle were ordered to enclose the whole of Clarendon park with a hedge, instead of the paling with which it had previously been enclosed, and to remove forty perches of paling that stretched from the top of the park to the bottom, near the lawn.

The Clarendon grounds were horticulturally concentric: there was the outlying parkland, within that the lawns, and within them the herb gardens, and quite possibly flower gardens, near the chapel and the Queen's chamber. Somewhere there was a wooded pleasance, for in 1271 saplings were brought to be planted in it, and there was also a fish-stew. This was a regular feature of both palace and castle grounds, even if there were no gardens, for it was almost as integral to the grounds as a well. Stocked with bream, roach and carp, it provided the main flesh item of diet, but took up little room.

Artistically sited, and perhaps surrounded by trees and walks, it could make a water pleasance, like the one at Woodstock which we shall encounter a little later on.

At Westminister palace, which was the chief royal residence, and which emerged by the late twelfth century as the home of the Exchequer, and thence as the home of most government departments, there was room in the midst of all the administrative and royal household buildings for a sort of fishpond. In fact it did not take up any extra space because it was the moat.

William de Husseborne, Keeper of the Privy palace under Edward II, died after eating a pike he had caught in the moat, to the delight of the monks, who considered the moat their rightful property.

The Privy palace of which poor William was keeper shared with the Prince's palace a wealth of lawns, paved walks, pear-tree gardens, vine gardens and fruit gardens. Water was supplied to these, and to the gardens attached to the chapels and government buildings, like the 'great herb garden between the chapel and the Receipt Exchequer', by means of cisterns, lead pipes and taps. They needed constant maintenance from skilled plumbers, who also constructed an aqueduct to take water to the Royal Mews built for Edward I at Charing Cross. Falconry was Edward's favourite field sport, and he had two chambers, one for falconers and the other for chaplains, built there in 1274 and 1277 respectively. They were made of earth and thatched with reeds, and enclosed a turf garden in which there was a leaden bird bath with the metal image of a falcon in the middle of it. Water poured into the bath through four brass spouts in the form of leopards' heads. This was a rare instance of hunting coming in from park to garden. As a rule hunting and parks were fenced off from the outer orchards and vineyards, which were themselves fenced off from the inner gardens. A park was uncultivated, and the bigger it was the better. A garden was cultivated and enclosed, the more completely the better.

There is one medieval royal palace with records that give an unusually evocative picture of both its park, which was probably the first one ever made in England, and of its gardens. It is the palace of Woodstock, in Oxfordshire.

It was an ancient royal meeting-place in the heart of a forest, where Aethelred had held council before the Conquest. In 1110 Henry I had a park made there by enclosing part of the forest within a stone wall, and stocking it with lions, lynxes, leopards, camels and a porcupine sent from Montpellier. This menagerie was too exotic to be hunted, and in Henry II's reign it was replaced by another exotic device, Rosamond's Bower, in which the unfortunate Rosamond was hunted, first romantically by the King, then fatally by his wife. The Bower was a maze, in the centre of which Henry II made love to Rosamond Clifford, his mistress, where Queen Eleanor could not discover them.

The maze at Woodstock was the only one in medieval England that was part of a palatial estate. Mazes and labyrinths are probably almost as old as man, and there were plenty of them in the Ancient World, but these, like the medieval ones, were generally in the green fields. They were cut out of stone, rock and turf, and made out of hedges and bushes. All the chroniclers attribute antique origins to Rosamond's Bower, calling it 'a secret chamber of Daedalian workmanship', and it was presumably like the classical hedge and bush mazes, since it had to be tall enough to hide Rosamond and Henry. It was removed shortly after its central prize was removed by Queen Eleanor, and Henry III used the park as a hunting ground.

If the King ran short of game, there was always a good supply of fish from the royal stews. There was a series of stews at Woodstock, each on a different level, for the records mention the upper and lower stews, and ponds, bays and sluices, all in the best monastic tradition. Each of the two stews consisted of several ponds, and the stews were joined by a causeway. The whole pond area was pretty extensive, and it was somewhere near the inner gardens, for the lower stew is described as being 'near the closarium'.

In 1248 Henry III had two gardens made, one on each side of his chamber, and one of these contained a stew. The records refer to it simply as a 'stew', not a 'fish-stew', and though it may well have had fish in it, it seems to have been primarily a sort of water pleasance. In 1250 the Queen's garden was enclosed 'by two good high walls so that no one can get in, and a suitable and pleasant garden made by the King's stew, in which she can walk, with a gate leading to this garden from the garden which adjoins the chapel of Edward, the King's son'. Two years later a stew was made in the King's other garden and for years later it too was hedged in.

The walls and fountains of the King's courtyard were mended in 1240, and an iron trellis made on the step in front of the King's chamber, facing towards the garden, to match its iron-bound windows, and possibly to support some rose bushes whose foliage would match the green wainscotting within. More than likely this was an enclosed rose garden.

In 1245 the level space between the Queen's chapel and the larder was walled in and made into a fair garden, and in 1249 the apartments of the chaplain, William, were 'uprooted and new built between the hall of Amis and the stable, so a new garden may be made in their stead'. Thirteenth-century Woodstock was made into a mass of gardens, most of them walled or hedged in, and entered through locked doors. There were gardens at Everswell, next door to Woodstock, the centre of which was the wellspring that gave it its name. This garden was joined to the Woodstock gardens by means of a lead-roofed alleyway, which led into a covered walk round the spring. Everswell was a cloistered water pleasance, its springs used to make ornamental pools in the centre of the cloisters, wells, fountains and 'leaden spouts about the passages of Edward's [the King's son] chamber'. There is no mistaking the exotic, romantic feel about the gardens at Woodstock and Everswell. The memory of Fair Rosamond lived on to enhance this. One of the wells at Everswell was called Rosamond's Well, and the whole group of buildings near it was known simply as 'Rosamond', one of them being Rosamond's Chamber, which was, like Rosamond, fragile as well as fair. The King had it repaired in 1249 because the roof had blown off.

Its location near the springs and water at Everswell may well have been in conscious imitation of the popular Tristan and Iseult legend, of which the central motif is the fountain and cistern. The similarities of this legendary setting with the Rosamond gardens at Woodstock are numerous, and include: the proximity of the ladies' chamber to the stream, the adjacent orchard (in 1264 one hundred pear-tree saplings were planted in the King's hedged and palisaded garden at Everswell), and Rosamond's gardens and pools. Given the popularity of the Tristan story in the courts of Europe, particularly that of Henry II and Queen Eleanor, for whom Thomas of Britain wrote his own version of it, it seems probable that the Rosamond gardens were indeed designed to echo it.

Allowing for a little poetic elaboration, the garden Chaucer describes in his *Parliament of Fowls* could be the Everswell Garden at Clarendon:

> A garden saw I, full of blossomy boughs,
> Upon a river, in a green mead
> With flowers white, blue, yellow and red;
> And cold well-streams, nothing dead,
> That swommen [swim] full of small fishes light,
> With fins red and scales silver-bright.

Palace gardens, like castle, manor and any other pleasure gardens, were designed to appeal to the taste of their owner, or more often their owner's wife, who gave them personal attention and made them distinctively her own. Henry I's garden at Havering, Essex, was looked after by a gardener called Solomon, who also looked after the paling round the park there. Then it was looked after by Solomon's son, Ralph Fitz Solomon, then by his grandson, Geoffrey Fitz Ralph, who was still in charge of it in 1200. There is no way of knowing what the gardens were like. The Solomonic association with sweet-smelling herb gardens in *Ecclesiastes* makes it just possible that the gardener at Havering took this name because he was a herb specialist, perhaps hired by the King for that reason. When Havering was extended and smartened up in 1251, a herb garden was made between the King's chamber and that of his son, Edward.

Less conjecturally, the gardens at Langley Manor in Hertfordshire showed some distinguishing characteristics. After Langley came into the Crown's hands in the reign of Edward I, its gardens were very much the plaything of the Queen, and were designed as she wanted them. Edward I's Queen was Eleanor of Castile, and she brought gardeners with her to Langley who were trained in the Moorish tradition of paved courtyard and fountain gardening. In 1280 she imported grafts of Blandurel apple-trees from Aquitaine for the orchard at Langley, and made a new vineyard garden, complete with a gardener's house. She had the garden wall and the old ditch filled in and new ones made. The gardens were still the Queen's special pride in Edward III's reign, when they were improved again. In 1388 Queen Anne of Bohemia had her own private garden at Langley, and a lodge which she called 'Little London in the Park'.

Medieval castles and palaces, like medieval monasteries and all big medieval houses, were made up of a lot of buildings, some joined to each other by covered walks, some separate, so that their gardens were naturally enclosed between them, and were designed as extensions of the most decorative of them, usually the Lady's Chamber and the Chapel.

The man in charge of the gardens at Guildford Palace in Surrey in the 1280s was William Florentyn, whose name suggests Italian origin, and who was also in overall charge of all the works and buildings there at that time. To give just a few examples of his horticulturally sensitive architecture, or architecturally sensitive garden design, depending on which way you look at it, he built a little staircase down from the Queen's apartments to her garden, a popular device also used at the royal palace at Kennington, and in many noble houses. (Criseyde's garden in Chaucer's *Troilus and Criseyde* was just below her chamber, so that 'A-down the stair anoon right she went into the garden . . .') Florentyn built a herb garden and cloistered it with marble columns; he added a stone porch to the hall, overlooking the hall garden. Horticultural design of this sort, or at least a sense of its place within building design, was part of every good architect's repertoire.

Fortunately for us, one medieval gardener architect left us a unique record of his work, showing this combination in haunting detail. He was not a royal architect, but one of a family of Northamptonshire squires who earned themselves a measure of architectural repute in the late thirteenth and early fourteenth century. His work on the manor of Harlestone, Northamptonshire, a property given him by the King as a reward for his work as a royal officer, shows the ideal combination of house and garden skills required of architects at that period. His name is Henry de Bray (*ca* 1269-1340), and he kept an 'estate book' of his work on his Harlestone manor in the 1290s. It is true that he was designing a gentleman's manorial estate, not a royal or even a noble one, but some of the gardens belonging to manors like Harlestone were pleasances, like those of noble estates. What differentiates manorial from palace and castle gardens is the addition, indeed preponderance, of utility gardens and yards, as a look at Henry de Bray's estate makes clear.

Manor House Gardens in the period from the Conquest to the late fourteenth century

The hall and north chamber at Harlestone, the two residential basics of any residence, cost £12, excluding the cost of the stone and the beams. Stone was so rarely used for domestic building at this period that stone houses were singled out by names like 'The Stone Hall'. A year after building the hall and north chamber Henry added a south chamber. In 1292 he built the third most important part of Harlestone – a new grange, and then a garden called 'The New Yerde', and a wall along the path that joined them, so that he effectively walled in the outbuildings and their gardens within the manorial enceinte. In 1293 he made some ponds in the courtyard below 'Bereweldyke', and changed the watercourse between two other courtyards. Water engineering was a department of horticulture and of architecture, and a lot of estate architects designed ponds and watercourses. Henry de Bray made watercourses between the ponds at Harlestone, to power the water-mill which he built there.

He put gates and doors in the garden and estate walls, and in 1295 added a poundfold to the farmyards. In 1297 he made a new, walled herb garden, and built a whole series of walls near it, so that the garths near the central buildings were all walled, though the accounts do not disclose whether the walls were made of mud or stone. Nor do they disclose whether the herb garden was laid out as a pleasance, with the paths between square beds edged with flowering herbs, or whether it was just a functional patch, and only incidentally a pleasance. It and all its walls cost 62s.4d., which was a lot of money and suggests that it was well, if not ornately, made.

There is an interesting entry in his book for the year 1300: '30s. for making a tower in the lower yard', which yard must have been the one outside the ladies' bower or chamber. It is doubtful whether this tower was a defensive one, for though defence and pleasure were the two priorities, their comparative importance varying according to local conditions, Harlestone was not a strategic centre, and pleasure was more important than defence. Two years after building this tower, Henry built a mound and a bakehouse in the courtyard opposite Saltwell, and then walled in that courtyard. It is possible that the mound was a defensive look-out point, and the tower a defensive extension to the ladies' chamber. But it is more likely that the mound was an earthen one, built as a seat against the outside of the wall, faced with stone and covered with turf, like the one which Chaucer says he had in his own garden, 'y-benched new with turves fresh y-grave', and that the tower was a shelter or a domestic outbuilding of some kind: it could not have been a very substantial tower, costing less than half the price of the herb-garden.

Grassy mounds like the one which Henry seems to have made against the courtyard wall were really part of an arbour, or 'privy-playing place', as the poet William of Palerne, writing in about 1350, calls it. The word 'arbour' comes from the Old French *herbier*, meaning a place covered with grass or herbs, and appears in Middle English in many different forms, the most common being 'erber' and 'erbier'. Garden walls, banked all round and the banks covered with turf or sweet-smelling herbs, were punctuated by recesses containing seats shaded by branches woven over lattice frames, and by grassy mounds such as the one at Harlestone. Such arbour enclosures were probably originally defensive, and developed later into 'playing-places', so the Harlestone mound may have had both a defensive and an aesthetic purpose within the space of a few decades.

The year after it was built, Henry added considerably to the domestic amenities of the manor, in accordance with the pattern of castle and palace development at that time. He made a new kitchen, and a fountain near it, which suggests that it was a functional fountain, though Henry could easily have made it decorative as well. He then built a dove-house at the corner of the herb garden. It was an expensive one, costing more than the kitchen, and its position suggests that part of its purpose was to enhance the herb garden's pleasant appeal, for the cooing of doves was a popular medieval delight, full of symbolic importance for romantic and religious love.

> I passed through a garden green,
> I found a herber [arbour] made full new –
> A seemlier sight I have not seen,
> In each tree sang a turtle [dove] true.

This is the opening of a fifteenth-century religious pop song, *Verbum Caro Factum Est*. Dove-dung was a useful bonus for the garden soil and doves were good eating for humans and falcons, but these were not the only *raisons d'être* of dovecots, and the impression that the Harlestone one was primarily for pleasure is strengthened by the fact that two years after building it Henry built another one, next to 'the Newyerde garden'. This garden may well have been a pleasance of some sort. It was certainly big enough to have been like the yard in *Troilus and Criseyde*:

> This yard was large and railed all the alleys
> And shadowed well with blossomy boughs green,
> And benched new, and sanded all the ways,
> In which she walketh arm and arm between.

Henry enclosed his new Harlestone yard with twenty four perches of wall in 1307. A lot of the Harlestone walls were mended and ditched, and in 1309 a new short wall was built from the sheepfold to the 'Abbot's courtyard.' As one would expect of a farmhouse, there were more courtyards than gardens at Harlestone. Some of them were closes for livestock, but others, like the Newyerde, were probably gardens, or were subdivided into crofts like the Leycroft, which Henry planted with oats, and others were simply referred to by Henry as courtyards. In 1309 he spent 7s.4d. on levelling his main courtyard, which was presumably the entrance yard.

Henry's estate book was written for architectural purposes, and does not give details of the trees and plants in the gardens, but it does give an idea of the close relationship between gardens and buildings in the medieval period, both in design and construction. Henry refers several times to 'building a garden', and this is a common entry in medieval accounts. Gardens were walled, fenced, hedged and palisaded much more closely then than they are nowadays, so there was a good deal of stonework, carpentry, hedge-making, locksmithing and painting to be done in the making of them, and more of the same in the making of their mounds, fountains, benches, railings, paths and raised beds. Well-to-do gardens had to be built before they could be cultivated (see illustration p. 80).

Garden walls were a medieval pride and joy, and a status symbol. Disputes about them were rife, and there is one fourteenth-century agreement, made between the two parties to one such dispute, John of Laufor, a clerk, and William of Auverne, a citizen of London, which shows in a few lines the medieval relationship between architecture and horticulture, and the important place of garden walls within that:

> Because William had removed the earth in his garden, next to a stone wall in front of John's solar [first-floor chamber] without John's consent, he shall construct three buttresses to support the said wall, and keep them in repair; the water running off the said solar he shall catch in his garden. John shall have two windows going on to the same garden, but so barred with iron that William may incur no loss therby. William may not block the view of the said windows by buildings.

Buildings could indeed be gaudy eyesores for they, like garden walls and fences, were usually brightly painted. Henry de Bray whitewashed his great hall and grange, probably both inside and out, and this was standard practice as far as halls and chambers were concerned. The royal palaces looked at in this chapter were painted inside in green, red and white, some of them with silver- or gold-spangled ceilings, and were whitewashed outside. White was the favourite outside colour, and was used on garden palings, fences and gates, though in the later Middle Ages there was a fashion for painting doorways in the garden hedges green, to disguise them and so give the garden the appearance of a complete enclosure without an entrance.

Stonework was necessary in the construction of fountains, cisterns and conduits, and it was the hallmark of affluence. By the late thirteenth century the socially ambitious were putting as much stonework into their buildings and gardens as they could afford. Henry de Bray built Harlestone out of stone, and Paul Piper, who designed Odiham Castle for the Countess of Leicester, was denigrated as a parvenu and a new bourgeois by the chronicler, Matthew Paris, because he was so fond of buying up estates and building stone manor houses and pleasure gardens, enclosed and embellished in stone, on them. He was a new-rich steward of Henry III, and a leader of the mid-thirteenth century cult of stone housebuilding and pleasure gardening, in imitation of the royal properties, which led Matthew Paris to describe him as 'an unrivalled builder of manor houses . . . he so beset one, named Toddington, with a palisade, chapel, chambers and other houses of stone . . . and with orchards and pools, that it became the wonder of beholders . . . displaying to them the wealth and luxury of earls'.

After civil servants, the next most ambitious estate gardeners at this period were Church dignitaries, who were often civil servants themselves. Bishops built themselves palaces and palatial gardens; abbots built themselves luxurious private apartments and gardens, not only within the precincts of their monasteries but also in the countryside near by, as weekend homes, and in London.

They had been building estates and gardens of this kind since the mid-thirteenth century, especially those who had come to England straight from France, where it was already a well-established fashion. William de Colerne, Abbot of Malmesbury from 1260 to 1292, was one such Norman abbot, who brought his taste for country houses and gardens to England with him. He made new gardens on his estates at Crudwell and at Porton, in Wiltshire. The latter had two pools, a mill and a millpond, and William planted a vineyard and new yards and orchards at his monastic residence.

The Abbot of Westminster, who was one of the most important churchmen and politicians in England, had a castellated, moated manor at Neyte, in Middlesex, only a mile from his abbey, which he, and occasionally the King, used as a country house. So frequently did he stay there that his monks talked of him as being 'at home' when he was at 'La Neyte'. It had five gardens, for which the abbot's gardener bought lettuce, savory, borage, chervil and violet seeds in 1327. Besides a herb garden it had turfed alleyways and walks, and quite possibly an orchard and a flower garden as well. The Westminster Abbey accounts are full of references to the abbot's stays at 'La Neyte' and of the King's visits there. The King's gardener from 'le paleys' went there in 1345 to cut some small willow twigs to tie up the palace vines, from what was obviously a willow plantation, part of a nursery and vegetable patch containing willows, flax, hemp and peas. The gardens, though doubtless kept nice for the abbot, received extra attention just before royal visits, particularly tidying and planting sessions. The news that Edward II was going to stay there in the early fourteenth century caused twelve men to be hired for two days to weed the gardens and get the walks into top condition.

Abbey manors and gardens that were not on the royal circuit like 'La Neyte', and belonged to less important houses than Westminster, were more steadily maintained in the style which their abbots chose to set off their manors to best effect. By the fourteenth century these manors were often very grand, and fitted with suitably luxurious gardens. Thomas Horton, Abbot of the Benedictine monastery of St Peter's, Gloucester from 1351 to 1377, enlarged his abbatial residence there by extending its chapel towards the infirmary garden. The residence was already substantial, with a lead-roofed stone hall and adjoining apartments for the abbot and his household, and a large fish-stew. The abbot's private rooms consisted of a large bedchamber, a buttery, pantry and cellar, a withdrawing room and a number of adjoining bedchambers and galleries for his close associates and relations. Other visitors stayed in a separate set of apartments and had their own hall, with a gallery where they could exercise in bad weather and look down on the flower garden below, where they could walk in good weather. There were three stables, two slaughter-houses, a woodshed and a dog kennel, and there was another walled garden, probably for medicinal herbs. Besides this mansion, the abbot had a rural residence at nearby Over, which had originally been no more than a vineyard, and was made into a home by Abbot Staunton, who had built a chamber and garden there, surrounded by a wall, a few years earlier, to which his successor added a parlour.

This Norman style of landscape gardening spread through English society, from the Crown to its courtiers, barons, civil servants and churchmen, thence to those of the lesser nobility and gentry who could afford to adopt it. These, however, were few. Manorial lords of a humbler sort than Henry de Bray and Paul Piper only kept practical, productive gardens, like the ones kept by monastic cellarers and kitcheners, with the same aim of providing fruit, vegetables and herbs for the household kitchens. Many of these manorial gardens were several acres big because they included an orchard; indeed this was often all there was to the garden. An orchard was the most rudimentary sort of garden a manor, palace or castle could have, just as an onion patch was the basic sort of cottage garden. The thirteenth-century manor of Old Soar, in Kent, consisted simply of a hall and a two-storey block set in orchards and woods: the basic essentials of a primitive manor and its grounds.

The terms 'orchard' and 'garden' were often used interchangeably by manorial accountants, who called any more closely cultivated garden 'the little garden' or 'the inner garden'. Orchards were easily maintained and yielded big cider, perry and nut crops in return for a little tenant labour. For instance, on the manor of Crawley, in Hampshire, in 1282 tenants holding half a virgate of land[1] got ten apples a day each and a mid-day meal. This kind of manorial labour service was very common, as was the kind of manorial orchard it maintained.

We can see an example of one distinction between orchard and inner gardens in the first entry of the 1296-7 minister's accounts for the earldom of Cornwall. They deal with the earldom's manors all over England, and therefore make an ideal survey of English manorial gardens. The first account is for Oakham in Rutland, where 10s. worth of grass from the big park, 10s. worth of grass and fruit from 'the big garden' and 2s.4d. worth of grass from 'the inner garden' was sold. The accountant noted that no nuts had been sold that year, which means that there were nut trees, probably in the outer 'big garden', with the fruit trees.

The next manor to be dealt with is Little Weldon, in Northamptonshire, whose sole agricultural item was a profit of 2s.3d. from the sale of nuts. At Glatton, Huntingdonshire, garden fruit brought in nothing, but sales of garden hay brought in 3s. At Knaresborough, Yorkshire, the northyard fishery brought in a profit of 4s., and at

---

1 The virgate was the standard servile land-holding, and was usually thirty acres big; a half-virgate fifteen acres, though this was subject to much local variation.

nearby Harden the sale of grass and fruit brought in 20s.; at Rikehale 4s.6d. These gardens have obvious similarities with the big, rough, orchard gardens of monastic kitchen gardeners who, like manorial gardeners, were supplying big household kitchens.

On the Earl of Cornwall's manor of Bradninch, in Devon, there was an eel fishery which made 18d. profit a year; some beehives, from which the bulk of the honey was put into store and 4½d. worth sold; a park, from which the pasture was sold, along with grass from the garden, for 100s., and the old hedges for 1s., and a big orchard, from which 5½ quarters of apples were sold for 5s.6d. On Monesk manor, in the parish of St Clements, Cornwall, 4s.4d. worth of honey, 7s. worth of garden fruit, 1s. worth of garden grass and 11s.1d. worth of turves were sold. Turf was a common fuel in fen and moorland areas, and regional specialities like turf cutting and eel fishing overlie the basic orchard and grass cultivation detailed in the survey.

Isleworth, in Middlesex, was the Earl's biggest manor, and its speciality was viticulture. Generous expenditure on the many works necessary to keep up the vineyard rewarded the Earl with 124 gallons of verjuice and 3 dolia 1 pipe[1] of wine. The orchard yielded 102 gallons of cider, which the Earl sold. Though Isleworth was obviously an important manor, the weekend retreat of the Earl when he was in London, there is no sign of any sort of pleasure garden there, as far as one can tell from the accounts.

Other manors belonging to the earldom sold cherries, 'big nuts' (walnuts as opposed to filberts and hazelnuts), pears, fallen branches, doves and nettles. These last appear as an item of sale on other manorial accounts. When young, they are like spinach to eat, and when old their fibres are strong enough to be made into coarse thread and woven into coarse cloth; when applied to wounds they help to staunch bleeding.

With such rough gardens as those shown in the survey, expenses were few, and were made up for the most part of payments to hired fruit collectors, cider makers and wall builders and repair men. Only about half the Earl of Cornwall's manors had even this kind of rough garden, and only one manor, that of Wallingford, in Berkshire, had any suggestion of something more sophisticated. The Earl had three manors in the bailiwick of Wallingford, but Wallingford itself, to which the account quoted refers, was actually a castle, so its gardens

1   One dolium = 252 gallons; one pipe = 126 gallons.

cannot strictly be counted as manorial. They included a vineyard, with vines supported on palings; an apple, pear and cherry orchard; a large swannery, with thirteen of the swans feeding in one of the castle courtyards, and a 'herbarium', which was cleared of leaves and tortoises (!) in 1296.

This herbarium may have been a lawn, for a workman was paid to 'reap' it, but it could equally have been a herb garden, from which the herbs were 'reaped'. Near it were some little apple and pear gardens, separated from the orchards. These were ditched and hedged, as were some rose-gardens, of which at least one was entered through an outer door and then an inner wicket gate, for which the constable bought hinges, screws, hasps, latches, locks and keys: a real *hortus conclusus*, this one.

The constable had his own walled garden, which shows the extent to which the castle had developed into a domestic complex, not unlike a fortified manor such as Harlestone, except that Wallingford had a moat instead of ponds, to supply it with fish. This froze over so solidly in 1296 that 12d. worth of labour was needed to break the ice on it so that the fish could be caught. There are two curious entries in the account: one is for repairs to the door of 'the blind-house', which must have been just what its name suggests – a hut for a blind beggar, like the anker huts in some castles; the other is a payment of 6d. for gathering stones and 'roofing them with herbs in winter, for a penina'. This word never appears in medieval accounts, and it would be pleasant, though somewhat unscholarly, to think that it is a unique reference to a medieval rockery.

In general, manorial gardeners were concerned to get the rocks and stones out of their gardens rather than into them, so that plants could grow. But by no means every manor had a cultivated garden, and those that did grew the same plants as cottage gardens: some to fill the pot and others to flavour its pottage.

At Cuxham, in Oxfordshire, the manorial garden was a sprawling collage of garden and orchard, which adjoined the rectory grounds for a distance of at least 66 yards, and extended all along the west, and perhaps also the south, of the manorial curia, or enceinte. The manorial account rolls use the terms 'garden wall' and 'curia wall' interchangeably, which implies that the garden surrounded the curia (see Fig. 6). Not all the garden was intensively cultivated: men were hired occasionally to dig thorns out of it, mow the grass, plant acorns and fruit trees and fell timber. The fruit trees at the southern, orchard end of the garden produced mainly apples,

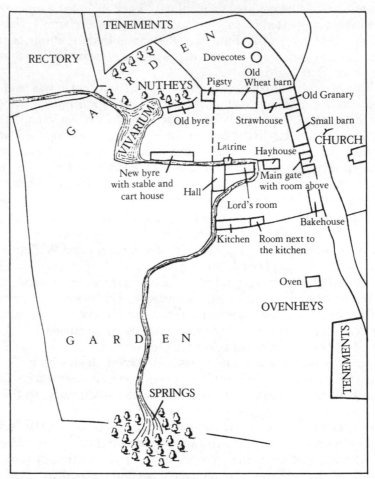

Fig. 6: The medieval manor of Cuxham, Oxfordshire.

which were made into cider, but also some pears and cherries. In the other tree-filled part of the garden, the north-west corner, shading the fishpond which also served as a duckpond, there was a close of nut trees, and somewhere, presumably facing south, were some vines. It looks as if there was a curtilage set apart for the famuli (manorial servants) to grow their pottage cereals, for in 1297-8 they were supplied with four quarters of oats to make meal for their pottage 'because of the failure of their curtilage that year'. The rest of the manorial garden was either left as grass and timber or planted with beans, to make the manorial pottage, and with onions and leeks to flavour it, and with hemp. It was a typical manorial fruit and vegetable garden.

Just as bishops and abbots built themselves houses and gardens befitting their status as members of the nobility, so vicars and parsons lived in houses which, alone in the village, approach manorial gardens; they were often built in stone, and had large gardens. The Vicar of Eardisley was assigned an extra piece of glebe land by the Bishop of Worcester in 1357 because his house was in such a confined position that he had no room 'to walk or grow leeks or other herbs'. A good vicarage, like a good manor, deserved a kitchen garden. A vicarage was nearly always described in medieval records as 'a house and garden', often about an acre in extent, midway between a cottage and a manorial property. Like every kind of relatively well-to-do residence, vicarages grew more comfortable and elaborate as time passed, while their gardens, being of the same type as manorial and cottage gardens, remained basically the same.

Fourteenth-century accounts of vicarages and manors show an abiding pattern of building and gardening, so it would be repetitious to quote them. A quick look at the late fourteenth-century accounts of the east Devon manor of Bishop's Clyst, three miles east of Exeter, is sufficient evidence of its horticultural continuity with the Earl of Cornwall's manor in that area a century before. Bishop's Clyst had one park, called Chelspark, and the lord made two more there in 1382: one planted with alders, the other stocked with animals. There was a fishpond within palisaded banks, for which the lord had two boats built and waxed. There was a dove- or pigeon-house, and those of its inmates which were not consumed on the manor were sold for 5s. or 10s. each year. Broom, alder, brushwood and straw from the parks was sold, and occasionally the garden produced enough apples and pears for some to be sold. In 1372 two pipes of cider were sold for the good price of 20s.; in 1375 1 dolium 1 pipe for 15s. The set-up is familiar. So is it with more grandiose manors, of which there were considerably more by the late Middle Ages, and with palaces.

Late Medieval Pleasure Gardens in Castles, Palaces and Wealthy Manor Houses

Since wealthy manor houses, palaces and castles all developed according to one basic pattern in the late medieval period, and grew more alike as social distinctions blurred, the late medieval gardens of these types of residence can be discussed together.

Their gardens all belonged to fortified houses built according to the quadrangular plan, or at least the rudiments of it, and they all belonged to people who could afford and were interested in fashionable pleasure gardening. These people, broadly speaking the upper reaches of society, lived in homes designed primarily for delight, domestic only in the most indulgent sense. These houses were designed according to a pattern that had already become formalized by the late thirteenth century, and was basic to English stately homes from the mid-fourteenth to the seventeenth century: that of a private wing and a kitchen and service wing, separated by a hall.

Some gardens were enclosed within the walls; orchards and vineyards were generally, but not always, outside them. Wanswell Court in Gloucestershire is a small fifteenth-century manor house, surrounded by a large, wide moat, which used to enclose all its house and farm buildings and its orchards and gardens.

Those who lived in castles made them into fortified mansions, indistinguishable from manor houses like Haddon Hall and Wanswell Court. By the mid-fifteenth century this transformation was complete, but castles had been steadily tending towards it, both architecturally and horticulturally, as the age became less warlike. Jousting became more popular as it became more histrionic, leaving the real, bloody tournaments of the twelfth and early thirteenth centuries behind. By the mid-thirteenth century, tournaments usually took the form of Round Table, a military game and a social gathering at which people watched jousting with blunted weapons, wrestling, skipping, stone- and lance-casting, dart-shooting, bowls and other sports. John Yoland, the Earl of Huntingdon, and the half-brother of Richard II, was a passionate devotee of jousting, and built his great mansion of Dartington, in south Devon, around a central quadrangle of private apartments, and made the quadrangle into a tiltyard.

[114]

Other leisure activities were also on the increase. Clare Castle, Suffolk, in the late fourteenth century interim period between the building of the huge, concentric Edwardian fortresses and the building of the fifteenth-century fortified manors, already had many features associated with the leisured domesticity of the latter. It had three towers, the names of which were Constablestower, Auditorstower and Maidenstower, names indicative of its military, domestic and romantic life. The moat had been made into a swannery and the castle was full of gardens. There were vines at the Great Gate, as there had been since early Norman times. There was a close-garden, which had its own pool, and there was a Lady Walk, which was near the Maidenstower, and sounds as if it was part of a feminine quarter for the castle's few female residents. By 1450 the castle accounts refer to new paling being put round 'Le Maydengarden'. Castles had come a long way since the days of the single keep.

Yet the keep survived until the close of the Middle Ages in the form of the pele tower. This was a defensive tower to which a quadrangle of residential buildings was added, and it was the most common type of fortified building along the Scottish border in the late fourteenth and early fifteenth centuries. This was a reversal of the trend in the rest of England, which from the late thirteenth century onwards was towards the building of manor houses, with fortifications attached.

The records of late fourteenth and early fifteenth century domesticated castles and fortified manors and palaces give some hints about the appearance of the gardens they contained. The records of Sheen Palace, in Surrey, for instance, which reverted to the Crown in about 1313, catalogue its development by Edward III. Between 1358 and 1361 he spent the kingly sum of £25.19s.0d. on the cultivation of the garden and the planting of vines in it. In 1366-7 he had the cloisters paved, and a herbarium made in the middle of them, in the monastic style which we have already seen in use at royal palaces, and which became very popular at this period. After a hiatus in Henry IV's reign, perhaps because Sheen had been the favourite palace of his deposed predecessor, the vast works at Sheen were renewed in the early fifteenth century, and expanded still further after Henry VI's marriage in 1445, in order to accommodate the new Queen graciously. The clerk of the works was ordered to 'new make the water-bridge' and 'a great quadrangle with a gatehouse' and 'a brick wall to enclose the garden'. A number of royal and baronial palaces had cloister gardens and vineyards like the ones at Sheen.

There was a vineyard at the royal palace of Rotherhithe, in Surrey, from which the grapes were to be carried to the King, wherever he was, in panniers specially bought for this purpose in 1363 and 1366. The gardens at Rotherhithe were extensive, and expensively maintained. In 1354 the gardener there, whose name was Philip, kept a detailed account of his expenses, which gives us an idea of their size and cultivation. He spent 5s.10d. on 14 lbs. of parsley seeds, 'for sowing in the King's garden in February'; 1s. on 12 lbs. of onion seeds to be sown in the same month; 3s. on 12 lbs. of leek seeds; 2s.6d on 4 pecks 1 gallon¹ of hyssop seeds, and 7s. on 3 gallons of vegetable seeds. Besides these seeds for the kitchen and the King's garden, Philip bought 3s.4d. worth of 'various plants for various trees, from John of Preston on January 4th', and 22d. worth of plants from John Aleyn and his companion. The gardens were enclosed by fences and plaited hedges, for Philip bought 'a thousand gross of twigs to enclose the King's garden, at 2s. per hundred gross, costing altogether 20s., and 8 bundles of small twigs with which to bind the big twigs, at a cost of 16d.' He also paid labourers 14s.8d. to cut and collect a cartload of old branches from the Isle of Thanet, and bring them to Rotherhithe in a hired cart. There was a huge force of hired labour working in the gardens, most of them working only in spring and summer. In 1354 the wages bill for the gardens came to £34.8s.11¾d., out of a total expense account for the castle and grounds of £386.15s.2d.

There were often eighteen labourers working together in the gardens in March and April, at the generous wage of 4d. a day, and many of them were clearly palace workmen borrowed from their usual work: they were surnamed Carpenter, Baker, Smith, Garlic-monger, Larderer, Hayward, Wallmaker, etc. Many of them were women, and they all worked under the direction of Philip and, in 1355, a second gardener called Richard Beansmith. There must have been more than one wallmaker working at Rotherhithe, for in 1354 one Thomas Cook, a mason, was paid £17.10s.0d. for making seven perches of stone wall around the moat of the manor, the stone being the King's sandstone and limestone. The whole place was moated and walled; its gardens were enormous, well kept, and productive, and they may have included pleasure gardens that are not

1   i.e. 9 gallons or 72 lbs., altogether

mentioned in the garden accounts because they are accounted in the building accounts, which are lost to us. Pleasure gardens such as must have existed in many university colleges, palaces and castles at this time are described in a series of accounts for the gardens of Winchester College between 1394, when the college was occupied by William of Wykeham's fellows and scholars, and 1437. The first reference to plants in Wykeham's gardens is the reference in the 1396 account to the purchase of 1 lb. of onion seed for 9d., and it is followed by the purchase of 4d. worth of garlic, which shows that the garden had the right, alliaceous priorities. The gardener bought a long cord for measuring the garden, at the very high cost of 2s.6d., which implies that it was specially marked or knotted in some way, and was probably used to measure and mark out the pleasure garden. It might even have been a special decorative rope that was laid out along the borders of the garden, instead of railings. In 1397 some thread for measuring the garden was bought at the much more reasonable cost of 1d; this was obviously plain thread or string.

In this same year work began on the pleasure garden. An assistant was hired to help the gardener 'make the garden ordained anew'. The next year one Henry Knyght spent six months surveying the new garden and supervising the men working on it, and in 1399 it was ready to be planted: 7s.6d. worth of 'little plants' were sown by the gardener, who had the enchanting name, of which a medieval gardener had every right to be proud, of Thomas Daisy. Daisies were very popular flowers in the Middle Ages, not persecuted trespassers on bare lawns as they are today.

With the help of workmen, the gardener planted 1s.6d. worth of little plants in 1400, and 4s.2d. worth of seeds in 1401, but the account does not say whether they were for the pleasure or the vegetable garden or for both. The accounts for the next two years are lost, and the next surviving one is for 1404. It mentions a big payment (9s.7d.) made to two labourers for clearing and cleaning 'les alures' in 'le Bour'.

'Les alures' at Winchester may either have been alleys within an extensive arbour, or raised seats within a small one. In 1419 eighteen cartloads of rubbish were bought to raise the 'alures', and the number of references to 'alures' in the garden, outside as well as inside the arbour, suggests that they were alleys, garden counterparts of the allures on castle ramparts.

We are given a clearer picture of the arbour itself. In 1406 the gardener bought rods and canes 'for the Rosemondesbower', an interesting proof of the fact that Henry II's Rosamond garden at Woodstock begat a whole genre, and a name which suggests that the 'alures' in the arbour were indeed alleys, and made a sort of labyrinthine pleasance in imitation of the maze at Woodstock. This pleasance, whatever it was like, was hedged in and entered through a gate. Inside it were a lot of railings, some of them quite substantial, for branches were frequently bought to make and repair them, and also rods and osiers. These probably enclosed beds of flowers and sweet-smelling herbs – the Rosamondesbower often needed weeding. In 1408 an expensive new knife was bought for 1s.8d., to cut and trim the hedges, and an ell of linen cloth for 5d. to make an apron for the gardener, and two labourers were hired to weed the bower for six days.

Another possibility is that flowers were planted straight into the turf, to make a 'flowery mead', which was one of the simplest and most popular types of formal garden in the medieval period. This is, however, unlikely to have been the case. Arbours were generally enclosed areas within flowery meads, and also, such meads needed re-turfing every three or four years, and there is no mention of this in the Winchester accounts. In 1418 some rods were bought 'for making les traylinges', which suggests lattice structure. Similar lattices of sweet-smelling flowers and blossoms may also have overhung the alleyways in the outer garden. The railings which bordered these walks were always being repaired and replaced, and the walks themselves measured and raised, so the garden was obviously used a lot. Such gardens always were. They were a place to play, to relax after the evening meal in summer, and to talk. Love-trysts, battle plans and prize givings were made in gardens. Then, as now, they were havens of repose; at Winchester probably of scholarship too, and of refuge from it. In 1437 the accounts specify for the first time the length of thread bought to measure the garden: 14 fathoms (84 ft.) Even if this measurement is exclusive of the vegetable patch, and a measurement of length only, not perimeter, the garden was a small one to accommodate an arbour and so many plants, trees and walks. It must have been very much like the garden shown in the fourteenth-century manuscript illumination opposite p. 80.

This was an arbour, complete with seat, and a couple using it as a 'privy playing place' for checkers. It has railings and a railed alleyway, flower beds, flowery turf, trees and a surrounding wall, all within a very small enclosure so close to the chambers of the house that the householder could do what Lancelot did in the *Romance of King Arthur*: 'he awakened of his swoon, and leapt out of a window into the garden.'

A gardener was an essential member of staff in households like the one in the illustration. At Winchester there was always a full-time gardener, who could have extra help when necessary, and had the woodwork, of which there was a lot, done for him by a carpenter. There was a new gardener every few years, paid an annual salary of anything between 13s.4d. and £1, which means that there were a lot of gardeners in the Winchester area, of varying ability and perhaps with varying specialities.

Sometimes they were simply called 'William the Gardener' or 'Philip the Gardener', but usually their names were more particular, albeit rather enigmatic: Thomas Daisy, John Springold, John Park, William Park, John Polwegge (pull wedge), John Attwater, Nicholas Drake. Their special cares were 'les alures' and 'le bour', names which betray the French influence on gardening at this period. This was a genuine horticultural, not just a linguistic, influence, for these two items are the only ones in the accounts written in French, and they are specialist horticultural items.

4

Love Gardens

'Paradise', said St Augustine, 'is a place where there are trees growing.' He had some other things to say about it, but this simple statement gives us a crucial insight into the medieval vision of Paradise. According to St Augustine, it was generally thought of in three ways: materially, as a place somewhere on the earth; spiritually, as a state of the soul, and in both ways at different times. He himself thought of it in this last, double way, which was the one that appealed most to the medieval mind. The basic image of it which each of the views interpreted was the one described in *Genesis* 2: 8-9: the place with trees to which St Augustine alluded; the Garden of Eden.

This retained its original features, as described in *Genesis*, throughout its medieval career: luxuriant, shady trees, including the Tree of Life and the Tree of the Knowledge of Good and Evil, abundant fruit, and a river which parted into four streams. Some early Church Fathers took the location given in *Genesis*, 'eastward in Eden', quite literally, and preached that the Garden was in the East, somewhere between the Tigris, Euphrates, Nile and Ganges, though this presented them with the insoluble problem of finding a spot where these four rivers joined. Others preached that the Garden was on earth but had something of heaven about it, and was therefore on a mountain or some high place, somewhere in the east. A few placed it near Jerusalem, but most interpreted it allegorically.

Origen (185-254), and Cyprian (200-258) saw in it the likeness of the Church, whose trees were its saints, watered by the four rivers of the Gospels. St Ambrose (340-391) saw in it the allegory which has been the dominant Christian one for Paradise ever since: that of the interior of the soul, the *anima fecunda* of Ambrose's *De Paradiso*. St Augustine, being blessed with the greatest intellect in the early Church, interpreted it in his *De Civitate Dei* as an allegory of the

Church, as Origen and Cyprian had done, and in his *De Genesi* as an Ambrosian allegory of the soul, with the tree of life representing wisdom, and the four streams the four cardinal virtues. St Bonaventura distinguished the earthly from the heavenly Paradise as the Church militant from the Church Triumphant. All the interpretations with which their symbolism was concerned concentrated on the Garden of Eden, as described in *Genesis*.

But there was one other garden which shared with Eden this central position as the medieval image of Paradise. Sometimes, especially in the early part of the period, it was distinguished from the Garden of Eden; more often it was amalgamated with it to make a single Biblical archetype of Paradise. Throughout the whole of Judeo-Christian history it has been the most popular image of Paradise and love because of its matchless beauty, and it was this which earned the name *The Song of Songs* for the poem about it which tradition attributes to King Solomon.

It is a love poem, made up of a series of exchanges between lover and beloved, and its central image is a garden, which is the symbol of the beloved, the bride:

> She is a garden enclosed,
> My sister, my promised bride;
> A garden enclosed,
> A sealed fountain.   (4:12)

In sensuous, erotic language, the poem describes this sealed garden, watered by a well or fountain of living water; a garden of lilies and of the Rose of Sharon; fragrant, breezy and full of the rarest fruits.

> Breathe over my garden,
>   prays the bride to the north and south winds
> To spread its sweet smell around.
> Let my beloved come into his garden,
> Let him taste its rarest fruits.   (4:16)

This garden was the model for all the medieval romance gardens, both sacred and secular. Its rhythms, language, images, symbols and meaning recur in the art and literature of the whole period; by the twelfth century it had overshadowed its archetypal partner, the Garden of Eden, and became the dominant image of Paradise and love. For it was an earthly garden as well as a heavenly one and, like Eden, was interpreted both representatively and allegorically, as an image of human and of divine love. Within these two interpretations there were five different ways of understanding it.

The most popular interpretations understood the *Song* as an allegory, either of the individual soul and its creator, whose marriage was the *hieros gamos*, the mystical union, towards which every soul aspires, or of Marian love, wherein the bride was the Blessed Virgin, beloved of Christ.

'A garden enclosed is my sister, my bride,' wrote Gregory of Nyssa in the fourth century, at the start of one of his treatises on the soul.

Hugh of St Victor made a list of its trees and flowers and their allegorical values; his disciple Richard of St Victor, gave a detailed tropological description of it, which included instructions on matters like how to weed it and how to keep the fountain of the devout soul supplied by the spring waters of the Holy Spirit's graces. Such is the *Song*'s beauty that its appeal never faded; it was even more dominant as the image of Paradise in the later medieval period than it had been in the earlier.

It was the favourite text of St Bernard, who understood it in the same way as St Thomas Aquinas, as an allegory of the soul's union with God. St Bernard was one of the great apostles of love who enthralled twelfth-century Europe with the chivalrous devotion of their love. His prayers are troubadour love songs dedicated to the Blessed Virgin Mary and, like those of his contemporaries and those of St Anselm (1033-1108), who was really the founder of the whole movement of 'affective piety', are often indistinguishable from the secular love songs of the period. St Francis (1182-1226) actually nicknamed himself 'God's wandering minstrel', and dedicated himself to Lady Poverty, in the best tradition of courtly love, which is central to an understanding of symbolic gardens from the twelfth century onwards because it sees the garden, the bride, as the Blessed Virgin Mary, beloved of Christ, her marriage with him being the miraculous one of creature and creator, and also mother and child, which resulted in the birth of the Saviour.

The Marian interpretation is the key to the medieval rose-garden, the main subject for discussion in this chapter. In the interpretative chronology of the *Song* it first comes to the fore in the seventh century, at the same time as the cult of Mary the Virgin and the Mystical Rose, with both of which it was intrinsically bound up. Like them, it flourished in the twelfth-century enthusiasm for courtly love, in the grip of which the Cistercians first gave Mary the title 'Our Lady'. Thomas the Cistercian's commentary on the *Song* reads like a classical *florilegium*, and mixes the images of Latin love poetry with those of the Christian *Song*. The association of Our Lady with the rose and with the sealed garden of roses and lilies described in the *Song,*

I am the Rose of Sharon,
The lily of the valleys,

lasted in England until the Reformation, and in the Catholic Church it exists to this day.

It has an exact parallel in secular love, the word 'secular' being used here as distinct from 'mystical'. The love between man and woman, bridegroom and bride, was sacred, despite being merely human, because love was reckoned to be a divine gift, and in its married form, consecrated by Christ. In view of this, it is easy to see how Our Lady and a human lady could become interchangeable objects of devotion. But the human lady could only be the rose, the sealed garden of the *Song*, if she was loved with the love of Charity, which was the new love brought to the world by Christ so that man could be saved. It was St Augustine who expounded Charity as the law governing every kind of true Christian love, and as the opposite of Cupidity, which was the love of any creature, including oneself, for its own sake.

The *Song* is vibrantly sexual; its language and images are erotic. According to Augustine, if it is used for the purposes of idolatrous sexual love, it is made into a symbol of extreme Cupidity, ruled by worldly wisdom. But if Christ is its gardener, and it is used for the purposes of married or chaste love, it is a symbol of Charity, suffused by warm, Charitable breezes and ruled by divine wisdom. Charity was at the heart of the *fin amour* of courtly love; its reverend nature raised the lover above himself, and so was the means of his achieving perfection. It was his route into the very paradise garden from which his fallen nature excluded him, into the *hortus conclusus* of the *Song* and into Eden. For by the late twelfth century these two gardens had been amalgamated, and infused with classical, Eastern and other Biblical traditions to form one single, supreme, medieval image of Paradise.

The classical *locus amoenus* was very similar to the Garden of Eden. It was a beautiful land full of trees, flowers, birds, rocks and rivers. It was just what its name suggests: a pleasant place for the souls of the blessed to inhabit. The important thing about it for our purposes is that it was a place, not a garden. The classical world liked open vistas. Secure within the walls of its villas and towns, and within its imperial hegemony, it enjoyed looking out on to the steep slopes and far distances beyond. Not so the medieval world, which liked to ward them off and to enclose itself within the safety of walls. To the medieval mind Paradise was definitely an enclosure, which is why the enclosed garden of the *Song* made a stronger appeal to it than the relatively expansive Garden of Eden.

Eden, however, was never completely abandoned. No Biblical image of Paradise could have been in the Middle Ages. To late Antiquity it was a Christian version of the Roman *patria*; to the Celts it was the longed-for homeland to which one was always striving to return. Associated with the *locus amoenus* which the Medievals inherited from the Ancients, and Christianized, it was frequently used as a sort of periphery for the enclosed Paradise garden which lay within it: an earthly paradise attendant upon the heavenly one. If the *locus amoenus* element in it was uppermost, it appeared as a flowery, riverside meadow, usually in the middle of a wilderness; if the Eden element was uppermost, it appeared as an orchard or grove, often affording the lover entrance to the sealed garden within it by means of a tree overhanging the garden wall.

There was no firm distinction made between the earthly and the heavenly Paradise. Some, like St Bonaventura, did distinguish the two; the majority were content to have both of them united in one Paradise, and if they made a distinction it was only an implicit one, in the shape of a sealed garden within a meadow or an orchard. In the early Middle Ages in particular, there was often no distinction made between orchard and Paradise garden.

As time passed, the *locus amoenus* meadow element and the Eden orchard or wood element tended to be let slip to the fringes of the enclosed Paradise garden, and by the thirteenth century the latter had become the absolutely dominant Paradise image, absorbing the features of a distinctly peripheral Eden. The more the wilds and the woods were confronted and tamed, which they were in fact and in romance from the twelfth century onwards, the more important walled gardens became. The womb-like, sheltering quality of flowery meadows and groves was diminished when the wilderness around them was diminished. In a dark forest, a meadow ranked as a sanctuary; in a flowery meadow or a pleasant wood, only a walled garden ranked as one. And so it was that such meadows and wood, *loci amoeni* and Edens, came to be used in later medieval literature as settings for the central action, and often for the central gardens of romance. By the late fourteenth century the flowery meadow in Maytime, and the stream by the grove of trees, were absolutely standard openings for love poems.

The Eden version of that Paradise had one important asset which made some medieval writers prefer it to the sealed garden of the *Song*, and which continued to win it support throughout the period, despite the dominance of the *Song*. That was the mystical Tree of Life which is common to all the major religions.

Eden was a tree garden, and the mystical trees of good and evil which grew in it never lost their appeal for the Medievals; indeed it increased throughout the period. The New Testament constantly uses trees as symbols, the greatest of them being the Tree of the Cross itself. Because of its rôle in the Redemption, it was depicted as the opposite of the Tree of Sins. As the Tree of the Cross became a more and more popular theme from the twelfth to the fourteenth century, so did the theme of the two opposing trees of good and evil. Whole systems of vices and virtues were worked out on these symbolic trees. The shade of the Tree of Good was generally represented in the Middle Ages as Sapientia – the true wisdom of Solomon, *Ecclesiastes*, the *Book of Wisdom*, and the shade of the Tree of Evil as scientia – the false wisdom of the world. This was in accordance with the Augustinian dichotomy between Charity and Cupidity, which was the basis of the whole iconographical scheme of the opposing trees.

In the late fourteenth century, when the sealed garden of the *Song* had been the Paradise Garden for over two centuries, Langland still chose the Tree of Charity 'which groweth in a garden that God made Himself' (an echo of 'the garden planted by the Lord God' in *Genesis* 2:8) as the central symbol of his vision of Middle Earth, which was a compound of Eden and the *locus amoenus*, in his work *The Vision of Piers Plowman*. The tree symbolism of Eden was its most enduring symbolic asset, and as Eden came increasingly to be enclosed within the walls of the *hortus conclusus* in Paradise symbolism, its Tree of Life became one of the central motifs of that garden, as it had always been of Eden.

An Image of Reality

The amalgamation of these two symbolic gardens, though never absolute, was pretty well accomplished by the thirteenth century. It was due not only to the natural medieval liking for enclosure, which achieved solid expression in the castles and palaces of twelfth-century Europe, but also to the influence on Europe at that time of Persian culture, by way of the Arab conquests of Spain and Sicily, and the Crusades. The Persians were exquisite gardeners. They were cultivating roses even before the time of Christ, and considered them to be flowers of great luxury. When the Moslem Arabs conquered Persia and Syria in the sixth century, they were impressed with the beautiful rose-gardens they found in both countries, and set about imitating them.

Aristocratic Persian gardens were quadrangular enclosures, often divided into four equal squares by streams flowing from a central fountain, which was one of the two indispensable features of a good garden in their desert society. The other one was shade, and this was provided by a tree positioned next to the fountain, or by a group of trees making a shady walk. The similarities between these Persian gardens and the Garden of Eden, as described in *Genesis*, are obvious, and indeed the very word 'paradise' comes from the Persian word *pairidaeza*, meaning a walled garden. The poetry, art and courtly rituals of medieval Persia are full of garden imagery, and its high society was full of paradises. Sometimes they were tiled; often they were turfed and planted with flowers.

They first came to Europe, along with the name 'paradise' for this kind of garden, through the agency of the Byzantine Church, and first found a western European home in the cloister gardens of monasteries, which were a combination of Persian paradises and classical courtyards.

It was a combination of monastic influence on early medieval society; the Arab conquests, first of Persia and Syria, then of Egypt and southern Spain, and the middle Eastern influence on Europe which resulted from the Crusades, that freed paradises from monastic enceintes and spread them abroad as the rose-gardens of courtly Christendom.

Monasteries were the refuges of early medieval culture in Europe. Many of them contained flower gardens, which supplied flowers for the decoration of the church and the altar, for medicinal purposes and for the spiritual and aesthetic delight of the monks. Monastic gardeners spread the cultivation of flowers to the gardens of Merovingian and Carolingian castles, palaces and cities, expounding its three fold value as they did so. Monastic women made a particularly important contribution to the spread of flower gardening for medical purposes; its spread for symbolic reasons, also by monastic brethren will be elucidated in the course of this chapter.

While it is probable that monasteries got the paradise format for their rose-gardens from the Middle East, by way of Byzantium, it is certain that they got Middle Eastern help, by way of influence on the Crusaders, in spreading that format through Europe in the twelfth and thirteenth centuries. Thibault IV, Count of Champagne, for example, brought the rose of Provins back to Europe with him from Syria, and it soon became a European favourite. The Christian monks were helped by Moslem as well as Christian warriors in their work of horticultural education and dissemination. Influenced, like the Crusaders, by Persian paradises, the Moslem Arabs spread them through their European dominions, starting as early as the eighth century.

They took up the culture and veneration of the rose which they learnt in Persia, and made the rose a sacred Muslim flower, just as it was a sacred Persian one. One of the most popular early Muslim legends tells how the rose was born out of the sweat of Mohammed's brow. Persians and Arabs alike celebrated roses as 'a messenger of the garden of souls'.

By the twelfth century the influence of the Moslems on Europe had gone far towards identifying rose cultivation with the keeping of walled paradise gardens. The paradise garden captivated the romantic imagination of Europe, already possessed as it was by the sealed garden imagery of the *Song*, and confirmed the final supremacy of that garden as the image of Paradise.

In order to understand the full subtlety and intricacy of medieval rose-garden symbolism, which is too often looked at superficially, it is necessary to examine briefly the symbolic importance of the rose, and all the connotations of that, from the beginning of its history. This coalesces naturally with the examination of the history of garden symbolism, and makes it fully understandable.

The Place of the Rose in Medieval Symbolism

The rose first appears as a European garden flower and romantic symbol far back in the oldest monuments of Hellenic poetry. According to Herodotus, roses were brought to Greece by Midas, whose rose garden in Macedonia was famous for many centuries for its beauty and fragrance, and was visited by Herodotus himself.

They were definitely cultivated in Asia Minor and Greece in the seventh century BC, and Greek colonists took them to some of the islands in the eastern Mediterranean and to Sicily and meridional Italy, where they flourished and were valued as highly by the Romans as they had been by the Greeks.

They became the top flowers of the Roman deities, as they had been of the Greek deities before them, and in particular the deities of love. Roman legends linking Venus with the first roses are significant for our medieval interest because they establish two connections which lasted, in a Christianized form, throughout the Middle Ages: one between roses and the God of Love, and one between red roses and the blood of a divine victim or a martyr. In fact the Romans described their red roses as purple, and the adjective 'rosy' became synonymous in late ancient poetry with purple, then with brilliant, beautiful or gilded. In like manner medieval poetry celebrated (as in this fifteenth-century carol to the Blessed Virgin)

> the purple rose
> That whylom [once] grew in Jericho,

and used the rose as a synonym for beauty.

Joy, beauty and love were the main classical associations of the rose and its Goddess, Venus. But there were three other classical associations of the rose, which also continued to exist in the medieval period, and were linked with the rose's romantic symbolism in both periods. The first is the association of the rose with fertility and the season of Spring; the second the association of the rose with pleasure and enjoyment; and the third, because love can be painful as well as pleasant, and because the rose was the classical symbol of love, the association of the rose with death. Along with lilies and violets, roses were laid on the tombs of the beloved, and in graveyards. Their romantic significance contained a reminder of the evanescence of love, and of life itself; the more complete the bliss of love, the more melancholy the knowledge that it must fade and die, just as the spring and summer seasons fade into autumn and winter. Time is of the essence in a temporal world; there is neither time nor the passing of time in Paradise. This was the one inescapable difference between secular and sacred medieval love gardens.

Gardens, being Biblical symbols of love and Paradise, were eagerly taken up by the early Church Fathers. The rose, by contrast, was an object of suspicion because of its place of honour in pagan society. The fourth and fifth centuries were ascetic ones in the Christian

Church. In fact it was their very asceticism, and the dogmatic resolution of their religious quarrels, that eventually gave birth to the cult of Mary, the Mother of God, and of the rose as her symbol. The desert Fathers and early monastic communities found the femininity and comfort they needed to sustain them in devotion to Mary, and satisfied their asceticism by emphasizing her personal excellence and the purity of her motherhood. She became the protectress of penitents. After the Council of Nicæa in 325 Mary was frequently spoken of as Theotokos, the Mother of God, and at the Council of Ephesus in 431 her motherhood was declared a doctrine. According to the Christian poets, Mary's motherhood enclosed the whole of heaven and earth within her womb, within the space of a single round rose. The all-in-one, one-in-all rose of love, once praised in pagan poems, became a Christian rose.

The rose had freed itself of initial Christian disapproval by its own irresistibility and had become, even before Mary, a symbol of decorative and mystical devotion. Paulinus of Nola (345-431) and St Jerome (342-420) revoked their bans on roses and encouraged the faithful to decorate their churches with them. Sts Basil (329-379) and Ambrose (340-397) allowed their instincts to overcome their formal reservations, and declared the rose the most perfect of flowers – one which had been without thorns when it grew in Paradise, until the disobedience of Adam and Eve gave sharp spikes to its beauty.

As had been the case in classical antiquity, the rose became not only the symbol of the Goddess of Love but, when red in colour, the symbol of the blood of a martyr. The greatest martyr of them all was, of course, Jesus Christ, who thus had a double association with the rose: as the child and creator of the Marian rose, and as the supreme rose of martyrdom. Christ was the *sol æquitatis, fons bonorum, flos dei* ('sun of justice, fount of all good, flower of God') according to Paulinus of Nola, and his five bleeding wounds were the five petals of the red rose, his crown of thorns the thorns of the rose bush.

The Gospel accounts of the life of Christ, coupled with the garden images of the Old Testament, offered a range of symbolic possibilities to Christians that far outstripped the range available to their classical predecessors, and medieval Christendom exploited this offer to its furthest limits. As far as the Marian rose was concerned, it was greatly helped by the early medieval promulgation of doctrines about Mary, who had received comparatively scant attention from the evangelists, and needed fuller treatment to establish her as the supreme symbol of Christian femininity. It was the doctrine of her motherhood that first inspired devotion to her as the Mystical Rose, and it was the doctrine of the Virgin Birth that expanded Mary's rose symbolism into the most important, complex and elaborate motif of medieval art and literature, both sacred and profane. Soon after the acceptance of the doctrine, the early Church Fathers began to make the obvious allegorical identification of Mary's inviolate womb with the sealed garden of the *Song*, penetrated only by God. A closed gate, through which only Christ could enter; a precious stone, through which the sun of Christ's light shone; a sealed fountain; an enclosed garden – these were the early images of the Virgin Birth. Wreaths, crowns and garlands were hung on church statues, especially those of the martyrs and of the Virgin, in her month of May, just as they had been hung in Greek and Roman temples. The medieval cult of the Virgin Mary brought the virginal and the triumphant together in this one symbol, the age-old defence of the closed circle against evil, the symbol of perfection, nobility, virginity and victory, and completed its Marian dedication by weaving that symbolic crown or wreath out of roses.

The early identification of Mary with a red and white rose, which symbolized both her love and her virginity, was never a poetic success because there was no such rose, and the image was too artificial; the double image of rose and lily was much more popular. Both flowers are mentioned by name in the *Song*, and the fact that the Rose of Sharon was probably the crocus or narcissus, and the lily the Palestine anemone, didn't detract from their significance. The Rose of Sharon appears several times in the Old Testament. The lily appears in both the Old and the New Testaments as a symbol of purity and innocent beauty; it was a common healing medicine in the Middle Ages, and soon became a symbol for spiritual healing and a cure for sins. It was also an ancient fertility symbol, and this complement to its healing purity made it the ideal complement to the rose of the Virgin Birth. The little, pale, gently fragrant violet secured itself a place as the symbol of Mary's humility from the start, though its very virtue prevented it from ever having the charisma of the lily and the rose.

With the cult of the Virgin and the rose growing to include such a wealth of symbolic meanings and flowers, it was not long before Mary began to be hailed as the Flower of Flowers. Nor was it long before she figured in many stories of saints' lives, especially those in which she intervened directly to help her faithful, taking the form of miraculously appearing roses. Rose legends proliferated, and reached the peak of their popularity in the twelfth century. Perhaps the most famous of them was the legend of Josbert, a monk who recited the five psalms that begin with the letters of the name Maria every day. On the feast of St Andrew, 1156, the Prior noticed that Josbert was not in chapel with the rest of the community at prayer time. He went to look for him in his cell, and found him dead, with a rose in his mouth, one in each ear and one in each eye: one for each of the five letters of the name Maria. This little story has all the favourite ingredients of twelfth-century religious symbolism: monastic devotion to Mary; her intimate, rosy reciprocity; the sacred number five, reminiscent of the five wounds of Christ, and the rose as the token of love for the departed.

Like all the facets of the rose cult once associated with paganism, the use of roses as tokens of love and grief for the dead was at first condemned by the Church, then adopted and expanded. Monastic burial grounds were often planted as rose-gardens, in prefiguration of the Paradise garden to which it was hoped that the departed had gone, and to bless them with the image of Mary, so that they might continue to love it in death as they had done in life.

The Beginnings of Earthly Love

Amor (love), *dilectio* (pleasure or delight), *caritas* (charity), were the basic elements of monastic love, both fraternal and divine, in early medieval Europe, and became the basic elements of the courtly love cult which swept western Europe in the twelfth and thirteenth centuries, applying all the devices of love for Mary in heaven to the love of a woman on earth.

The quintessence of Mary's perfection was her virginity, just as the perfect love between a troubadour and his lady was above all 'pure'. St Augustine's doctrine of Charity was the inspiration of this pure secular love, which was the love of the troubadours, Minnesingers and other courteous lovers. The more deeply religious the language of divine love, the closer it was to the language of courtesy.

The old German word for this inspirational harmony of divine and human love was *minne* – Aristotle's 'love of friendship' which he says is based on the love of what is noblest in oneself and, since a friend is part of oneself, what is noblest in him or her, so that the two selves come towards wholeness. This wholeness is the closed rose garden of the *Song of Songs*, the rose wreath, the inviolate rose, serenaded by the Minnesingers and all the earthly love poets, who were intoxicated by it.

'A beautiful melody of spirit sang within him, and sometimes burst out, and the divine murmur of his soul broke out in transports in a song,' wrote Thomas of Celano (ca 1200-55), a biographer of St Francis. Collections of such songs, and of prayers, hymns and devotional works began to be called flower gardens. People said the prayers of a *hortus deliciarum* (garden of delights), a common alternative to the *hortus conclusus* as a symbol for the Church, the New Jerusalem and the individual soul; a *hortulus animæ* (little garden of the soul), a *gilgengart* (lily garden) or, most commonly of all, a *rosarium* (rose-garden), which is the origin of the word rosary.

The connection between the Christian rosary beads and the medieval rosary or rose-garden was made in Europe some time in the twelfth and thirteenth centuries. It began much earlier, when the Irish monks first gave psalter singing an important place in religious devotion, and divided the psalms into three sets of fifty. They incorporated the saying of 'fifties', which is what they called the Little Psalter, into their devotions, and made strings of beads, usually in circlets, but sometimes open, to help them keep count. The repetition of a single prayer as a background to meditation is an age-old prayer technique, and the fifties soon came to consist entirely of Pater Nosters, and in the eleventh century, in accordance with the cult of the Virgin Mary, Hail Marys.

The Hail Mary first appeared in about 1050, and was already popular by the twelfth century. It was a particular favourite of the Cistercians. At the same time hymns of praise, the majority of them dedicated to Mary, were being written and sung in great numbers, and a collection of these was known as a rosarium or rosary. It was only a short time before the collection of Hail Marys recited on the beads was also called a rosary, and soon afterwards the beads themselves. They were first called a rosary by Thomas of Cantipre in the thirteenth century. Inside this garden of prayer is the mystical rose, enclosed by five decades of prayers to Mary, each decade devoted to a divine mystery on which one meditated while praying. There are five joyful, five sorrowful and five glorious mysteries, and from the thirteenth century onwards they were one of the most popular forms of prayer and meditation in Europe, particularly in England.

Images of Christ in The Garden

The rose-garden belonged to its queen, be she heavenly or human, but she had to be loved and served by a knight if its secrets were to be known to anyone besides herself. Mary is shown in rosary paintings as a madonna with her child, just as the earthly beloved in the rose-garden is shown, at some stage of her stay in the garden, together with her lover (see illustrations p. 81). The figure of Christ as the knightly lover of Mary and mankind was a familiar one in medieval literature, and the Ambrosian image of the blood he shed for man as a red rose was taken up with fervent elaboration from the late thirteenth century onwards. Christ's wounds were also a highpoint of affective devotion from the thirteenth century onwards, and they were most commonly symbolized by a fountain or well, by which means they found a place in the more agonized art and literature of garden symbolism.

Less bloody, more restful images of Christ's wounds were less popular with artists than with poets, who wrote some of the most sophisticated poetry of the period in some of its most restrained language. The fourteenth-century mystic, Juliana of Norwich, called the wound in Christ's side 'a fair, delectable place, and large enough for all mankind that shall be saved to rest in peace and love', in a prose meditation which used the arbour image in preference to the more usual image of the wound as a window in Noah's ark.

Christ himself only made the occasional appearance in such literature, as the gardener cultivating the herbal virtues of the soul. His presence in medieval symbolic gardens is almost always invisible and mysterious. It is implicit, not explicit, in the choice of the garden as the prime symbolic setting. The two turning-points in the Gospel story: the agony and arrest of Christ, which mark the beginning of his passion, and the resurrection, take place in gardens, fulfilling the sense of promise that blows in the breezes of the *Song of Songs* garden and flows through the streams of Eden. A garden is a secret place, enclosing within it the mysteries of the Old and New Testaments.

The later Middle Ages, however, did find one way of giving Christ a figurative presence in the symbolic garden, in its most common usage as a metaphor of the Virgin Birth, and it was a way which had a secular as well as a religious application. The device in question is the unicorn legend. With the efflorescence of devotion to the Blessed Virgin in the thirteenth and fourteenth centuries, this legend became a symbol of the whole life and death of Christ, foreshadowing the whole plan of the Redemption, and Mary had a vital part in both these. But it began in the early Middle Ages as a much simpler allegory.

The legend is a very old one, which first appeared in Christian history in about AD 300, in the *Physiologus*, a collection of animal stories made at Alexandria, and later called *The Bestiary*.

The legend said that the unicorn was a small but fierce animal, resembling a kid, but with a sharp horn on his head. He was solitary and fleet of foot, running so fast that huntsmen could never catch him, unless a virgin was near by. If that was the case, the unicorn would lay his head in her lap and fall asleep, while she stroked it. The huntsman could then catch him and lead him to the king's palace.

The unicorn's small stature symbolized Christ's humility, and his fierceness the wrathful strength of the Messiah: 'God brought them out of Egypt; he hath as it were the strength of the unicorn.' (*Numbers* 23:22) His resemblance to a kid symbolized Christ's association with sinful men. The horn in his head was a symbol of Christ's power. The unicorn's solitary life was a feature that had been emphasized from the earliest times – by Pliny, Aelian, and in their turn by the Church Fathers, who made it a symbol of the monastic life. It also explained the unicorn's ability to avoid capture, unless brought into the company of a virgin, who symbolized the Blessed Virgin. Less obviously, the huntsmen were interpreted as Gabriel and his angelic associates, acting through the Holy Spirit at the Annunciation. It followed from this that the unicorn's capture symbolized the incarnation of Christ. 'The God whom the whole earth could not contain did Mary contain and carry,' according to St Ephrem of Syria's fourth-century Homily on the Nativity.

This is how the unicorn legend was fitted into Marian devotion. In the late thirteenth and fourteenth centuries the purity of the unicorn because of his association with the Blessed Virgin was stressed more than any other aspect of this story. In the fifteenth century, the period from which nearly all the medieval pictures of the unicorn survive, he was shown in a closed garden, his head on Mary's lap, in a double allegory of the Virgin Birth, like the double allegory of the rosary, also shown in many late medieval pictures.

Christ was contained within Mary's womb both physically, by the unicorn's head in her lap, and also by the traditional use of the sealed garden as a symbol of Mary's virginity, inside which he lay. The unicorn was introduced into late medieval art precisely in order to preserve the religious meaning of the symbolic sealed garden, which was being encroached upon by the purely decorative, and by scenes from secular life. But it was only by being strongly secular itself that the unicorn legend could achieve this preservation. Its picturesque imagery and narrative appeal were ways of captivating the artist's liking for the beautiful, decorative and courtly, and keeping it within a scheme of religious symbolism. Being a story of hunting and of a fair maiden, it could satisfy the increasingly intrusive late medieval taste for both of these, and so keep them out of allegorical portrayals in which they had no place.

As far as the unicorn's secular popularity was concerned, this was successful. But as far as the portrayal of Paradise Gardens was concerned, it was only partially so, for in the late fourteenth and fifteenth centuries delight crept remorselessly into them at the expense of mystery. In some late paintings one is distracted by rabbits, hunting scenes and extraneous decorations, and the enclosure motif, central to the Virgin Birth allegory, has been reduced to a minor ornament. Such changes of setting are symptomatic of more than a sense of understandable boredom with a symbolic scheme that was centuries old, and a desire to embellish it a little; they suggest a quite different, secular scheme. For it is in the nature of the religious symbolic garden to keep the same setting: an unchanging enclosure within which the eternal has scope to change, transform, establish or what it will. There is no need for formal change when the spirit is divine. But if the spirit is secular, formal change is needed to prevent tedium and repetition; it puts new life into old symbolism.

Sacred and Secular Love Gardens

The difference between sacred and secular love gardens is not one of appearance; it is one of longevity. After the expulsion of Adam and Eve from Eden, gardens were testing-grounds of man's ability to see through their physical delights to the creative divinity that lay behind them. Fallen man, of course, could not do this without the help of God's grace, and the gardens in which he did not find this were fallen paradises, secular rosaries.

This is the theme of the *Pearl* romance, and of Chaucer's satires, *The Parliament of Fowls* and *The Merchant's Tale*, which are the great garden poems of the late fourteenth century, by which time sacred and secular paradises were more clearly distinguished than they had been in the twelfth and thirteenth centuries. Allegory had degenerated a long way from the picturesque subtlety it had been for the troubadours; in literature, as in the rival arts, it now displayed its sanctity or secularity didactically. One must go back to the early thirteenth century, to the *Romance of the Rose*, that mammoth romance which brings together all the descriptive and allegorical conventions of the Middle Ages into an allegory of man and the enclosed garden, to verify Augustine's proposition that the more heavily Charity is disguised in an allegorical work, the more beneficial its detection is for the reader. The poem is a humorous retelling of the Fall, so heavily disguised that it would have greatly pleased Augustine. Its very setting is an idyll of conventional courtly love. The poet is twenty years old at the time of his dream, and the season is spring, the month May,

> the time of love and jollity,
> When all things waxen gay.

And yet the idyll is its own danger. May does not last, nor do its roses. In the words of a thirteenth-century English lyric,

> Now shrinketh rose and lily flower,
> That whilen bore that sweet savour,
> In summer, that sweet tide.

The garden in the *Romance* must fade and die, as must all earthly gardens, when summer is gone. For medieval Christendom the passage of the year recalled the loss of the original Paradise garden of everlasting life and spring.

The *Romance* opens with the conventional courtly delight in Maytime love, hints at its vulnerability, shows that the rose-garden and its summer delights are an 'insubstantial pageant', and contrasts that pageant with the fields of bliss which are the reward of those who keep the law of nature. Not the law of man's fallen nature, but that of the God-given force governing life on earth.

> For nature hath not taken his beginning
> Of no party or cartel (portion) of a thing,
> But of a thing that perfect is and stable.

The *Romance* shows the testing rôle of earthly gardens both elliptically, in the Augustinian manner, and openly, in the fourteenth- and fifteenth-century manner, bringing together all the allegorical and descriptive traditions of the centuries before it and inspiring those of the centuries after it. Chaucer translated it, and used its ironic language and imagery in several of his works, most obviously *The Merchant's Tale*, which is a pointed satire, full of references to the Charitable Biblical gardens that had inspired the courteous art and literature of earlier generations, and were easily and frequently falsified.

Chaucer was nostalgic for the garden cult of those earlier generations. But not just for its Charitable gardens; also for its beguiling, delicious Cupiditous ones. Like most of his contemporaries, Chaucer enjoyed satirizing false paradises, but was not so self-righteous as to be immune from their appeal. Part of the fun for a good writer was to make such gardens appealing, just as the discerning reader's fun consisted partly in penetrating that appealing disguise to find out the doctrine beneath it, and partly in enjoying the appeal. The older he got, the more Chaucer delighted in the fleeting appeal of Venus's love gardens, only condemning them if they pretended to offer more than that.

Late fourteenth- and fifteenth-century poets did not find it unbearable to write about the short life of love; on the contrary, they dwelt on it with wistful enjoyment, and none more effectively than Chaucer. Early medieval works stressed the opposition between such delights and spiritual ones; later works stressed the co-operation between the two if they were fully, that is physically and metaphysically, understood.

By the fifteenth century this long tradition of simultaneously sacred and secular garden symbolism, which had dominated the arts in Europe since the efflorescence of courtly love lyrics in the twelfth century, was pretty well ended. Realism replaced symbolism in art and literature. Narrative replaced philosophical settings, the artistic potential of which was deemed to be exhausted. Painters favoured narratives, such as the unicorn legend, and detailed realism, such as can be seen in the illustrations to fifteenth-century books of hours and psalters. The Van Eyck brothers and their associates and contemporaries showed the subtle power of nature's forms, and so emancipated landscape painting at the expense of garden painting, in which landscape had been little more than a backcloth for most of the period. Taken out of its traditional medieval philosophical setting and put into a narrative one, it found the freedom outside the symbolic garden that it had always been denied inside it.

Poets, like artists, largely abandoned flower and garden symbolism, either in favour of Gothic exoticism or in favour of the realism favoured by artists. The poem 'I have a Flower', written in about 1500, is typical of that late medieval and early Tudor realism; its flowers constitute a garden inventory, not a symbolic scheme.

> Marjoram gentle, or lavender?
> Columbine, golds of sweet flavour?
> Primrose, violet or fresh daisy?
> Gillyflower gentle, or rosemary?
> Camomile, borage or savoury . . . ?
> The rose it is a royal flower.
> The red or the white? – show his colour!

With the Tudor rose of poems like this we have left the Middle Ages behind us. Love gardens are now no more than places to make love; the philosophical discussion and the symbolism of garden love are gone. What remains is the question whether medieval love gardens existed in fact or just in art and literature. Did people make rosaries and sealed gardens with symbolic flowers, trees and fountains?

The few records that survive reveal the existence of paradises in some medieval monasteries, at least some literary romance gardens, and several palace and manor rosaries. As well as these, there were the symbolic gardens of no fixed abode, mentioned in contemporary references to manorial households and in manorial and household records. Writers like Chaucer would not have referred to symbolic gardens so often, sometimes in realistic detail, if they had not expected them to have evocative power for their readers. There seems no reason to doubt that well-to-do and fashionable medieval society used its natural medieval aptitude for horticulture to make its fondest dreams come true.

5

'Many a Fresh and Sundry Flower'

Full gay was all the ground, and quaint,
And powdered, as men had it paint,
With many a fresh and sundry flower,
That casten up full good savour.

The casting up of full good savour is a good starting-point for this chapter because it is one of the things Medievals valued most about their flowers, as the above quotation from Chaucer's translation of the *Roman de la Rose* suggests. They liked their savours the same way as they liked their food and drink: strong enough to assault the senses, indeed to completely overwhelm those of modern man. In the stinking, pre-toilet world of medieval England, fragrance was understandably esteemed, the more so the stronger it was. Medieval literature celebrated it as one of the most perfect forms of beauty, and women of all classes sought to enhance their beauty, and that of their homes, with it. Medieval fragrance was both mystical and practical to an extent that we find it hard to understand today.

Its mystical power was established by the Old Testament, wherein it played a mediatory role between God and his creation. It persuaded the Lord to bless Noah and his sons, when he smelt 'the soothing savour' of Noah's sacrifice (*Genesis* 8:21). It is the first thing the bride praises about her love in the *Song of Songs*:

Your love is more fragrant than wine,
Fragrant is the scent of your perfume,
And your name like perfume poured out;
For this the maidens love you.

(*Song* 1:24)

The *Song* is full of sweet fragrances, which came from the tender grapes, apples and spices, the ointments, garments and the very love of the lovers. Fragrance was one of the mystical, erotic delights the Middle Ages inherited from the sealed garden of the *Song*, and never ceased to praise and cultivate, in the literature of symbolism and reality, and in reality itself.

Medieval gardens were much more sturdily enclosed than modern ones, and in summertime the fragrance of their flowers was captured for the delight of the men, women, bees and small creatures that moved in them. All the favourite medieval flowers were strongly scented and were doubtless planted so as to mingle or concentrate their various scents to best advantage, as the gardener wished. The evocative powers of their scents gave flowers an important place in medieval romance. So did their visual beauty.

This chapter seeks to find out which flowers the Medievals most liked to see appearing on the earth, what they said about their beauty and its associations, and what symbolic importance they therefore attached to their flowers, comparing them in some cases with the same flowers in the present day.

Medieval flowers were used far more variously and in far greater quantities than they are today for decoration, present-giving, tryst-making, the celebration of all kinds of sacred and secular festivals, and for personal adornment. Garland-making was a major feminine pastime in the Middle Ages, and so was the drying and strewing of flowers, making flower perfumes and air fresheners, ointments, oils, cosmetics, dyes and medicines, and cooking with flowers. The ideal medieval flower was not only beautiful and fragrant, but useful in all kinds of ways that are lost to us today, and a large number of flowers we think of as merely pretty fulfilled all three of these requirements.

It was not only pleasure gardeners, but also the strictly utilitarian cottage gardeners and monastic kitcheners and infirmarers who grew flowers in the Middle Ages. They domesticated those wild flowers which had a wide range of domestic usefulness, and this survey begins with a look at these humble but valuable flowers.

Useful Flowers

Few wild flowers were more common than those of the artemisia family, but they were brought into cultivation early in the Middle Ages because they were in constant household use. *Artemisia abrotanum*, better known as southernwood, has 'well nigh as many virtues as leaves', according to Walafrid Strabo, and that is a great number, for southernwood has a mass of hairlike leaves. But it was grown mainly for the ability of its leaves to soothe fevers and wounds. It was also dried and put into lavender pot-pourris to give them bite.

Its near relation *Artemisia absinthum*, better known as wormwood, was equally common and equally well thought of, as a flea repellent. Late medieval legend attributed its bitter taste to the fact that it grew on the path where the serpent went in the Garden of Eden, but the practical value of its bitterness lay in its power to expel worms (hence its name) and poisons from the system; most English medieval medical writers recommended it as a cure for constipation and stomach-ache.

Artemisia vulgaris has a more pleasant taste, which earned it the name mugwort, for it was used to flavour home brews and wines.

Another flower which was thought to repel flies and bugs was the tansy, which has been a favourite in cottage gardens ever since the early Middle Ages. In the early nineteenth century John Clare wrote of the 'golden rods and tansy running high' in the gardens in his Suffolk village; tansy was still being widely used in his time, and indeed until very recently, to make tansy cakes. All parts of the plant are aromatic and bitter-tasting, and were commonly used in medieval cookery. The bitter taste of medieval tansy cakes, which consisted of little else besides tansy juice and eggs, may have been intended to recall the bitter herbs eaten at the passover, for tansy cakes were eaten at the end of Lent, just before Easter. If nothing else, they were useful for getting rid of wind and working up an appetite for better fare to come when Lent was over. Tansy leaves and juice were put into omelettes as the sour part of sweet and sour fillings, and into herbal sauces and salads.

Like the tansy, the marigold is now primarily a decorative flower, but was a culinary and medicinal bitter herb in the Middle Ages. It is one of the many medieval flowers that were named in honour of the Blessed Virgin Mary, and in medieval records it appears under its full title: St Mary's Gold. It was widely used as an antidote to pestilence and painful stings.

> Gold is bitter in savour,
> Fair and yellow is his flower . . .
> Draweth out of ye head wicked horrors,

wrote one fourteenth-century physician.

Dried marigold flowers were a stock household medicine and were also useful for cooking in winter, when there were no fresh flowers. They were put into stews and pottages as a sort of petal pepper, rubbed into cheese to keep its colour bright, and sugared into a conserve which was both delicious and efficacious against the plague. Native over most of Europe, the marigold was grown by many a medieval kitchen gardener alongside the leeks and onions that went into the pot with it.

The two native sorts of anemone—*Anemone hepatica*, known as liverwort, and *Anemone pulsatilla*, or pasque-flower, were almost as popular. John the Gardener, a fourteenth-century Kentishman who wrote the first practical guide to gardening in the English language, listed the liverwort as a herbal flower in his treatise, and it was taken, as its name suggests, as a digestive drink and to ease liver troubles. The pasque-flower is now rare in England, but it is a native, and used to be so common that it was only occasionally grown in gardens, usually by those who wanted the bright green dye it yields. This was a favourite medieval colouring agent for Easter eggs; hence the name pasque or Easter flower. At one of Edward I's Easter court festivities four hundred eggs were dyed with it. The pasque-flower was a delicate Easter adornment for candles and statues, and a soft heart for posies, being what the twentieth-century gardener, Vita Sackville-West, describes as 'soft as the suffle of a kitten's fur'.

The daffodil was common in the wilds, but was only occasionally cultivated. Ladies, however, sometimes grew the asphodel in their gardens because its flowers yielded a yellow dye with which they dyed their hair and eyebrows. The roots could then be eaten, and were so well liked by those who developed a taste for them, notably the trend-setting royal court gourmets, that the plant was nicknamed *cibo regis* (food of a king). Because of its early flowering it became generally known as the Lent Lily, lentil or Lent rose.

The foxglove is native to Britain, and was occasionally cultivated because it was very pretty and useful. The thirteenth-century Welsh physicians of Myddrai used it externally against scrofula, and it continued to be used in this way throughout the medieval period. Its shape, reminiscent of a *gleow* (the Anglo-Saxon name for an arched instrument containing a row of bells), gave it an association with fairy music. Its Irish name means fairy-bell or fairy-cap, and this may have had something to do with its continuing use as a vaguely charismatic, magical, superficial healer.

Milfoil – the plant with a thousand leaves, was also known by its Anglo-Saxon name, yarrow, and its old country nicknames tell us what its main use was, and why it was sometimes grown in cottage gardens: sanguinary, staunchgrass, bloodwort. It was reputed to have been used by Achilles to staunch his soldiers' blood, and was certainly used in that way in medieval England. If you are bleeding because of 'vermin in the womb', wrote one fourteenth-century physician, 'take millfiore, flour and cumin, and mix them with eggs or vinegar. Bind this on to your nowele (hole) in a cloot (cloth), and the vermin will out dead.'

There is not much one can add to that, and one is best to pass straight on to a flower that is a little less bold in its uses.

The iris is one of the oldest cultivated plants. Its original habitat was probably Syria, whence it moved to Egypt, thence Europe, between about 1501 and 1447 BC. The yellow water-flag iris was the emblem of the sixth-century Frankish king Clovis, who is said to have seen it growing in a river, realized that the river was therefore shallow enough to cross, and saved his army by leading them across it, away from a disastrous battle. In the twelfth century it was taken up again as the French royal emblem by King Louis VII, when he went on crusade. He called it the fleur de Louis, and from that time on it became the French royal flower, under the name fleur-de-lys. The white fleur-de-lys was a symbol of virginity and was often used as a background in paintings of the Virgin Mary.

But the English were not to be outdone by their French rivals, and in 1339, when Edward III claimed the throne of France, the fleur-de-lys appeared in the Royal Arms, where it remained until it was displaced by the Irish harp in 1800. From the thirteenth century onwards it had appeared in English manuscript illustrations, embroideries, seals and wood carvings, like the misericords at Exeter Cathedral, executed in about 1255, and it was clearly one of the most popular and most widely cultivated of English flowers.

The blue iris, the oldest cultivated variety in Europe, was as widely grown as the water-flag. *Iris foetidissima* was also common, known as the gladwyn. The iris was one of the top medieval all-purpose flowers. Its leaves were used to cover chairs and repair thatched roofs and strew on floors. Its roots yielded a fairly strong ink and, when dried and either bruised or powdered, a strong, sweet smell similar to that of violets. The roots were extensively used as air fresheners and deodorants and the medieval name for them, orris, became a household word. Blue iris flowers were not only beautiful and fragrant, but also productive of a purplish juice which turned green when mixed with alum, and was much in use in the fourteenth and fifteenth centuries as a clothes dye. Iris juice was good for removing spots and freckles too, and was rubbed into the teeth and gums as a kind of toothpaste and tooth-adhesive combined. Being such a useful flower, the iris was included in a lot of rather vague remedies for rather vague disorders such as 'workings in the chest' and 'evil breathing'. It made a pretty church, house and garden decoration, and amply fulfilled the three requirements of beauty, fragrance and usefulness which qualified a flower as a medieval favourite. It was grown in cottage, flower and herb gardens.

A much less versatile flower, which only just edged its way into the borders of English gardens, is *Nepeta cataria*, or nep for short, which is the same as wild catmint. It was an ideal border flower, growing low and giving off a strong scent, like a herb; it was in fact often grown in herb gardens and used as a seasoning, and is one of only two members of the mint family that were grown in flower borders commonly enough to be included in this chapter. Perhaps because of its strong scent, it was reported to make meek people fierce, and therefore to have been eaten by hangmen when they had a job to do. It was popular with cats and bees, and made a fragrant border round the sweet scents of a flower garden.

Calamint was a garden occasional in the Middle Ages, and is the second of the mints included in this chapter. It was taken against colds and fevers, and calamint tea remained a cure for colds in some country areas until the beginning of this century.

Another herbal flower that was popular with bees and paid the occasional fragrant visit to flower gardens is *Polygonatum multiflorum*, or Solomon's seal, a British native which was cultivated at an early date, and was included in a fifteenth-century list of 'herbs for savour and beauty'. Its strong point was beauty rather than savour, for its roots were used to clean the complexion and soothe away bruises.

Celandines, nowadays uprooted as weeds, 'groweth in garths and by the way' in the Middle Ages, according to one fourteenth-century medical writer, who goes on to say:

> In time of summer yellow is his flower.
> Full bitter to drink is his savour.

But drunk it was, as it had been ever since the time of Aristotle,

The *peony mascula*, which still grows on the island of Steepholm, where it was first planted by Augustinian monks nearly seven centuries ago.

One of the giant alexanders of Steepholm, once grown by the monks there as kitchen herbs.

Picking flowers in a flowery mead, which is enclosed by a fence but opens directly on to the countryside.

A rose-garden enclosed by a high wall. The central rose-bush is enclosed by a wattle fence.

when it got a reputation for healing sore eyes and improving the eyesight. Celandine juice was applied to the eyes all through the medieval period, and belief in its efficacy was so deep that draughts of celandine juice, and even proximity to the flower, were reckoned to bring relief:

> And if it be taken as is said*
> And under each man's head laid
> Soreness leaves the eye.

Because of its bright colour, simple shape and bitter taste, it had powerful, primitive medicinal associations. Its yellow colour was thought by some to be a divinely sent hint of its power against yellow jaundice, to which end its bitter juice was swallowed in quantities of honey and ale. Its colour also appealed to artists, who mixed it with mercury and egg yolk to get a goldish paint. Celandines were well-known, well-respected flowers in the Middle Ages, and have declined sadly to become the weeds we consider them today.

Herb Robert (*Geranium robertianum*), by contrast, only began to become at all popular as a garden flower towards the end of the period because it is brightly pretty, and becomes more strikingly so under cultivation. It was used as a remedy for stone and kidney diseases.

The meadow cowslip is closely related to a flower that established itself earlier and more firmly in gardens: the primrose. The Saxon Aelfric refers to the 'cuslippe', a name which means 'breath of a cow', as a native of English woods and meadows, and in the mid-fifteenth century John the Gardener still called the primrose 'the cowslip', but it had been cultivated as the primrose in English gardens, and by Tudor times had long been known on the Continent as an English garden flower. It is easily transplanted, and so was brought into cottage gardens early on. Both it and the cowslip were commonly made into wine, and used to make sweet waters and dessert decorations. Primrose leaves were rubbed into the skin to keep it free of blemishes, and into wounds to relieve their soreness. The leaves and petals were eaten to relieve aches and pains, and the petals were put into soothing baths and into tansy cakes and pottages. The meaning of the name primrose is apparent in its Italian form, *prima verola*, the first flower of spring. Chaucer echoes this when he says of the fair lady in *The Miller's Tale*, 'She was a Prime-

* [i.e. on Lammas day (August 1) with 3 Pater Nosters and 3 Ave Marias]

Role.' The primrose has remained a popular wild and garden flower to this day, and was used as a skin cosmetic and pot herb right up until the eighteenth century. Primrose and cowslip wine are still made in some country areas, and are greatly to be recommended.

Cowsloppus of Jerusalem was one fifteenth-century name, and an eccentric one at that, for another old English plant which was brought into cultivation and used in pottages: *Pulmonaria officinalis*, known as lungwort. It got its name because its spotted leaves were interpreted as a sign that it was a cure for spotted and diseased lungs. The belief that a plant's appearance directly indicated its useful purpose in this way is known as the doctrine of signatures. The modern attitude to the old doctrine of signatures is patronizing to the point of seeing the Medievals as a gang of indiscriminately credulous simpletons. In fact there is little evidence in their medical writings, superstitious and unrealistic though most of them are, of signatures having much doctrinal power. In a few cases, where the shape, colour or design of a plant was particularly distinctive, as with the liverwort, celandine and lungwort, these were seen as signatures, and the plants used accordingly. But such uses were seldom exclusive. Lungwort was much less commonly used for the treatment of lung diseases than sweet syrups and hot sweet drinks, which were the sovereign remedies for 'bad phlegm'.

One flower that does turn up with indiscriminate universality in medieval medical prescriptions is the plantain or waybread (*Plantago major*). It didn't have a signature save that of its abundance, according to which it was used. John the Gardener recommended growing it in the garden, though there were masses of it growing wild, and we have no way of knowing whether anyone bothered to follow his advice. Waybread was an important ingredient in ointments to cure wounds and festers, belly-flux and costiveness; to thicken the blood, rub into red testicles and warm a cold womb. It is never mentioned as a garden plant in medieval literature, and probably belongs with the multitude of flowers that were widely used in medieval cookery, medicine and decoration, but grew wild and were only occasionally cultivated in gardens.

To name just some of the better known of this kind of flower: monkshood, the dried roots of which yield a drug that slows down the nervous system and so numbs pain; bell-flowers; horehound (*Marrubium vulgare*), used against fevers; meadow saffron; lilies of the valley, used to adorn Lady Chapels and statues of the Blessed Virgin; rose-bay willow herb; wallwort or pellitory, an all-rounder, like waybread; sea holly; maidenhair fern; St John's wort (*Hypericum perforatum*), which had an age-old aura of pagan magic because it flowered on St John's day, June 24, at midsummer; golden rod; honeysuckle; globe flower; broom, the emblem of the Plantagenets; great yellow loosestrife, which was dried and hung from ceilings to keep flies away; mullein, its leaves soaked in tallow and burnt like wicks; pansy, also called herb trinity because it had three petals; marsh mallow, its leaves and roots rich in starch and aspargin mucilage which is an emollient and so well thought of by the ancients that the Greeks gave it a name meaning heal-all (these flowers figure in the supporting foliage on the fourteenth-century misericords in Wells Cathedral); meadowsweet, the leaves of which are full of wintergreen; brionies and snowflakes.

> And then they took the flowers of the oak, and the flowers of
> the broom, and the flowers of the meadow sweet, and from
> these they called forth the very fairest and best endowed maiden
> that mortal ever saw and baptized her with the baptism they
> used at that time and named her Blodevedd [Flowers].

This Taliesin tribute to Bromwyen, daughter of Llŷo, must be our only tribute to these flowers, as we pass on to deal with fully garden flowers.

Useful and Pretty Flowers

Many medieval flowers were also herbs; many herbs were also flowers and vegetables; many vegetables were also herbs. By the same token, many herbs, vegetables and flowers were pretty enough to embellish gardens in which they were grown for utilitarian reasons, or useful enough to be picked for household use out of gardens in which they had been planted for pleasure. The group of flowers to be discussed now consists of those which, for one or other of these reasons, cannot be categorized exclusively.

The utility flowers discussed so far were only occasionally cultivated, and then only in infirmary and kitchen gardens; they had no place in flower gardens. But flowers that were beautiful *and* useful found a place in all these kinds of garden.

The periwinkle is one such flower. It is now an ordinary garden flower; in the Middle Ages it was an outstanding one. It was brought to England by the Romans, who used it to make wreaths, and named it vinca because of its long, supple stems, which could be intertwined like links in a chain (*vincula*). It was made into wreaths and garlands all through the Middle Ages, particularly death garlands. In England it was the traditional crowning flower for criminals on their way to execution:

> Crowned one with laurer [laurel] high on his head set,
> Other with pervink, made for the gibbet.

So, according to the poet, Simon Fraser was executed in 1306, with a garland of periwinkles on his head. But the medieval Englishman was not easily cast down by such associations. 'Men call it joy of ground,' wrote one fourteenth-century English physician, going on to give this cheerful little description:

> Perwynke is an erbe green of colour.
> In time of May he beareth blue flower.
> His stalks are so faint and fay
> It never more groweth him high.
> Ye leaf is thick, stiff and green.

Its faint and fay stalks made it low and wide-growing, the ideal cover for banks and lawns. It grew wild in England all through the medieval period, and one only needed to build a little enclosure in the midst of a periwinkle patch to have a flowery mead garden.

Alongside the periwinkle grew the beautiful, fragrant, symbolically important and very useful violet.

> Whose virtue neither the heat of the sun has melted away
> Neither ye rain hath wafted and driven away,

as Bartholomew Anglicus put it in the thirteenth century.

The medievals used both its fragrance and its healing power medically. It was put into baths and washing waters, which its oil scented and softened. It was eaten as a cure for 'heart straitness', stone and inflamed liver. Syrup of violets was given to children and those with 'wasting fever', both to purge them and to whet their appetites. Violet petals are emetic and purgative because they contain an alkaloid, but unlike most medieval purges, this fourteenth-century violet one sounds like a simple sweet comfit, especially as the physician notes that it should be taken after a good meal: violet or rose sugar, to be taken in rose-water. The lucky patient was then to be rubbed with violet or rose oil, dried, wrapped in clean linen and put in a sweet-smelling place with no window open. A cloth sprinkled with rose-water was to be left near his bed, together with a vessel of cold water and sally, rose and vine leaves. For once, medieval medicine sounds bearable, even pleasant.

Syrups made of cowslip and violet blossoms were used to colour dishes and flavour custards and omelettes, both of which were savoury in the Middle Ages, and therefore ideally complemented by sweet crushed flowers. All kinds of dishes were garnished with violets, and sweet violet water was a popular gift on birthdays and saints days – the more so because violets are esteemed for their immediate and symbolic beauty as well as their practical uses. Chaucer only mentioned the violet once, but his phrase, 'the violet all new', captures something of its fresh, fleeting, unpretentious appeal.

The Menagier of Paris (the Parisian Householder) was a fourteenth-century Paris merchant who wrote a treatise for his young wife, telling her how to run her new household, including its gardens. This treatise is an invaluable source of information on well-to-do middle-class life. The Menagier was very fond of violets, as flowers and as herbs, and gave his wife instructions on their growth and transplantation, telling her to bring them in as pot plants during the winter, but to accustom them gradually to the indoor heat, and to accustom them in the same way to the cold when putting them out again in spring. Like periwinkles, violets made good ground cover, and were planted in the turf of arbours, banks and flowery meads. Medieval poets often included them in lists of the most common garden flowers, and medieval artists often included them in pictures of Paradise Gardens. This was because their closeness to the ground and quickly fading perfume led to the adoption of violets as symbols of humility in the early Church.

> O fragrant rose, lily chaste,
> O violet of purity,
> Thine eye of grace upon us cast,
> *Noster misericorde*,

runs one medieval carol to the Blessed Virgin, showing the pure and humble violet as the third in the great trinity of medieval symbolic flowers.

Its symbolic connection with the Blessed Virgin increased its symbolic association with purity, but even without this connection there is a natural association between humility and purity, and the white violet might well have become a symbol of the latter in its own right. Poets often coupled it with the primrose or the daisy, both of which were flowers of freshness and pure innocence. They often grew next to columbines, which were pretty enough to have a place in flowery meads, though too abundant in the wilds to be cultivated much. They were welcomed if they intruded into flowery meads and cottage gardens. The columbine was one of the eight herbs used against the plague in 1373, and it continued to be used against measles and the pox until the eighteenth century.

A much more important flower was the gillyflower, the modern pink. In his only two references to it, Chaucer first calls it a spice in his translation of the *Roman de la Rose*, then a herb, in his *Tale of Sir Thopas*. An attractive, aromatic flower like the gillyflower, which was in wide culinary use, could be categorized at will. The gillyflower often appears in recipes alongside cinnamon, with which it blended well because of its aroma and taste of cloves. Medieval gillyflower sauce, made with 'great portions of gillys (clove pinks) and canel' (cinnamon) was later known as clove sauce. The gilly-flower is the nearest we have to an English medieval spice, though it is native to southern and central Europe, not England, and is only thought of as English because it came to England early on and did very well there.

It looks as if the Normans brought it with them from their monastic gardens, for it is naturalized on the walls of Rochester Castle and some Norman monastic ruins, both in England and Normandy, notably in Falaise, where William the Conqueror was born. Carnations, which are descended from gillyflowers, still do best on limestone banks and rocks, old lime rubble such as is often found in these ruins, and on sand and shell mixtures.

The botanical name of the gillyflower is derived from the Greek. It is *Dianthus caryophyllus*, meaning the divine flower (*dianthus*), with nut-(clove nut) shaped leaves (*caryophyllus*). This suggests that it had been esteemed as a spice since ancient times. Its English name, gillyflower, may be a corruption of July flower, one of its medieval names, others of which were sops-in-wine, queen of delights and, by the end of the period, carnation, the name of the darkest variety. This name may derive from the cut flesh colour (the Latin *carnis* means flesh) of that variety, or possibly from the Latin word *corona*, meaning crown, which would suggest that gillyflowers were one of the flowers medieval women liked to weave into fragrant crowns and garlands.

By the reign of Edward III there were three different-coloured varieties in England: flesh pink, crimson and white; by the fifteenth century the bloody clove, or clove pink as we know it, the most strongly coloured and scented variety of all, had established itself as the most popular because of its usefulness in flavouring wine and ale. It was also used to flavour after-dinner syrups, sweet tarts and preserves, and to spice pot-pourris.

All the gillyflowers had a minor medical value, mainly as disguises for the unpleasant taste of bitter potions, and as strengtheners for sweet syrups. Gillyflowers improved sweet waters in which rheumatic patients soaked away their aches and pains and, according to John of Gaddesden, writing in about 1314, heart patients soaked their shirts before putting them on.

> Virify the heart with a powder made of roses, liquid aloes, saffron and gillyflower, all in rosewater. Soak the shirt of the sufferer in this.

In medicine, as in cooking, gillyflowers were essentially spices, which explains their popularity in the spice-loving Middle Ages. In 1652 Julian Fenbow planted a nutmeg clove carnation in his garden, to use as flavouring for his wines. It survived into this century, when its flower was observed to be small (¼ in. diameter) and semi-double, with sharply serrated, dark red petals. The stems were slender, the grass small, bluish and upright. This flower seems to have been a direct descendant of the medieval clove pink, developed by two centuries of breeding into a double form and a less sweet smell, more like nutmeg than cloves. Its long life is in the medieval tradition, for gillyflowers were hardy and easy to grow, even in poor soil. The Menagier grew them in his flower garden, and instructed his wife on their cultivation even more carefully than he had instructed her on the cultivation of violets.

They should be sown in March, he said, or planted, presumably as pot plants, on St Rémy's day (October 28).

> When the frosts draw near, you should replant in pots, at a season when the moon waneth, in order to set them under cover and keep them from the cold in a cellar, and by day set them in the air or in the sun and water at such time that the water may be drunken up and the earth dry before you set them under cover, for never should you put them away wet in the evening.

Because they were potted and kept indoors during the winter and were therefore on hand all year round, gillyflowers were used as a form of currency. Medieval property rents were paid in a number of complex ways: by means of exchanges, the performance of works and services, a large money payment followed by a token annual rent, and many other devices. Token rents were usually quitrents, and they were often paid in gillyflowers. 'One clove gillyflower, to be paid in the spring', or in the autumn, or both, is a common entry in medieval charters and property documents.

Dianthus barbatus is native to the same southern areas of Europe as its relative, the gillyflower, and it probably came to England in the same way. *Dianthus carthusianorum* was probably introduced by the Carthusians, which would explain the flower's name. Like all kinds of gillyflower, it grew well on walls. One other variety, the yellow stock, March or winter gillyflower, showed such a liking for walls that it earned itself the name wallflower. It was a great favourite with bees, so it was also known as the beeflower, and because of its sweet smell, sweet William. It may be a Norman introduction, like the true gillyflower, possibly even a Roman one. Either way, it was as popular as the true gillyflower all through the medieval period, as the number of names given to it would suggest. They include bellflower, gerafleur, jilliver and Jack. Its botanical name, *cheiranthus*, abbreviated in the Middle Ages to chare or cayry, means hand-flower. Wallflowers were often carried in the hand to festivals, and given as gifts because they lasted well and kept their sweet, comforting smell. Another of this flower's medieval names conveys a similar idea: heart's ease.

Yet the wallflower had a symbolic importance which was far from easy or comforting to the heart. It became the symbol of faithfulness in adversity, and in courtly circles was commonly worn in the caps of those who had been disappointed or crossed in love but were courteous enough to remain faithful; hence its still further nicknames: bleeding heart and bloody warrior. The most popular English version of its legend tells of a maiden called Elizabeth, the daughter of a northern Marcher earl, who was betrothed to King Robert III of Scotland (*ca* 1400), but in love with Scott of Tushielaw, the son of a border chieftain. One day Scott came, disguised as a minstrel, to sing of his love for her under the window of the castle where her father had imprisoned her. Listening to his song, Elizabeth threw down a sprig of wallflower, which must have been living up to its name and growing out of the wall, to show that she had heard, understood and accepted him, for his song was an elopement proposal. When the time to elope came, however, the rope by means of which Elizabeth was lowering herself to the ground broke, and she fell to her death. Scott spend the rest of his life minstrelling all over Europe, wearing a wallflower in his cap. From that time on, the wallflower became the symbol of faithful and undying love in Britain. Anyone who was anyone in fashionable circles wore a wallflower in his cap. To be a wallflower at a medieval dance was an honour, not a disgrace. Wallflowers were grown along the walls of monasteries, where their symbolism was given a religious dimension. Some monks wore wallflower crowns and carried wallflowers on feast days, as symbols of their religious faith and devotion.

Another flower that grew in monastic flower gardens and had some religious symbolism, but on a much smaller scale, is the snowdrop. It was also called Candlemas bells in the Middle Ages because of its bell-shaped flowers, which open at Candlemas, February 2, the feast of the Purification. This flowering date and the white fragility of the snowdrop explain its association with virgin purity. Its monastic association is speculative, based on its liking for the sites of old monastic gardens. If monks brought the snowdrop to England from Italy, where it was an old favourite, it was not until the fifteenth century. St Francis called it an emblem of hope, presumably because it is the first flower to break through the winter snow, but its main symbolic importance was virginal. Alternatively, the monks brought it into cultivation from the damp woodlands of the north country and Herefordshire, where it was native. But it never became a garden favourite or a cult flower; it was never much painted or written about. Chaucer does not mention it, nor do his medical, horticultural or culinary contemporaries. The snowdrop remained a tiny, pretty, untouched medieval virgin, cultivated only where there were Lady Chapels to decorate at Candlemas.

The saffron crocus did just the opposite. It made a romantic entrance into English medieval history and became one of the most sought-after and expensive of English flowers. The secret of its desirability was the yellow dye contained in its pollen, which was strong enough in colour and flavour to make it very useful in cookery as well as cosmetics and manuscript illumination. The word saffron is an Anglicized form of a Turkish corruption of the Arabic word 'zà-farán', meaning yellow, and the flower's introduction to England may have been as direct as its etymology. The Arabs grew saffron croci in their southern Spanish provinces, whence saffron was exported along the Mediterranean trade routes to Germany, the

Netherlands and Britain; the crocus itself may have travelled the same routes.

But there is a strong tradition that it was bought directly to England from its native Holy Land by an Englishman, not by the Arabs, whose saffron was sold to the English at such fantastic prices that it was the main reason for the Palestinian saffron bulb being smuggled through the Arab customs in the Near East by an Englishman. The Tudor geographer, Hakluyt, was quite certain that this was the case, and he even gave the name of the smuggler: Sir Thomas Smith, secretary of state to Edward III, who hid a saffron bulb in the head of his walking cane, and so brought it back secretly to his home town in Essex in about 1330, on his return from a pilgrimage to Jerusalem. Saffron croci were certainly grown around the town of Walden at an early date, and when Edward VI granted the town its arms in 1549, the design chosen was three saffron crocus flowers.

A less popular tradition holds that the saffron crocus was brought to England from the Holy Land by the Hospitallers, a century earlier than it was brought to Saffron Walden. Whatever the date of its establishment, the saffron crocus proved very difficult to cultivate and harvest, and oriental saffron continued to be imported into England throughout the medieval period.

Pereira, the eighteenth-century Portuguese scholar of Islam, wrote that the stigma of nine flowers were required to make one grain of good saffron, which means that 4320 flowers were required to produce one ounce of saffron. So even if it had been an easy plant to grow, saffron would still have been very expensive. But it is very hard to grow, and even harder to harvest and dry. John the Gardener wrote of it:

> Saffron will have without lesying [lying]
> Beds y-made well with dyng [dung.]
> Forsooth, if they shall bear
> They should be set in the month of September,
> Three days before St Mary day nativity [8th September]
> Or the next week thereafter; so must it be.
> With a dibble you shall him set.
> That the dibble before be blunt and great:
> Three hands deep they must set be.

For all the hazards of its production, English saffron was considered among the best in the world. One fifteenth-century manuscript, written in England, mentions the production of English saffron 'in field and garden', and claims that it can be used just as well as oriental saffron to make yellow dye.

If a pinch of saffron was infused with glair (egg-white glue), the result was a transparent, strongly yellow glaze, which was sometimes used as a substitute for gold colour in manuscript illumination, but more often mixed with blue colour to give a good green, or mixed with verdigris to improve an existing one. Saffron was also ideal for colouring food. A lot of medieval sauces and pottages were coloured and flavoured with saffron; quince jelly was fortified by the addition of clarified honey, almond milk and saffron; apple moss and pears in syrup were powdered with saffron and spices; the batter for apple and parsnip fritters was made of flour, eggs, ale, saffron and salt. Medieval cooks liked the strong flavour of saffron, and they loved its colour. Brilliant, long-lasting, saffron made an excellent medieval hair dye, though one that would be a bit too drastic for modern taste.

Monastic infirmarers sometimes grew saffron in their gardens; more often they were too busy to spend time on it, and bought it instead to use sparingly in the sweet spiced cordials they gave to heart patients and those whose humours had 'fallen evil'. Saffron cordial was considered sudorific and generally beneficial, its sunny colour helping to cheer the patient up. It had a reputation for making people happy; so much so that one or two people were said to have died of laughter after taking English saffron. Jobst Findaker of Nuremberg definitely died as a result of saffron. In 1444 he was burnt in the same fire as the adulterated saffron he had sold. Laws were passed against the adulteration of saffron, and inspectors appointed by city councils to enforce them. Saffron was an infirmary, market and kitchen garden flower cultivated by and for the affluent minority, just very occasionally in their pleasure gardens.

Like the saffron crocus, *Lychnis chalcedonia*, a kind of campion, came from the Holy Land, and it was a pleasure garden flower, albeit a very minor one that was usually picked for garland-making, its chief use. It was probably brought to Europe by Louis IX of France on his return from the crusades, and was named after its place of origin: Jerusalem Cross.

The hollyhock is also reputed to have come to England from the Holy Land during the crusades, whence its name. Holy hoc means holy mallow in Anglo-Saxon and old English. The flower does grow profusely in Palestine, and is not a British native, so the theory may well be correct. The alternative is that it is a much older import, hence the Anglo-Saxon 'hoc' part of its name, the 'holy' simply reflecting the respect in which it was held because of its medical efficacy. It is only mentioned medically, however, as a herb to be infused and taken against lung diseases and bladder inflammations, and as an ingredient of herbal baths, scarcely enough to merit the epithet 'holy'. It seems best to accept the Holy Land theory, and regard the Anglo-Saxon 'hoc' as a linguistic anachronism, of which there were many in Anglo-Norman, or a reference to one of the native British mallows. The hollyhock never appears in literature as an inhabitant of flower gardens, and seems to have preferred the wilds or the walls of cottage yards. The Menagier didn't grow it, but recommended its crushed petals for colouring white wine red.

The peony can be much more freely located in the horticultural imagination: it grew in every kind of infirmary and kitchen garden, and in a few pleasure gardens. The ancients used its seeds to flavour meat, and its seeds, roots and petals to make infusions against melancholy, as the medievals did after them.

> 'Hast thou,' quoth he, 'any hot spices?'
> 'I have pepper and peony and a pound of garlic.
> A farthing worth of fennel seeds, for fasting days I bought it,'

replies the old woman to her questioner in *Piers Plowman*, which suggests that peony seeds were eaten raw, like fennel seeds, as well as in casseroles. They made a good hot mouthful when one had nothing else to eat. They were also drunk in hot wine and ale last thing at night, as a precaution against nightmares and unhappy dreams.

Neckham recommended the dried roots as a cure for epilepsy, a recommendation based on his reading of classical medical literature, but one that was not medievally adopted to anything like the extent of the consumption of the seeds. When it came to satisfying the medieval taste buds and temperamental fluctuations, there was nothing like a good seed. If things got bad enough to produce a heart attack, the best remedy, according to the surgeon, John of Arderne, was to press a hot paste made of smallage roots, fennel, ground ivy and peony to the heart, keeping the poor patient cool all the while by sprinkling his face with rose-water.

The infirmarer at the Benedictine abbey at Winchcombe, in Gloucestershire, grew peonies in his garden, the seeds of which have been found on the abbey site. They are particularly interesting because they are the seeds of *Paeonia mascula*, which only became naturalized in one place in Britain: Steep Holm, which is a small island with cliffs 250 ft. high, midway between the English and Welsh coasts, five miles off Weston-super-Mare. It says a lot for medieval monastic intercourse and hospitality that somehow the infirmarer of the Augustinian priory on Steep Holm contrived to pass some of his peony seeds or plants to the Benedictine infirmarer at Winchcombe.

Paeonia mascula is an exceptionally beautiful variety of the flower, with pink, red and white flowers, the most common colour being purplish crimson. These flowers can be over 4 ins. in diameter; they have gold-tipped stamens and rose-red seeds, looking like coral, that are exposed when the seed vessels open in autumn; hence its alternative name, *Paeonia corallina* (see illustration p. 144).

We have the rare privilege of seeing *Paeonia mascula* just as it was in the Middle Ages because it has survived for over seven centuries, and still thrives on Steep Holm today, along with several other medicinal plants, under the protection of a nature trust. It is a native of southern Europe, and was taken to Steep Holm by the Augustinians who crossed from France to establish a priory there in the late twelfth or early thirteenth century, the micro-climate, milder and drier than that of the mainland, making the island an exceptionally successful herb farm. The priory appears to have been short-lived, but its services to English horticulture were both enduring and excellent.

Paeonia officinalis, also found in southern Europe, was more common in medieval England, though how it got to England is not known. Aelfric was familiar with it in AD 1000 and it appears in later medieval documents: the infirmarer at Durham Cathedral Priory, for instance, paid 3s.2d. for 3 lbs. of peony seeds in 1299.

It is appropriate to follow the peony with the Christmas rose, one of the family of plants named hellebores, or poisoners, by the Ancient Greeks. Though it is not strictly native to Britain, traces of it have been found on British neolithic sites, and it was certainly known in Roman Britain. The ancients had surrounded it with a magical aura, probably because of its poisonous properties, which survived into the Middle Ages, when it was credited with purgative powers. In some areas it was planted outside cottage doors until recently, as a protection against evil spirits. Christmas roses are traditional cottage garden flowers. They are not in John the Gardener's list of cultivated flowers, but if they seeded themselves near the trellising of a formal flower garden, they were welcomed.

So were poppies, both the native red and the opium poppy brought by the Romans. Most of them grew wild, and were early escapes from garden cultivation. Wild and garden poppies were very common, and they may have been allowed to grow in flowery meads, alongside periwinkles and violets, to make red and white, and blue and violet flower carpets. In one of the twelfth-century Arthurian romances, that of *Eric and Enid*, the author begins a simile by saying, 'As the lustrous gem outshines the brown flint, and as the rose excels the poppy . . .' A humble flower, the poppy, despite its bright colouring.

The native sweet woodruff does not have spectacular flowers, but its leaves are sweetly scented; hence its name and its medieval nickname, 'sweetgrass', and hence its success in medieval flower gardens. When dried, it smells of sweet hay, and was used as a strewing herb for floors and as a freshener for clothes. When fresh, it was used to decorate and scent houses and churches. It was at its best round about St Barnabas's day (June 11), at which feast it was garlanded with roses to make red and white wreaths of fragrance for the statues and candles that filled medieval churches.

Sweet woodruff was one of the Blessed Virgin's most common garland flowers, and it was used to garland many an earthly sweetheart, too, on summer festival days. Summer drinks and wines were infused with it, and its sweet white freshness was the essence of summer and all its delights.

> Away is here winter woe
> When woodruff springeth,

opens one fourteenth-century love lyric, which sums it all up, and in doing so brings us to the third class of garden flowers to be considered in this chapter: those which were cultivated for their beauty. They had all sorts of practical virtues, but it was their beauty that made them 'the pleasures and delights of the garden' (*Eric and Enid*.)

Beautiful, Flower Garden Flowers, and Flower Gardens

They were of very few kinds, far fewer than we grow in our flower gardens today, but each kind grew more abundantly and fragrantly. In most cases they were more delicate than their modern hybrid descendants; their colours were fewer; they were more uniformly loved as romantic symbols, more celebrated in songs and poems, more picked, woven, walked upon, given and received. The flowers we are about to consider were the idealized images of poetry, prayer and art, the very stuff of romantic symbolism. They are the flowers we must picture to ourselves when we picture medieval pleasure gardens, and in order to do that, their appearance and perfume, and the appearance and perfume of the gardens they grew in must be described as exactly as possible.

The flower gardens in which the most beautiful medieval flowers were grown were formal but lively. The medieval love and understanding of nature gave them an exuberance that combined with the conventional formality containing it to bring perfect satisfaction to the medieval heart. The simplest type of flower garden was the flowery mead, wherein low-growing flowers were planted in turf lawns, sometimes walled, sometimes left open, to make a beautiful domestic meadow. (See illustration 10). The flowery mead was the *locus amoenus* of God's beautiful world, enclosed by man as his own and, insofar as it was possible, improved upon by the addition of more meadow flowers.

> There sprang the violet all new,
> And fresh periwinkle, rich of hue,
> And flowers yellow, white and red;
> Such plenty grew there never in mead.
>
> (Chaucer's translation of the *Roman de la Rose*)

We have already looked at the violets, periwinkles, primroses and gillyflowers that filled such meads; we need only look at the way they were planted and enjoyed to complete our picture. As usual, Chaucer gives us what we need, in this case through his description of the flowery mead in *The Franklin's Tale*.

> This garden full of leaves and flowers;
> And craft of man's hand so curiously
> Arrayed had this garden, truly,
> That never was there garden of such prys
> But if it were the very paradise.
> The odour of flowers and the fresh sight
> Would have made any heart for to light . . .
> So full was it of beauty with pleasance,
> At after dinner gone they to dance,
> And sing also . . .

They danced, played chess and tables (a kind of medieval back-gammon), told stories, walked and rested. Ladies went into the garden to play with pet squirrels and monkeys, talk with caged magpies and popinjays (parrots) brought back from the Middle East by the crusaders, and listen to the songs of caged larks and nightingales.

None of these activities were restricted to flowery meads. They could be done in the secrecy of an enclosed garden, usually a rose-garden, with its fountains, walks and arbours. There are no definite records of how big these sealed gardens were; just occasionally we get enough information to make a guess, as with William of Wykeham's garden at Winchester, which seems to have been very small. There is no reason why a rosary shouldn't have been tiny, with one central rose bush and perhaps a few more surrounding it. Equally, there is no reason why a rosary should not have been very big, (like the one in the *Romance*), with avenues of roses, long paths and big, shady trees full of birds. Gardens varied as much in size in the Middle Ages as they do now.

They adjoined the south walls of castles, palaces and houses. Such gardens might stretch down to a stream or flowery mead or they might be walled in 'strict and close' within the enceinte, as in one romance *Aucassin and Nicolette*.

Whatever their size and position, medieval sealed gardens and flowery meads seem to have offset what we might consider their excessively stereotyped formality with a refreshingly naturalistic way of growing their flowers. There were no flower-beds of the sort familiar to us. In the few cases where flowers were planted in soil beds, these were raised anything from 2 ins. to 2 ft. above the ground and surrounded by palings and walls. Usually flowers were planted in the turf which covered the ground, benches, banks and abundance of seats that were arranged along the garden walls or next to a central tree or fountain (see illustrations pp. 145 and 160). Some-times they were planted in pots, which stood on the turf and the seats. Trees were often planted in raised turf mounds, surrounded by wattle fences, which doubled as seats. Medieval lawns, unlike modern ones, were luxuriously long, and full of flowers and herbs; they were fragrant carpets to be walked, danced, sat and lain upon. What modern lawn could find a poet to write about it as Chaucer wrote about the one in the *Legend of Good Women*?

An enclosed flowery mead, with flowers growing out of the turf on the ground and on the enclosing wall.

A lady gathering roses, probably to garland, from a trellis. They are typically medieval, with big flowers, leaves and thorns.

A lady making a white rose garland in a turfed, banked rosary.

'Many a Fresh and Sundry Flower'

Upon the small, soft, sweet grass,
That was with flowers sweet embroidered all,
Of such sweetness, and such odour overall . . .

Arbours and the railings that enclosed them were trellised with climbing flowers. Wells and fountains were surrounded with flowers. The borders of the gravelled and sanded paths were lined with herbs and aromatic flowers. The overaii effect was one of perfumed profusion and of colour. The colours, like the varieties of garden flowers, were few but brilliant. Periwinkle, violets, primroses and daisies made carpets of 'fresh flowers blue and white and red' (*Troilus and Criseyde*).

Daisies were very popular in medieval gardens, especially flowery meads. The word daisy comes from the Anglo-Saxon word 'daezeseye', meaning eye of day.

For fear of night, so hateth she darkness!
Her cheer is plainly spread in the brightness
Of the sun, for there it would unclose
(Chaucer's *Legend of Good Women*)

The daisy has the same aura of innocence and freshness as the violet, and was grown alongside it in flowery meads, just as it grew alongside it in the meadows of the countryside. Legend has it that when St Augustine of Canterbury first came to England he spent a lot of time walking in the woods and meadows, and compared the daisies that he found here to the spirits of the blessed in the courts of heaven. Children came to him with daisy chains, and he taught them about Paradise by showing them the sun at the centre of the flower, symbolic of the sun of righteousness which should shine out from every heart with its white rays of purity and goodness. In Paradise all righteous souls would be united, like the daisies that grew together in the meadows.

All kinds of daisies were made into crowns and garlands, and daisy crowns were celebrated for their fresh, meadowy appeal, which many preferred to the appeal of brighter and more exotic flowers. Ox-eyes were the favourites, and were so called because they were large in size and white in colour. 'As white as a daisy' was a popular medieval simile and compliment, which was considered especially suitable for queens, since it implied that they had retained their freshness and innocence despite their worldly fortune. The emblem of Margaret of Anjou, who married Henry VI of England at the age of fifteen, incorporated three daisies.

[161]

Troubadour romances recommended daisy buds for those hungry with Charitable love. One of the oldest nicknames of the daisy is 'measure of love': its petals were pulled off to tell whether one was loved or not, and the medievals went to a lot of trouble to make daisy lawns, as much like meadows as possible, where one could make daisy crowns and chains, and reckon up one's measure of love. Daisies had some peripheral utility as anti-bilious medicine and salad herbs, but they were meadow garden flowers above all else. The medievals would be horrified at our iconoclastic attitude towards one of their favourite flowers.

The lily seems always to have been described in formal moral terms, just as the daisy was in poetic ones. Neckham wrote in the twelfth century:

> The stalk of the lily, when it is green, produces a most splendid flower, which changes from green to white. So must we persevere in the best of behaviour so that, immature plants as we are, we may attain to the whiteness of innocence. Furthermore, the whiteness of this flower does not turn back into green, and even so our continence must not succumb to the enticements of this dissolute life.

The lily's symbolism predates Christianity and is found in all the ancient religions. It is one of the two flowers named in the *Song of Songs*, which explains its adoption by Christian symbolists, who began writing about it as a symbol of the Blessed Virgin in the second century.

> As a lily among the thistles,
> So is my love among the maidens.   (*Song* 2:1)

The old fertility symbolism combined with the Marian purity of the lily to make it the perfect Annunciation symbol, and it was painted and written about in that role throughout the Middle Ages. Artists and poets alternated between the rose and the lily in their symbolic portrayals of the Blessed Virgin, the rose being the favourite symbol of her love and the lily of her purity. The lily is, as medieval poets never tired of pointing out, 'white as milk', and therefore symbolic of womanly chastity. 'Lily-white' was a stock poetic cliché, and became a commonplace of speech.

The development of the lily from green to white, which Neckham used as the basis for his moral allegory, had given it mystical significance as the flower of light even before Christian times, and the promulgation of the doctrine of the Assumption in the second century gave that light a Christian, specifically Marian, focus that surpassed even the Annunciation in its mystical purity. The Assumption is the ultimate taking up of matter into spirit. Its very completeness meant that there was no evidence left behind to enlighten humanity about it such as the living evidence of the Annunciation embodied by Christ. Before long the early Church had supplied itself with an image, in default of evidence, of the Assumption.

In the second century the legend grew up that when Mary was assumed into heaven lilies and roses were found in her tomb. This was not accepted in the West until the fifth century, when the white lily became known as the Madonna lily and began to appear in almost every picture, poem and prayer connected with the Blessed Virgin, particularly those about the Assumption and the Visitation, which is celebrated on July 2, at the height of the lily season.

St Catherine, whose name signified purity, was credited with a vision of Paradise in which she was met by angels wearing wreaths of white lilies. Her popularity increased when the crusaders brought her home town of Alexandria under Christian rule, and one of the many legends that grew up around her at that time was that lilies had been without scent until the fourth century, when God rewarded her holiness by miraculously scenting them, thereby converting her father, the Emperor Costis, to Christianity. When she died her veins flowed with blood as white as milk or, one could just as well say, as white as lilies.

The real white Madonna lily, *Lilium candidum*, is native to the Holy Land and may have been brought to England by the crusaders, along with the Turk's Cap lily, which is naturalized on a few sites in Kent, Surrey, Devon and Scotland. But this was probably a re-introduction, since the lily was certainly well known to the Anglo-Saxons, who seem to have liked it better than the rose. St Etheldreda, the foundress of Ely Abbey, is portrayed in the tenth-century Benedictional of St Ethelwold holding a single white lily almost as tall as herself.

The tall, solitary lily did not belong in a flowery mead along with the gregarious little violet or periwinkle; it belonged in a sealed garden, along with the rose. Such medieval garden pictures as we have show that this is indeed where it was grown, in accordance with Christian tradition.

> My beloved went down to his garden
> To the beds of spices,

[163]

To pasture his flock in the gardens
And gather lilies.   (*Song* 6:2)

Lilies were ideal for growing up the railings of such gardens, where they made a wall of white fragrance, dotted with red roses. They were grown in monastic paradises, and no doubt also in rectory gardens, and used by the clergy as Lady Altar and Lady Chapel decorations.

Castle, palace and manorial gardeners likewise supplied them to the lady of the house, as decorations and as sources of perfume, oil, medicine and food. The Menagier grew lilies and roses in his garden. The 'flowers white and red' which grew in the paradises of medieval poetry are lilies and roses, both of them e'.ery bit as useful as the utilitarian flowers with which this chapter began, but both blessed with the added glories of outstanding beauty and fragrance. Lilies and roses never lost their popularity in the Middle Ages; they appear as often in literature and art at the end of the period as they do at the beginning of it, and their religious symbolism made them as popular with peasants as they were with princes. So did their usefulness.

In the Middle Ages lily roots were usually ground and mixed with wormwood, mint, camomile, cumin, betony, roses and mastich, soaked in vinegar and applied to the stomach on a sour bread plaster. They were used in the same sort of way, mixed with 'swine's grease', to break boils and soothe burns. Lily-root syrup was taken to purge colic and to clear the lungs of pleurisy. Lily snuff was used as a decongestant right up until the nineteenth century.

The main domestic use of lilies, other than the medicinal one, was as a source of fragrance. They perfumed people and clothes, and were one of the flowers used in still-rooms to make scent. Lily pollen was a minor source of yellow painting dye.

The two greatest medieval flowers, the lily and the rose, had no nicknames; their proper names were evocative of such riches that there was no need for alternatives.

Medieval Roses and Rose Gardens

Roses have grown wild in the northern hemisphere since the oldest times. Fossilized roses have been found all over Europe and the East, though the only fossil records of roses in Britain are a few from the neolithic and interglacial ages, and their precise identities are uncertain. By the sixteenth century BC the rose was an established garden flower in Crete. Ptolemaic Egypt was famous for its cultivated roses. The Babylonian King Sargon (2845-2768 BC) sent 'two species of fig-trees, vines, rose trees and other plants' to his capital at Akkad.

The oldest rose would appear to be the vivid red, semi-double *Rosa gallica*, the cultivated descendant of the earliest wild roses and the ancestor of all the roses of medieval Europe. But there were also other varieties of rose in ancient times, though the gallica was the most popular. They included the *Rosa centifolia*, so called because of its mass of petals, and better known as the provence or cabbage rose, reputedly one of the oldest species of cultivated rose, and the *Rosa bifera*, or autumn damask, a fragrant, free-flowering natural hybrid of the red *gallica* and the *moschata*. The *moschata* (moss rose) is a close relative of the summer damask, also native to the area around Damascus, and a natural hybrid of the red *gallica* and the Phoenician musk. This rose became known as the Holy rose because it was brought to Europe by Christian monks, and first appeared in its cultivated form in the courtyards of religious sanctuaries in the Christian province of Tigre, Abyssinia.

It is clear from the remarks made by Theophrastus, 'the father of botany' (370-280 BC), in his *Enquiry into Plants*, that the Greeks, who used roses extensively to make perfumes, cosmetics and medicines, thought less of them as garden flowers than the Romans, who used them in these ways with typical excess and also grew showpiece rose-gardens. The combined symbolic, aesthetic and house and garden value of the rose to the Romans was such that they must have cultivated it in their English gardens.

Pliny says that the Romans named England Albion because of the white roses they found there. *Rosa alba* grows wild all over central Europe and may indeed have been growing in England when the Romans arrived. Or it may have been brought to England as a garden rose by Roman traders before the first century, from the Crimea-Kurdistan area, which was its earliest habitat. *Rosa alba* became an English garden favourite in the Middle Ages, being especially popular as a hedge rose, and was incorporated into the great Seal of State by Edward I in honour of his mother, Eleanor of Provence, whose emblem it was. Edward's rose emblem has a green stalk and almost gold-coloured petals. The red *gallica*, also brought to England by the Romans, was adopted by Edward's brother Edmund, the first earl of Lancaster, as his emblem, in honour of his second wife, Blanche, whose emblem it was. It thus became the red rose of Lancaster.

The main varieties of garden rose grown in medieval England were the *Rosa alba*, the *Rosa gallica*, and the damask rose, which may have been brought to England by monks, traders or crusaders. It is first mentioned by name in Edward I's 1306 'Bill of Medicines'. The native *Rosa rubiginosa*, the sweet briar or eglantine, was widely used to make medicine and mead, and was trained along the walls of cottages and cottage gardens, and the fencing or railing of pleasure gardens, because it is a good climber and has a sweet scent that is very popular with bees. But strictly speaking, it is a wild rose and will have to be treated as such by being excluded, with fond apologies, from this chapter.

Medieval cultivated roses were different from modern versions of the same varieties. They were more like the wild roses from which they were descended, having smaller and more fragile flowers that were open to bees, and a gentler, more subtle fragrance. Only when their petals were dried, and this is particularly true of the *gallica officinalis*, the apothecaries' rose, did they smell really strongly; when fresh they gave off a fragrance too delicate and haunting to be called a perfume, and one which was the sole, magical exception to the medieval rule of the stronger the better.

> Wholesome in smelling be the sweet flowers,
> Full delightable, outward, to the sight;
> The thorn is sharp, covered with fresh colours,

wrote Lydgate in the mid-fifteenth century, drawing our attention to the other major difference between medieval and modern roses: medieval thorns were bigger and more abundant. Hence the emphasis on thorns in medieval rose symbolism. Most medieval roses were tall, rambling bushes with long, thorny stems; they are variously referred to by medieval writers as bushes, trees and flowers.

Albertus Magnus, the thirteenth-century encyclopaedist, wrote of the *Rosa alba*:

> It has often 50 or 60 petals. It is a tree of which the trunk often attains the thickness of one's arm; it is very bushy and the branches long and thin.

Most of the roses in medieval literature and art are red. Rose-red was an even more common simile than lily-white, and the only white roses in proverbs and poems are wild ones. The *Rosa alba* was the only widely cultivated white rose, and part of its appeal lay in its complementary role to red roses, which it set off to perfection in gardens, garlands and bouquets.

> 'She walketh up and down, and as her liste [as she wishes]
> She gathereth flowers, party [both] white and red,
> To make a subtle garland for her head,' (*Knight's Tale*)
> (See illustrations pp. 160 and 161)

The prototypes of the shaggy, bushy roses that shed their summer petals after one short season were the *Rosa alba*, with its extravagant foliage, and the damask rose, with its long, green branches laden with prickles.

The *gallicas* were the most upright and compact of all the medieval rose varieties, and were therefore the best variety for formal gardens. The single central 'rosers' of medieval rosaries were almost certainly *gallicas*. Even so, they were wilder and more like trees than they are in their modern form. The piquant transcience of that central rose, and of many such in medieval romances, was sharpened by the fact that, with very few exceptions, medieval roses flowered only once a year. 'All stand on chaunglis (change) like a midsummer rose,' wrote Lydgate, knowing that such a simile would strike straight home with a medieval audience. Numerous medieval proverbs dwelt on the same theme.

The *Rosa mundi*, associated with Henry II's Fair Rosamond, was so called because it united the rose colours of the world, i.e. red and white, given that white meant anything from pure white to pale pink or gold, in its striped petals. But if it was known to Rosamond's twelfth-century chroniclers, it was only elliptically so. It is a bud sport of the *gallica officinalis* and was not in general cultivation until the sixteenth century. It contradicted the medieval liking for the strong and simple, be it in flowers, smells or flavours. The true red and white rose is the York and Lancaster, a variety of the damask, and it is not so much striped as white with an occasional blush-pink blotch. Like the *Rosa mundi*, this was never a medieval favourite. It was a late medieval hybrid, and rare enough for Henry VIII to adopt it as an emblem of his unique kingly power; he had the Order of the Garter insignia remodelled to include a red within a white rose, alternating with a white within a red rose.

But the Tudor rose was only one in a long tradition of royal rose badges. Roses were royal insignia in England from the reign of Edward I onwards. The red rose of Provins, the *gallica officinalis*, brought to Provence from its native Phoenicia by the crusading count Thibault IV in the early thirteenth century, was adopted by Edmund of Woodstock, youngest son of Edward I, as his emblem when he returned to England from an embassy to Provence in 1320. Henry IV had as his emblem the red rose of Lancaster. Edward IV was nicknamed the Rose of Rouen because he was born in Rouen in 1441, and during his reign coins known as rose nobles were issued; his cognizance was a Rose en Soleil. The heraldic badge of his son, Edward V, was the white rose of York. The slipped rose, on a short stalk with two leaves, surmounted by the royal crown, was the badge of England.

Institutions too took roses as their emblems. The chapter house at York Minster, built in the reign of Edward I, had this inscription over its doorway:

> *Ut rose flos florum*   (As the rose is the flower of flowers
> *Sic est domus ista domorum.*   So is this the house of houses.)

Countless monastic buildings and churches were decorated with rose carvings in their stone and wood work, as well as bunches of fresh roses throughout their interiors. Rose windows, which became one of the great glories of medieval English architecture, were probably introduced into Europe by crusaders returning from the Middle East, where the rose was the favourite theme in Islamic art and poetry. Throughout the medieval period, roses were carved on misericords, screens and all kinds of church and palace furnishings. There were rose tapestries, embroideries and manuscript illustrations. Men, women and places were given rose names; endless poems and songs were written in honour of roses.

The Menagier devoted a whole little section of his treatise on housekeeping to the household uses of roses. He gave a simple recipe for red rose water and one for the best way to keep roses red. It is apparently to tie up twelve buds in linen and put them in an earthenware jug fully of verjuice. When the buds have drunk all the verjuice, refill the jug, and when the buds are full blown take them out of the bag and soak them in warm water for a while. Such was the medieval faith in verjuice. Or in roses. 'The rose of Provence is the best one to put into dresses to make them smell nice. The petals must be dried and sifted through a sieve in mid August so that the worms fall through the holes in the sieve', continued the Menagier.

Rose water, oil, preserves and petal garnishes were almost always made of red rose petals, those of the *Rosa gallica* keeping and intensifying their perfume when dried and powdered.

Roses are easy to propagate and are the best possible flowers on which to practice that favourite medieval skill, to which the Menagier was as addicted as every house and garden holder: grafting. While the Menagier grafted, pruned and clipped, his wife ground red rose petals into rose sugar for use in making preserves and fruit tarts.

Physicians recommended rose sugar for making comforting plasters for the heart, to be followed by 'a draught of wine that cleaneth the bowels,' leaving one ready for a draught of refreshing rose water. This was not only a tonic but a skin cleanser and an eyewash. Celandine, fennel, rue and vervain waters were used in the same way, but none with so much relish as rose water. 'Anoint your house with rose oil,' wrote one fourteenth-century physician. A royal recipe for scenting a room recommended that cypress wood be burned to remove the foul air; then twelve spoons of 'bright red rose water and fine powder sugar' be boiled slowly over hot embers, until the room smells as if it is full of roses. The humble cottager had to be content with 'anointing' his hovel more humbly by sprinkling it with rose water or making rose pot-pourris. Well-to-do medieval homes had a still-room, where the housewife made scents to 'anoint' herself and her house; cottage wives made scents and scented waters in their everyday household basins.

All medieval roses recipes were sweet. The flavour of the rose was too delicate to survive the rigors of a medieval pottage, for which the peppery taste of marigolds was better suited. Roses were used to flavour sweet puddings, preserves, especially quince jam, sweet jellies and white wines in need of a boost. Rose petals were confectioned in honey to make a sweet compote known as Melrosette, and rosewater was occasionally given to children as an alternative sweet drink to rose hip syrup, though its main use was as a salve for sore eyes.

Rose medicines, like rose foods, were essentially sweet and comforting; they were not strong purges or 'hot' or 'cold' cures. They were heir to the classical view of the rose as a comfit, cosmetic and medicine combined. Those who could afford John of Gaddesden's fees, and the oil to make the rose oil he prescribed against ephemera fever, a hot and dry complaint, rubbed themselves with rose oil after bathing, resting in a cool place and being fanned with cool air. If the condition was caused by too much hot food, which it probably was if the patient had been indulging in the best medieval dishes, he should eat cold things and drink vinegar syrup flavoured with roses. If it was caused by over-activity, he should rub camomile and violet oil into his joints, and apply fomentations of roses, violets, and camomile to them. Rose and violet syrups were commonly prescribed against fevers, and the simplest of all medieval prescriptions is John of Gaddesden's cure for 'a hot stomach': 1 oz. roses. Rose wine sweetened with rose sugar was one of the more palatable medieval electuaries.

The medical rose played just the role one would expect of it: that of a pleasant soothing agent, or else as a disguise for less pleasant medicines which were often drunk in rose water. The healing power of the rose lay in its fragrant beauty, as the author of the early fourteenth century *Lay of the Little Bird* implied in this passage from his romance:

> So sweet was the savour of roses and other flowers and singles
> that sick persons, borne within the garden in a litter, walked
> forth sound and well for having passed the night in so lovely a
> place.

This takes us back to the casting up of sweet savour which began this chapter. It is the subtlest healing power in medieval tradition and one which has been inherent in Christian imagery since Old Testament times. Divinely sweet breath like that of the beloved in the *Song of Songs* has been attributed to countless Christian saints over the centuries. The Anglo-Saxon St Guthlac was said to have had breath which smelled 'like mellifluous plants'. Padre Pio, the Italian Franciscan friar who died in 1968, is the most recent of a succession of saintly Christians whose bodies are said to have exuded the odour of attar of roses. To die in the odour of sanctity is a Christian ideal, which the medievals complemented with the ideal of living in the odour of the sweet flowers, in an earthly intimation of the paradise to come. Fragrance was the breath of God on earth, hence its holy and healing powers, and of course the scent of the rose made it irresistible to man and bee alike.

So this chapter ends with a rose story which should be added as a tribute to all those tributes made by the medievals to their favourite flower. Legend has it that Charlemagne planted a rose tree in the cloisters of Hildesheim cathedral over a thousand years ago. Historical evidence of its existence goes back at least five hundred years. In 1884 the tree began to weaken with age and three feet of rubbish was removed from around its roots, where it had accumulated over the years, and replaced with fertile soil. Gravel-lined pipes were driven into the soil at fixed intervals to give the tree an even, regular supply of rainwater, and it immediately put out suckers, which are now nearly a century old. The cathedral and most of the town were destroyed by an air raid on March 22, 1945, but the rose-tree's root-stock was undamaged. Some shoots were burnt down to a height of six feet, but six months after the fire the burnt shoots had regained their original height of twelve feet. The tree is thirty feet high. In 1950 it was subjected to an expert examination by the town clerk, who made an official statement to the effect that it is a common *Rosa canina Linn* and is indeed over a thousand years old. If we were medievals, we would believe it all without thinking twice.

6

The Herb Garden

The medieval herb defies modern classification. It might be a flower, vegetable, fruit or grass as well as what we think of as a herb. It usually had stronger qualities than its present-day descendants: an aromatic perfume, perhaps, or a pungent flavour; curative or preservative power; cosmetic or colouring juices, or a traditional magical association. It might have one of these qualities to a marked degree, or several of them, so that it was markedly versatile. Perhaps the best broad definition of a medieval herb is that it was a very useful plant, the best strict one that it was a plant used primarily for flavouring and medicinal purposes. So many medieval plants were so variously used that almost all of them were classified as herbs by the first definition. The herbs considered in this chapter are those which the medievals most commonly and consistently classified as herbs by either definition.

Most herbs were grown in with flowers, fruits and vegetables in the all-purpose gardens of medieval cottagers and smallholders. They were only separated into their own categorical gardens by well-to-do and institutional gardeners. Even then, most of the 'herbers' mentioned in medieval garden descriptions were not herb gardens but arbours, or sheltered pleasances planted with flowers, and possibly sweet-smelling herbs to add to their fragrance and prettiness. Herbal herbers were as rare as garden herbs and herb patches were common. They were by no means unknown in wealthy private households, but were much more common in institutions, particularly monastic ones, where there were large numbers to cook and care for.

The monastic infirmary garden was the archetypal medicinal herb garden. It sometimes included kitchen herbs, with which the infirmarer could make appetizing meals for his patients; more often such herbs were sent across to him from the cellarer's garden. Herbs that were both medicinal and tasty might be grown in both types of garden. They were the commonest, and could be accommodated even by the poorest.

The association of herbs with cooking is too obvious to need explanation, especially bearing in mind the unremittingly plain and starchy diet of the poor majority in the Middle Ages. But the rich, carnivorous minority were equally appreciative of herbs, which gave them the sweet and sour pungency that saved their diet from being simply a meaty expansion of the starch monotony. Pickling herbs were popular both for their taste and their preservative powers. A good many herbs were 'hot', which was an unfailingly popular thing to be, and some were 'cold', in case the hot, herbal enthusiasm of the cook had been too much for the medieval digestion, valiant as it was.

In fact, the 'hot' and 'cold' virtues of herbs were more medicinal than dietary. This close connection explains the medieval association of herbs with medicine, and needs to be examined alongside that association if both areas are to be properly, jointly understood.

The association of herbs with medicine may be as old as the very oldest gardens. There are suggestions of it in the fragmentary records of Egyptian and Solomaic herb-gardens, but it is not documented until the fifth century BC, in the works of Hippocrates, then those of Aristotle and Theophrastus.

The Hippocratic theory of the four humours, corresponding to the four elements of the human body and producing four complexions, was fundamental to medical botany throughout the medieval period, and underlay its 'hot', 'cold', 'wet' and 'dry' diagnoses and cures. The four humours corresponded and combined with the four elements, earth, air, fire and water, so that

1. blood was hot and moist,
2. phlegm was cold and moist,
3. yellow bile was hot and dry, and
4. black bile was cold and dry.

When the humours were evenly balanced, health was good; when one of them was in excess and the others deficient, complexions resulted:

1. too much blood made a sanguine complexion,
2. too much phlegm made a phlegmatic complexion,
3. too much yellow bile made a choleric complexion, and
4. too much black bile made a melancholic complexion.

Climate, diet and occupation all affected the humours and therefore the temperamental complexion, and it was the physician's job to work out the right antidotes to complexions and so restore a healthy balance. 'The temper of the hot and cold, moist and dry, should be joined together. Right as we see trees, corns and herbs do not grow without reasonable temper of the four,' wrote one late fourteenth-century English physician in a *Treatise on Distemper*, the very title of which is evidence of its foundation in classical theory.

Medieval English herbals, like those of every west European country, were reproductions of ancient treatises, their inaccuracy and irrelevance to English conditions only occasionally illuminated by a description or prescription drawn from life. As a guide to English herbal medicines and gardens they are of as little use now as they were then, when the vast, illiterate majority passed their traditional local herbal knowledge from generation to generation by word of mouth. Even those who could read the official herbals grew and used herbs as their own experience dictated.

Monastic infirmarers grew the herbs which their experience of caring for sick monks and neighbours had recommended to them. For every classical herbal copied out in their scriptoria, medieval monasteries dispensed and taught from their infirmaries a hundred home-grown herbal medicines. Nuns had fewer academic resources than monks to rely on, but a pre-eminently practical knowledge of the cultivation and use of herbs. Medieval monastic medicine was almost completely herbal and was scarcely affected by the lay development of surgery in the late Middle Ages. Medieval medicine, like classical medicine before it, looked to nature's plants to cure the distempers that its poisons, climate, accidents and abuse by the hand of man had caused.

If the humorous balance became upset despite diet and exercise, it could be restored by external 'simples', which were the botanical equivalent of humorous constitutents. When simples of one sort were compounded, they made a medicine with one pronounced characteristic: hot, cold, wet or dry. When several sorts of simples were compounded, they made medicines with double characteristics, such as hot and dry, and often with side effects connected with these, such as sweating or sleeping.

The correspondence between bodily humours and the world of nature made herbal medicines not so much cures in themselves as aids to the body in curing itself. Hence the importance attached by medieval physicians to confidence and, by monk physicians in particular, to faith.

The natural human preference for herbal over surgical medicine was especially pronounced in England, which was blessed with an abundance of native herbs. Monastic enthusiasm for God's healing herbs combined with the Church's fear of causing death by surgery to keep monastic medicine almost completely herbal. Pliny remarked on the enormous number of herbs known and used by the British. This was certainly the case in the Anglo-Saxon period, when English herbalists listed almost 500 plants that were familiar to them. Some of the later Anglo-Saxon and early Norman herbals contain a few good, naturalistic illustrations, obviously drawn from life, not from copies of classical or Teutonic fancies, as most illustrations were.

In about 1100 the monks at Bury St Edmunds wrote and illustrated a version of the popular, classically based herbal of Apuleius Barbarus, adapting his prayers into Christian form and copying all his plant descriptions, including those of plants which didn't exist in England. But where this was the case, and where illustrations had obviously become hopelessly far removed from the plant originals or had been damaged, they sometimes substituted drawings from life of a local plant. Instead of an African marigold they drew a peony; they didn't attempt an illustration of rosemary, which only came to England in the fourteenth century. Some of their drawings, like those of the thistle and the blackberry, were very accurate.

It is impossible to estimate how many of their herbs the monks cultivated. Their thistle looks like the cultivated European thistle, *Silybum marianum*, which the infirmarer may have grown along the outer wall or fence of his garden. There is hardly any direct evidence about what infirmarers grew in their gardens at this period.

The infirmary garden of Westminster Abbey survives to this day, and is a perfect example of the small, sheltered, enclosed, infirmary garden, though its healing herbs have long since disappeared. Like all infirmarers, the one at Westminster only accounted by name for the herbs and spices he had to buy, accounting for his expenses in growing 'herbs', 'seeds' and 'little plants' under these general names. Such expenses are not even a quantitative guide to the herbs grown because they do not include perennials, wild herbs brought into the garden, self-seeding herbs and gifts, all of which were free of expense and therefore of mention in the accounts. The only way to get an insight into the contents of infirmary gardens is to scour the works of contemporary writers for clues. The garden herbs which appear most frequently in the proverbs, pop songs, poetry and household accounts of medieval England clearly grew in its gardens; those which only appear in academic treatises must be treated with more suspicion.

One of the very few literary herb gardens in which individual herbs are distinguished by name is the one in *The Tale of Beryn*, written by a contemporary of Chaucer, possibly by Chaucer himself. It belonged to a tavern-keeper's wife, who said of it:

> For many a herb grew for sew [pottage] and surgery;
> And all the alleys fair i-paris [pared, trimmed], i-railed and i-maked;
> The sage and the hyssop, i-frethid [bound] and i-staked;
> And other beds by and by [full] freshly i-dight [dressed],
>
> For comers to the house, right a sportful sight.

This was an infirmary garden which was also a kitchen herb garden, planted with herbs like sage and hyssop that were both medicinal and flavouring, and also with separate beds of predominantly medicinal and predominantly flavouring herbs. The carefully tended beds made it something of a pleasance. They would have been planted according to herbal use, type, colour, fragrance and size, interspersed with railed alleys where the owner and her guests walked to admire the 'sportful sight' (see illustration p. 240). Not only were many medieval herbs useful in infirmary and kitchen alike, but they were also decorative and fragrant. Infirmarers supplied herbs to kitcheners, cellarers, sacrists and chamberlains, and received herbs, flowers and vegetables from them in return; on a cottage scale, many herbs grown in the garden were used in the medicine and kitchen pot and also as air fresheners, decorations, adornments and cosmetics. 'Sew and surgery' were always closely connected, with delight in close attendance.

As the best herb gardens were those of monastic infirmarers, and as medicine-making was the most important use of medieval herbs, infirmary gardens are the first sort of herb gardens dealt with in this chapter, which is about the carefully planted, tended and handled herbs of 'little cloister' infirmary gardens.

Infirmary Garden Herbs

The tavern-keeper's wife singled out sage and hyssop for individual mention, and just as hers is the model herb garden, so these are model 'sew and surgery' herbs, grown in every infirmary garden for use in medicines and cooking, to which they gave health and flavour.

The botanical name for sage, salvia, from the latin *salveo*, meaning 'I am well,' confirms that sage was an infirmary garden herb. The Romans used it in medicine and cooking, and brought it to Britain, where there is record of it as a garden plant by 1213. 'He that would live for aye must eat sage in May,' was one of a number of English medieval proverbs reflecting sage's medicinal reputation. Sage ale and sage tea were popular, slightly sedative health drinks.

Medieval physicians prescribed sage 'fresh and green to clean the body of venom and pestilence', and its digestive oils are used by homeopaths today to soothe nerves and convulsions, and were used in the early years of this century to remove traces of iron from the waters at Tunbridge Wells spa. Sage flowers yield a pale, dull violet dye that was used to colour desserts. The medievals chewed sage to whiten their rotting teeth, as well as swallowing masses of it in poultry and pottage dishes, along with the inevitable onions and garlic, which means that sage and onion stuffing has a medieval pedigree. As sage dries well, it was a useful strewing and pot-pourri herb, and as it grows easily it provided almost every medieval gardener with a bit of 'sew and surgery'.

Clary (*Salvia verbenaca*) was a medieval favourite, though it is hardly ever seen in gardens nowadays. It was called clary, clear-eye, or Oculus Christi, because its main medicinal use was as an eyewash, made by infusing its sweet scented leaves in water. It was a popular beer gruit, and was used in cooking in much the same way as sage. Both of them grew in kitchen as well as infirmary gardens.

Unlike the benign and soothing sages, hyssop is a metabolic stimulant, and has not survived in common use. It was probably brought to English gardens from its native southern Europe either by the Romans or by the Normans. It used to be found naturalized on the walls of the thirteenth-century Cistercian Abbey of Beaulieu in Hampshire, and was used by the monks, and indeed by many medieval householders, to strew on the floor because it releases a surprisingly orange-flavoured, resinous scent when walked on. This scent won it a place in the incomparable liqueur made by the monks at Chartreuse, and in medieval perfumes. Traditionally it is a holy herb, being one of the bitter purifying herbs eaten by the Jews at the Passover, its name coming from the Hebrew *Azob* (to pass by, leave). But though it was a good Lenten bitter, like tansy it was eaten as a bitter all year round and was not a particularly religious food, any more than it was an exclusively religious strewing herb.

'Sow hyssop in August,' wrote the Menagier, who went on to recommend its use in herb omelettes, pottages and pickles. These were its cooking uses, 'seethed, boiled or baked but never raw', as one fourteenth-century English writer put it. It was a hot purgative, suitable for hot pottages. It was drunk in oil, wine or syrups 'to warm away cold catarrhs and chest phlegms', and rubbed on to bruises, which it soothes. With its traditionally religious, generally purifying, astringent and stimulant uses, its bitter taste and sweet aroma, it is similar to another hot and dry herb which also grew in many medieval infirmary gardens and some all-purpose ones as well: rue.

Medieval physicians used it to remove ill humours and phlegms from any part of the body, because it is a strong purgative. Plague and poison were the most common targets for its purges, though it was also used as an eyewash when cooled down with rosewater. Its purgative powers did not stop at the intestines. Rue was used as a holy water sprinkler in exorcisms, as a strewing herb that expelled pestilential vapours with its aromas, being so used in the Law Courts until the eighteenth century, as an air cleanser, in nosegays that released germ-expelling perfume, and as an ale clarifier. It was not in general use in England until the fifteenth century, being restricted to the specialized infirmary gardens of monasteries, and perhaps the royal big households, but then it quickly became popular enough to earn the name 'Herb of Grace', which it retained in the form 'Ave Grace' in some parts of the country until the nineteenth century, and to appear in tangled herb and vegetable yards. Medicinally it was classified as a 'cup herb', taken as an infusion. In the kitchen it was used to make pickles that sharpened up broths and pottages. Being what Walafrid called 'puny in size', and happy with poor soil, it grew in poor gardens as well as the borders of infirmary gardens, where it often grew near a gentler, more decorative herb that was primarily useful in medicine, but also for purposes of fragrant and health-giving delight.

Camomile won the name 'the plants' physician' because it revives sickly and drooping plants growing near it. It is an exceptionally tough herb, thriving on poor, sandy soils and in droughts, but was usually only grown in carefully tended infirmary gardens because its flowers are so tiny that a lot of them are needed if they are to be of any use, and a camomile lawn takes a lot of work to establish. It was brought into English cultivation from the wilds by 1265, and was planted in plots or lawns because, as Falstaff put it, 'the more it is trodden the faster it grows,' and the more it releases its apple-scented aroma. Edward II's 1313 wardrobe account mentioned a purchase of camomile, to be used as a clothes freshener. Its flowers make a sedative, digestive, carminative infusion, and its blue oil was added to many a medieval bath for the sake of the same properties. The flowers were rubbed into sore skin and bites, and some cottagers could manage a little patch of camomile to provide them with this relief.

But for most of this period camomile was a relatively rare garden herb, grown in clumps by infirmary gardeners who wanted to revive their herbs as well as their patients with it.

Betony was almost as important a herb as sage in the Middle Ages; medicinally it was more so, and therefore worthy of proximity to 'the plants' physician'. The centuries have reduced betony to insignificance, probably because the medieval claims for it were so unrealistically wholesale that they were later discredited wholesale. 'At betony I will begin . . . better herb is there none in the world . . . Betony is ye best,' wrote herbalists from the twelfth to the fifteenth centuries, listing almost every disorder known to man, and a few more besides, such as 'violent blood', 'chilly need', fear and 'angry snake' bites, as curable by betony.

Dittany, like betony, fell into disuse. It was often used in conjunction with betony as a cure-all for all complexions. Camomile tea with dittany, scabious and pennyroyal added, was the favourite medieval 'herb water' against poisons, and variations on it were drunk as mild soporifics.

This last was the medical use of dill, its name being a derivative of the Anglo-Saxon *dilla*, meaning to lull. It was a kitchen as well an infirmary herb. Its spicey leaves added flavour to fish and pickles as well as pottages; its seeds flavoured dill vinegar and the aroma of its pretty yellow flowers attracted bees. It was the ideal spicey, cordial herb for an infirmary garden needing a bit of sunny colour to brighten its beds. Dill, cumin and anise were all aromatics that gave seeds eaten to help the digestion. Spice cakes made of these seeds were eaten after rich meals and after illnesses.

Cumin was more widely grown than dill, being a common item of peasant rents, alongside hens and eggs. Infirmarers grew cumin for the soothing complexion and eye ointment yielded by its seeds, which were also popular as a flavouring for poultry and pickles.

Anise was obtained from the oils of *Pimpinella anisum*, a native of the Near East which will only ripen in a few parts of England, notably East Anglia. This kind of anise was grown by a few dedicated infirmarers, along the south walls of their gardens, but was usually imported. Fennel was a more common home-grown source of anisic oil, which was also obtained from *Pimpinella saxifraga*, and was much revered in the Middle Ages as a digestive aid and anit-depressant. It was a constituent of all kinds of tonics and 'hot' drinks to combat spleen; it was 'good to every salve' and it grew like camomile,

> by ye earth low.
> Nigh every man well him know.
> (Fourteenth-century English
> medical manuscript)

The low-growing borders of infirmary gardens were the brightest and most aromatic parts of them, and visitors and patients walking up and down the paths were close to their delights. Perhaps surprisingly, pimpernel was described by one fourteenth-century herbalist as 'a noble grass'. Many herbs that we think of as grasses, weeds, or flowers, as well as many that we think of as too big and bushy to be counted as herbs, were grown in infirmary gardens, which had plenty of room for variations on the neat little enclosure prototype described by the hostess in *The Tale of Beryn*. There were often corners and walls that accommodated 'grasses' and tall and ungainly herbs.

Elecampane, for instance, grows to a height of four or five feet and has twelve inch leaves, a big tuberous rootstock and big, brilliant gold-yellow flowers. It was staked against the enclosing walls of the few infirmary gardens that accommodated it. The roots were taken up and dried each summer, part being used as a pleasant digestive for humans and animals (one of its Anglo-Saxon names was *hors helene*, horse healer) or a sweetmeat, and part replanted for the following year in a spot where delicate herbs would not be over-shadowed. The root has a fruity scent when freshly dug and a violet scent when dried, and was made into sweetmeats, candied cakes and sweets, to tempt sickly appetites and to indulge after-dinner ones. Medieval medical writers spoke of elecampane with relish; infirmarers with big gardens made sweets and cordials of it; household gardeners did the same, and between them they continued its existence from its probably Roman, possibly native, beginnings throughout the Middle Ages.

Bugloss is an equally unlikely infirmary garden herb because it is mild and insipid, the very things a medieval herb should not be, and had no marked suitability for healing any particular complexion, the very thing a medieval medicinal herb should have. But it was cultivated by as discriminating a gardener as John the Gardener, and was grown and used for 'sew' and 'surgery'. It was put into pottages and medicines rather in the manner of an inoffensive extra included for good measure, pale colouring and little else. It was a minor salad ingredient, usually under its French name, *langue de boeuf*, or ox-tongue, and was put into medicinal syrups under the general recommendations 'good against stiffness' or 'comforting'. Infirmarers must have had their own secret reasons for bothering with bugloss. The key to them may be the fact that bugloss is related to borage, which was grown along with most of its friends and relations in almost every infirmary garden.

Like bugloss, borage has a mild taste. This gets much stronger when the leaves are added to claret or cider, for which flavouring purpose it was cultivated in many English medieval kitchen gardens, as it had been in ancient ones. Its Greek name, *euphosynon*, alluded to the sense of well-being it imparted to those drinking borage-flavoured wine; its English name has a similar meaning, being derived either from the latin *cor* (heart) and *ago* (I stimulate) or the Celtic *borrach*, meaning glad courage. But infirmarers preferred the mild, unalcoholic borage, and grew it to make into cool cordials, plasters, bath oils and medicines for hot complaints. Only tavern-keepers, wine and cider makers, and infirmarers grew borage on any scale.

Only infirmarers grew its relation, comfrey. It still has its old nickname, boneset, in some parts of the country, indicative of its powers of healing wounds and stopping bleeding, but apart from infirmarers, most gardeners gathered it from the wilds and did not bother to enclose and tend it.

This is also true of vervain (*Verbena officinalis*), which was 'comely by way and gate', and only cultivated by the keen minority. In fact infirmarers tended to disapprove of vervain, which was a primitive sort of herb, accredited with vague, pagan powers of producing love. The ruthlessly practical infirmary gardeners distrusted such superstitious vagaries. Nevertheless, they didn't like to be too dismissive, and many infirmarers grew it, perhaps partly for its aromatic scent, while everyone gathered it from the wilds.

It was for the sake of its musky perfume, which intensified under cultivation until all parts of the plant were strongly aromatic, that angelica was brought into gardens from the wilds. It had a much more readily apparent claim to inclusion in infirmary gardens than vervain, being a major antidote to plague. Its full name is *Angelica archangelica*, said to be derived from the legend that an angel appeared to a monk in a dream and told him of its usefulness against the plague. Its cooking and delighting uses were, however, as apparent as its medicinal ones, and angelica was cultivated in all kinds of herb and in some kitchen as well as infirmary gardens. Hardly any herbs were confined to infirmary garden cultivation, since that was the occupation of a tiny minority, while healing, or at least soothing, was the occupation of every housewife. But the herbs considered so far in the chapter are ones that were primarily medicinal and therefore can justly be considered as infirmary herbs. The herbs in this next section are those that combined medicinal and luxurious household usefulness in such equal proportion that they can simply be considered as herb garden herbs.

Herb Garden Herbs

By virtue of the fact that only the rich, the leisured, the devotedly horticultural and the socially competitive kept herb gardens, these herbs are herbs of delight as well as 'sew and surgery'. The richer householders had time and space enough to grow these herbs in herb gardens, not just in kitchen garden amalgams. As far as 'sew' is concerned, the herbs in this section are those that flavoured meat, fish, elaborate pottages and confectionery. As far as 'surgery' is concerned, many of the herbs in this section were grown by infirmarers and cottagers as well as the ladies who looked after the health of their households. These ladies learnt much of their medicine from Benedictine infirmary sisters, the rest of it from their family, neighbours and personal experience. Some of them made little infirmary gardens, but more often they grew medicinal herbs in with kitchen and cosmetic ones, the three types often coinciding. Medieval literature is strewn with references to women herbalists, many of whom grew the healing herbs they used, gardening being a major feminine duty and pastime. Medicine was the one subject on which the Menagier's wife was able to turn the tables and give her husband some instruction; she probably made herself an infirmary patch somewhere in the garden he commended to her care.

Some women directed their gardening skills towards developing further skills as child nurses, hospital nurses, midwives, barbers, 'old wife physicians' and dietary experts. After monastic infirmarers, aristocratic and bourgeoise women were better endowed than anyone else with the responsibility, time, residential stability and knowledge to go in for medicinal herb gardening.

As far as delight is concerned, some of the herbs in this section were outstanding; others were just typically and incidentally obliging. Fragrance was the chief garden delight, fragrance and cosmetic usefulness their chief household delights.

> A chamber had he in that hostelry
> Alone, without any company,
> Full fetishly [skilfully, neatly] y-dight with herbs sweet.
> (Chaucer's *Miller's Tale*)

Sweet-smelling herbs were a summer enchantment. One of the favourite summer pastimes of medieval ladies was showing off the fragrance and neat prettiness of their herb gardens to visitors, as the hostess in *The Tale of Beryn* did. The best herb gardens were locked, walled enclosures, often set in a south-facing angle between two walls of a lady's chamber. They were laid out in beds, alleyways and perhaps herbal lawns, sometimes with fountains (see illustration p. 240). Most herbs like a lot of sunshine but are happy with quite poor, dry soil; their cultivation requires only light work such as weeding, raking, edging, trimming, tying up into little clumps and patterns, staking and hoeing, all of which could be done by women. Herb-garden paths and beds were bordered by small, sweet-smelling herbs, some of which we would call flowers, and many of which were grown by all kinds of gardeners for all kinds of 'sew and surgery'.

Angelica is the paragon of the versatile herb garden herb, grown by infirmarers for its anti-pestilential properties and by others for the same properties and also for its digestive, gastronomic and decorative ones. Its leaves were chewed to cure flatulence throughout the medieval period and long afterwards. Well-to-do ladies grew angelica in their herb gardens for a host of sweet reasons: the aromatic oil of its roots and seeds was used to flavour drinks (it was an ingredient of Chartreuse) and to make cordials, with honey and vinegar added; when distilled, it makes a musky perfume; the juice of the plant turns into a gum resin when dried; the stalks were candied and eaten as after-dinner sweets, much liked because of their sweetness and bright green colour; the seeds were burnt over a low fire to perfume rooms. Pretty, musky, sweet angelica gave sweet 'sew', strong 'surgery' and perfumed delight.

Lavender performed similar service. It is easily propagated, and after being introduced into England by the Romans, spread through countryside and gardens. All parts of the plant except the petals contain the oil that has been distilled in ancient, medieval and modern times alike into a skin perfume and bath oil, and in ancient and medieval times into varnishes, syrups, cordials and preserves as well. Like violet and rose water, lavender water was esteemed as a tonic and a heart cordial. Lavender flowers were eaten in salads, candied into sweets, and dried for pot-pourris and wardrobe bouquets; they were added to pottages and poultry stews as an alternative flavouring to mint. Lavender is attractive to bees, easy to grow and absorbent of the summer heat; not surprisingly it was grown by infirmary, herb and kitchen gardeners all through the medieval period.

Other members of the labiate family were popular for the same reasons. The strongest scented of them is balm, its botanical name, *melissa*, being an allusion to the honey secreted by its flowers. Like all the labiates, its leaves retain their scent after drying and were therefore made into pot-pourris and strewn about the house. They were also made into cordials, and balm tea was a popular restorative and comforter. Medieval taverners and monastic cellarers grew balm in their gardens, along with costmary, ground ivy and other gruits, to flavour their brews, and it was added to weak wines as a spice. It was the main ingredient of Carmelite Water, first made by the Carmelite nuns of St Just in 1379, which became the top cosmetic in late medieval Europe. As a 'sew' herb, balm was exclusively sweet, being eaten as a sweet comfit and drunk in sweet cordials, with angelica. It served, like lavender, to keep the garden full of bees, to such an extent that one of its ancient names was bees' leaf. It appears alongside lavender and the gillyflower in a late fourteenth century lyric in which the poet compares the beauty of his mistress to various sweet herbs:

> Your breath is sweeter than balm, sugar or licquorice . . .
> And yourself as sweet as is the gillyflower
> Or any lavender seeds strewn in a coffer to smell.

Sweet basil breathed a warm, clove-like perfume into the sweetened air of aromatic herb borders and beds. Like lavender and balm, it is a good strewing herb because it releases its scent when

The Herb Garden

walked on, and it flavoured medieval sauces and drinks sweetly. But it is a tender herb and needs rich soil to do well; the sweeter, tougher marjoram was more favoured. In warm weather its scent is beautifully refreshing and it makes a pretty, delicately pink patch of fragrance on the poorest of soils. Fresh or dried, it is one of the sweetest of herbs, and its oil was made into perfumes and waters, which had a slightly camphorous scent; its flowers made posies and pot-pourris, candied comfits, spices and preserves.

Pot or winter marjoram is even tougher, and was grown in kitchen gardens as a sweet and savoury pot-herb. Vulgar marjoram leaves made a soothing tea, and helped to soften the taste of over-acid beer. All the marjorams were added into salads, pressed against bruises and rheumatic swellings to relieve pain, and grown in infirmary, herb and kitchen gardens. Marjoram flowerheads, steeped in alum, water and a decoction of crab-tree bark, released a good purple dye that was used on linen. But sweet or gentle marjoram, as it was nicknamed, was the darling of sweet and aromatic gardeners. Its pink flowers make it virtually irresistible to bees, and it grew alongside all the other labiates in a hot bed of summer fragrance. Enclosed beneath the sun, overhung by sand, dust, the drone of bees and all-pervasive 'sweet savour' that never failed to intoxicate the medieval senses, the marjorams and thymes were every herb gardener's intoxicant delights.

Thyme does not appear as much as the marjorams in medieval garden, medicine or cookery books. It appears, under the name *serpulum*, meaning serpentlike, in one tenth century Anglo-Saxon work, which suggests that it is the low-growing wild thyme that medieval gardeners only occasionally bothered to cultivate and medieval cooks simply called 'a good herb'. It was used as a pot herb, in conjuction with savory and mint and, like most aromatics, infused into a soothing and digestive tea.

Thyme grows on very poor soil, and in between stones and patches of heath-land, and it was often planted in the poorest, out-of-the-way corners of herb gardens, where its little mauve flowers covered the ground, stones and walls and mingled their fragrance with that of the camomile, sage and lavender. Gaps in these fragrant little hedges were filled by purslane patches. Purslane has a very mild taste and no nectar, but its cool mildness made it a cool curative to 'hot' complaints, a thirst preventative, a salad extra and a source of one of the four 'cold seeds' of medieval medicine. It grows low and dense, and was a carpet for the strongly scented edging herbs.

Behind these grew the taller aromatics such as balm, the marjorams and mint. The medievals welcomed the bright green leaves and lilac flowers of spearmint, the hot, pungent aroma and dark pink flowers of pennyroyal, the strong, cool smell of water and corn mint as ideal contrasts to the dusky, musky border herbs beneath them. Refreshing and free growing, the mints were cultivated and used by all kinds of medieval gardeners.

Mint already had a high reputation in ancient and Biblical times, one of the reasons for this being its power to stop milk curdling, in the kitchen and in the stomach. The other reasons for its enduring popularity are its invigorating aroma, pretty flowers, delicious taste and pungent oil, which was the secret of the medieval preference for pennyroyal above all the mints. Pennyroyal appears in as many medieval medical as household treatises, under its part latin, part English name, pulogium (also pullial or pululogium), classified as 'a hot and dry herb of field and garden, to be taken against colds, rheums and coughs'. Infusions of its ultra-minty oil have been taken since ancient times to loosen the bowels, a service that always won medieval approval, and also to clear headaches and giddiness. Even without its medicinal usefulness, it was worth growing just for its repellent effect on flies and fleas, the resident scourges of medieval homes. Rooms, beds, tables, floors, churches, clothes and meals were strewn with pennyroyal to keep them flea-free, and sprigs of pennyroyal were tied or carried about the person to keep it similarly free and fresh.

All the mints, not just pennyroyal, have camphor in their flowers, which qualified them as bath, perfume and digestive herbs, besides being excellent flavourings for meat dishes.

Most herb sauces, salads, custards and meat dishes included some sort of mint picked from the garden of the housewife, be she a cottager or a countess. The round-leaved apple mint was not as common as the other mints, and was nicknamed 'Monks' Herb' because only monastic infirmarers grew it to any extent. It is milder than the other mints, which explains its relative unpopularity, but also its use by the infirmarers as a cordial and confectionery for the aging bowels and digestions of the older brethren.

'Savory is of the same savour to eat as marjoram,' wrote the Menagier, and it grew in the same herb beds. Like marjoram, it is strongly sweet-tasting, and was cultivated by those who could provide it with the rich, light, well-raked soil it demands. It made hot, sweet syrups and conserves, and hotted up cool salads, in which only the idle rich of the late Middle Ages had much interest. Savory was a herb garden, not a kitchen garden, herb.

Its aroma is milder than that of the labiates, and if it was not grown in with the marjorams, it was grown in with the other mild semi-aromatics and salad herbs by keen herbalists, gardeners supplying well-to-do kitchens, and infirmarers. These herbs didn't have the immediate aroma of the aromatics.

Coriander was one such small herb that needed special attention to be appreciable. Its pale mauve, almost white, flowers were overshadowed by those of taller and bigger herbs, and over-perfumed by the aromatics, unless it was planted apart from them, with other herbs of a mild disposition. Its virtue lies in its seeds, which have the same unpleasant smell as the rest of the plant until they are fully ripe, when they begin to smell sweetly of citrus. This smell intensifies when the seeds are dried, and the ripe seed oil that emits it was a much prized additive to liqueurs, sweets, preserves, like the Menagier's favourite nut jam, and cosmetics, including Carmelite Water. Dried coriander leaves gave a tangy flavour to soups and broth, turning them from savoury into sweet and sour.

Caraway is another crypto-aromatic. Its large, scented, parsnip-like roots lie deep underground, and its camphorous seed oil is, like that of coriander, only powerfully fragrant when fully matured and dried. It is a tall (2 ft.) glabrous plant, and aromatic seeds and oil are the last things one would expect of it and the only things the medievals really valued in it. Seedy herbs were grown by those who valued the peculiar appeal of seediness above that of scent and taste. Caraway oil was used like lavender oil; its seeds were used like coriander seeds. Indeed, in the *Form of Cury* King Richard II's cookery book, there is a recipe called 'Cormarye' which is, as its name suggests, a mixture of the two kinds of seeds. Coriander, caraway, pepper and ground garlic are mixed together, salted and put into red wine, and this is used to cover and baste loin of pork. A hot, sharp, seedy sauce such as this was a 'sew', a 'surgery' for the cold and phlegmatic, and a mouthful of delight, all at once.

Caraway was a rare plant, even in its native England, and few gardeners had a herbal seed-bed to provide them with the wherewithal for such a sauce. The Menagier had to explain to his wife what caraway was, it being even rarer in France than in England, and he did so by describing it as a 'seed eaten in comfits'. He included a great many of these seeds in his recipe for nut jam, rarity notwithstanding. Sweets, cakes, spiced wine, known as 'Compost Water', and roast apples, were filled with caraway seeds by those who could afford to buy them or were clever enough to grow them. People chewed coriander and caraway seeds to get rid of wind and make their breath smell hot and seedy. In an age when 'rotting and stinking teeth', 'cankers and worms in the teeth' and 'evil breath' were common complaints, and the remedies varied from toothpastes made of 'burnt roots of iris, aristologia, reeds, sea-shells, pumice-stones, stags horns, nitre, alum and cuttle bones, all ground together' to mouth-washes made of 'sage, cinnamon, mastich [resin], gall, cubeb, musk, juniper seeds, rosemary leaves and cypress roots', the tactic was clearly not to waste time trying to remove the smell, but to cover it up with a stronger one. In Chaucer's *Miller's Tale*, Absolom 'cheweth grain [cardamom] and liquorice 'To smell sweet, ere he had combed his hair,' so that he will win the favour of the carpenter's wife. Seedy herbs made up for their blandness without by their hot fragrance within.

Black mustard, for instance, is an English native with an Anglo-Saxon compound name which explains how and why it was used: must (grape-juice, with which it was often mixed) and ardens (hot). Mustard hotted up drinks, pottages, sauces, custards and capons. It was grown in mixed kitchen and in herb gardens throughout the medieval period. It is easy to grow, and John the Gardener recommended everybody to do so. Like most seedy herbs, it contains a medicinally useful oil, which in this case also made mustard paste and the dearly loved mustard sauce that made the medieval herring a fiery flesh meal. Mustard oil first irritates, then partially anaesthetizes the sensory nerves when applied externally, and stimulates the heart, respiration and digestion when taken internally, as it usually was in the Middle Ages. It was put into herbal plasters and baths for those suffering from cold and wet complaints, but was most frequently taken after a big, hot, spicy meal, to help with its digestion either by stimulating or by emptying the stomach, doses of mustard on the medieval scale being powerfully emetic. Neither pretty nor fragrant, the seedy herbs were a small minority with a big appeal.

One of them, however, was universally popular. It was not just a seedy herb, for seediness was only one of its attractions, and it was not just a herb-garden herb, for it grew in every single kitchen and infirmary garden too. In fact, it gives us the perfect introduction to the third section of this chapter, because it was everyone's 'sew and surgery' mainstay. Therein lay its delight, for though pleasant-smelling it is not aromatic, and it has no flowers, though its foliage is bright green, the way the medievals liked their foliage. The delightful thing about parsley was that it was the best kitchen herb.

Kitchen Garden Herbs

Like most of the herbs in this section, parsley was grown in herb and infirmary gardens as well as kitchen gardens, but its rich and constant kitchen use fully justifies its place in this section. It was John the Gardener's favourite herb. The author of the 'Fromond' household list, written in about 1500, described it as 'a sauce herb', in which capacity it was widely used, for its taste and its bright green colour, which elevated the humblest sauce into green sauce, or 'sauce verte', as the cookery books called it. The addition of parsley to pottages, pickles and casseroles was usually accompanied by the addition of sage.

Everyone used home-grown parsley in their cooking. 'I have porretts and parsley and scalons [shallots, chibolles],' boasted a cottager in Langland's *Piers Plowman*. Parsley went into the pot in vast quantities; the better off made 'the parsley, the parsnip, the porretts' into a sweet, sharp, green pottage or, if they had a sweet tooth and the Menagier's financial resources, a nice, bright green, November jam, made of parsley and fennel roots cooked in honey. The main medicinal use of parsley was diuretic, and it was commonly described as such under the classification 'hot and dry'.

'This herb is called petrosilium,' wrote a thirteenth-century English herbalist, 'because it grows in or near stones and stony places (petrosus is the latin for stony). It is warm and dry, very diuretic and aperitive. So says Ysidore.' (Isidore of Seville, 560-636, was a herbalist in the classical tradition.) Parsley does indeed prefer less rich soil, and often comes up in odd corners, eschewing the place where it has been sown. It is therefore a good, though unpredictable, edging herb, making thick, bright, pleasantly scented borders to beds of herbs and the paths that intersected them.

Its most valued family relation was fennel, but equally widely cultivated was another relation, chervil, which combined the assets of fennel and parsley, and was grown in many cottage gardens. 'Chibolles and chervils and ripe cherries many,' wrote Langland, in celebration of tasty cottage plants. Reaching a height of one to two feet, chervil was planted with its relations, fennel, angelica and coriander, some way behind the parsley borders. It grows quickly, easily and decoratively and, like parsley, grows again each time it is cut. Its foliage is feathery, tasting and smelling of aniseed. It was used in the same way as fennel, to flavour pottages, salads and sauces with the anisic warmth which was one of the most popular attributes of all the parsley herbs, and which gave chervil its botanical name: *cerifolium*, from *cheirei phyllum* – the leaf which warms or rejoices the heart. Hence its medieval nickname, fille. It was grown commonly enough to give rise to the saying 'not worth a fille', and provided 'sew', 'surgery' and a parsley-like delight to infirmary, herb and kitchen gardeners.

Chervil roots were boiled into 'sew', and in fact are only safe to eat when they have been boiled. Wealthier housewives candied them into sweets. Chervil 'surgery' is diuretic, like that of parsley, only milder. Its slender fruits, which appear when its flowers die, were little thought of because they did not have the aromatic strength of the seeds attached to parsley's seedy relations.

Of these, the least known and cultivated was alexanders. It was not a common kitchen herb, nor even a common herb-garden or infirmary herb, and does not belong in the sections of this chapter that deal with those herbs. It is included in this kitchen garden section because it was primarily a pot-herb, and because it is related to parsley. It is naturalized on the sites of several medieval abbeys, and its preference for the west coast, especially the island of Steep Holm, where it now covers the priory ruins and more than twenty surrounding acres, makes it a probable monastic import. Steep Holm is one of the few places in Britain where alexanders grow to their four feet tall, fully aromatic best (see illustration p. 144).

Their aroma and strong taste, somewhere between celery and myrrh, made their cultivation worth the effort required to keep them sheltered and supported. They have been replaced as a kitchen herb by celery, which also requires careful cultivation but is happier in the English climate. Alexanders have a much stronger flavour than celery, and were primarily used as flavouring herbs for pottages, meat casseroles and sauces to accompany fish, like fennel sauce.

The leaves and root tops were chopped into salads to enliven them, and their hot black seeds were chewed, like fennel seeds, to stave off hunger. Medicinally, alexanders had the standard parsley family use as a diuretic and flatulent. They were tall, garishly green and yellow-flowered, black-seeded occasionals in kitchen gardens.

Lovage was a more common celery-flavoured herb. It tasted so much like alexanders that the latter was sometimes referred to as 'black lovage'. Like alexanders, lovage was an occasional in kitchen and herb gardens. Its celery-scented leaves and stems were eaten like celery and added to pottages, but their main use was as a gruit. Many monastery, tavern and household brewers grew lovage in their gardens. Right up until the 1930s lovage beer was popular in England, as were lovage cordials and lovage tea, which had been drunk as a cure for jaundice, liver troubles and pestilence since the early Middle Ages. Lovage drinks were a familiar item of medieval household fare, as lovage was of medieval kitchen gardens.

More common still in medieval drinks and kitchen gardens was fragrant tansy or tansy balm, *Tanacetum balsamita*, called after balm because of its sweet fragrance, which also earned it its name of ale-cost. Like lovage and balm, it was an ale gruit, and it was used in cooking, having a taste rather like weak mint sauce. 'Take a foil or two of costmary and a clove of garlic,' begins one fifteenth century recipe, calling the herb by its most popular medieval name, the one that dedicated it to Mary, probably on account of its sweetness. Costmary was a common plant in tavern, cottage and all kinds of kitchen gardens.

Back Yard Herbs

Many of these were semi-wild intruders into back yards, used as purgatives if they had no other obvious value. Most of them were so common in the wilds that they were accommodated rather than cultivated in yards, and had no place in neatly planned herb gardens. Burnet was the most respectable of them, being slightly similar to borage and blessed with a boragenous cucumber scent and taste which won it some favour from salad herb gardeners. But for the most part it was a kitchen garden peripheral, hardy but uninteresting, chiefly valued for the attraction its little green, purple-tinted flowers exercised over bees. It survived neglect and showed itself in a lot of cottage gardens, alongside orpine, which was such a long-lived plant that it was nicknamed 'Live-long'. The pretty, reddish purple petals of orpine were useful salad coolers, like burnet, and soothed sore wounds. But neither orpine nor burnet were pungent enough to receive much attention from the medievals.

What the cottager really wanted was what every medieval wanted, indeed expected, of rough and ready herbs. None expressed it better than the widow in Chaucer's *Nun's Priest's Tale*, who explained the virtues of the herbs growing in the tangled patch behind her cottage thus:

> For God's love, as take some laxative.
> I counsel you the best, I will not lie,
> That both of colere [choleric humour] and of melancholy
> Ye purge you . . .
> And in our yard tho [these] herbs shall I find,
> The which have of their property by kind
> To purge you, beneath and eek [moreover] above . . .
> Of Lauriol [spurge laurel], centaury and fumeterre,
> Or else of hellebore that groweth there,
> Of katapuce [herbs with milky juices] or of gaitres beryis
> [dogwood berries]
> Of herb ivy [wart cress], growing in our yard.

These were the harsh, laxative, herbal equivalent of the wild flowers that were brought, or allowed, into occasional cultivation by cottagers. Spurge laurel, for instance, has poisonous black berries and must have purged with a vengeance. Other herbs of this sort were the yellow spearwort (*Ranunculus flammula*), that made a pleasantly hot and dry mouthful; the mildly digestive mouse-ear hawkweed (*Pilosella officinarum*); the native ferns, including hart's tongue fern, which was carved on one of the fifteenth-century misericords in Ripon Minster; bigold, the corn marigold; water pepper (*Polygonum hydropiper*); sanicle (*Sanicula europaea*); stitchwort, a member of the chickweed family, and a host of other, to our eyes, even weedier herbs.

Centaury was pretty enough to be deemed a flower as well as a herb. It was taken, as the widow recommended, as a tonic and purgative, to 'cast out humours of the head' and 'drive venom out of the flesh'. Centaury tea was drunk by those suffering from dyspepsia or wanting to purify their blood until the late nineteenth century.

Some of these field and garden herbs were very highly thought of. The agreeably resinous, faintly turpentinish, smell and taste of agrimony won it enough popularity as a general tonic to get it cultivated in a number of gardens. Like all herbs that lacked a specific application, it was recommended as a 'cleanser' and 'expeller', and was a constituent of umpteen herbal plasters and baths that soothed aches and pains. When dried, its flowers and leaves retain their aroma and were put into pot-pourris and on beds, to induce sleep. 'Lay it under head and sleep as if dead,' said a fourteenth-century herbal. Its flowers contain a certain amount of tannin and were used to dye linen and dress leather.

Valerian was hardly ever cultivated, though it had the same all-round healing reputation as agrimony, being nicknamed Heal-All. Where agrimony was sweet-smelling, valerian roots exude valeric acid, which smells of rancid perspiration. It was not welcomed in gardens, except by those who believed more in a nasty plant's power to harm disease than a pleasant plant's power to do one good. It was generally left on the wild side of the horticultural fringes, where the seedy but unassertive lunary (honesty) kept it company. Herbs that tasted as unpleasant as valerian could be sweetened by the addition of more agreeable herbs from the same fringes. The mildly honey-flavoured scabious, the mildly laxative ground-pine, the lemon-scented germander and the sweet gentians were all mentioned by John the Gardener as garden herbs, and all owed their occasional horticultural status to their sweetness, just as other herbs owed it to their purgative bitterness. They were as simple to grow as they were pleasant to drink and add to baths.

Adderstongue (*Ophioglossum vulgatum*) was one of these bath additives, since it makes an excellent infusion for washing sensitive skin. Sweet amber was known as tutsan (from the French *toute-saine*, meaning heal-all) in the Middle Ages because its antiseptic leaves eased open flesh wounds. It was cultivated in gardens alongside feverfew, which, as its name suggests, was taken against chest complaints, fevers and colds, and also to 'cleanse the kidneys and cheer the heart, when taken in wine', of over-indulgent eaters.

To the multitude of other wild and semi-wild herbs that grew here and there in medieval gardens and yards, but cannot be included in this book, we can only pay our respects, but there is one bush that must be considered before this chapter is complete. It was a late arrival in medieval England, and therefore cannot be considered along with the top-ranking 'sew and surgery' herbs, of which it was one. Its English childhood was tenuous and fragile, but having survived that, its life has been consistently and extraordinarily successful. Rosemary ends this chapter with appropriately versatile herbal panache.

A Perfect Herb

Dried rosemary flowers were probably imported into northern Europe from its southern home for some time before the plant itself arrived in about 1338. It was then that the Countess of Hainault send a copy of a treatise on rosemary, and probably a cutting or small bush of the plant, to her daughter, Queen Philippa of England. Rosemary's classical reputation as a 'sew and surgery' herb had spread all over Europe at an early date, and the herb itself spread in its wake, though much more slowly because, as one herbalist put it,

> The black frost, the northern wind,
> To this herb be unkind.

It was probably almost a century before English gardeners discovered how to thwart the unkind weather thoroughly enough for rosemary to become a common garden plant.

By about 1400 it had been sent to enough English gardeners for one of them to write a treatise on rosemary in English, the accurate details of which put it beyond doubt that the author had actual, not just theoretical, knowledge of growing it.

> It groweth but with mickle travail of man and with mickle watering in the first two years, but principally in the first year . . . His leaves are evermore green, and never falleth in any month . . . then if it shall be transplanted or taken up by the root, all to set, abide not long ere it be set, nor lay it in water nor in ground but it be a little while, nor the sun nor air take the root . . . never dung nor meynt [mix] manure nigh to it. It is tree and herb holy and clean kindly, and kindly it loveth not but clean.

As it was so difficult to establish and keep, it was limited to well-kept herb gardens and a few kitchen gardens until Tudor times, when it became much more common. As it was a 'tree and herb', taking up a lot of room, it was confined to the walls and corners of these gardens. It does particularly well on walls, which shelter it from frost. It grows up walls until, according to the medievals, it reaches Christ's age of 33 years. It never exceeds Christ's height, which the author of the treatise describes as the height of a man and a half; after that it grows in breadth instead, 'and that but little'. Its Christian reputation for holiness was based on its medicinal powers. It grew to the height of Christ; it healed with his compassion; and it purified like his grace. Rosemary flower tea calmed and 'cleansed the body within . . . and wash thy visage well therein, it shall make thee whole and clear . . . For it is kindly . . . for it is holy,' said a fourteenth-century herbal.

One of the pleasanter medieval toothpastes was made of powdered rosemary flowers and stems, and one of the pleasanter scalp treatments was to brush the hair with a branch of rosemary, an anticipation by five centuries of the modern use of rosemary as a hair treatment herb.

Rosemary's most direct classical inheritance was its association with remembrance, which lasted well into the last century. Rosemary was laid on the bodies of the dead to show that they would not be forgotten, and until a hundred years ago a sprig of rosemary was thrown into graves in many districts of England.

> As for rosemary,
> I let it run all over my garden walls
> Not only because my bees love it
> But because 'tis the herb
> Sacred to remembrance
> And therefore to friendship,
> Whence a sprig of it hath a dumb language

wrote Sir Thomas More in the early sixteenth century. Bees love it for its sweet smell and attractively pale blue flowers. Despite its bulk, it is an aromatic herb, like all the labiates, and found a place for itself as a fragrant hedge in late medieval English gardens. It tastes as good as it smells, and the medievals liked

> to see the rosemary in wine . . .
> And thou shalt be merry and lythe.

It was rubbed into roasting meats, dried for pot-pourris, wardrobes, strewing, and burning as an incense substitute in churches. Today it is almost exclusively a kitchen herb. The last word on it belongs to the author whose treatise helped to spread its culture in England nearly six hundred ago, and to give us an insight into that culture: 'And if you nourish him thus you shall have rosemary and great help and comfort thereby, with the grace of Almighty God of heaven.' Herbs gave so much 'help and comfort' that the medievals always thought of them as somehow given to man and blessed by an extra special 'grace of Almighty God in heaven'.

> For the same ground that beareth the wikke [wicked]weeds
> Beareth eek these wholesome herbs as full oft.
>
> (*Troilus and Criseyde*)

7

The Vegetable Patch

Our medieval ancestors didn't think much of vegetables. The ones that interested them were either starchy ones or ones that gave a good strong taste to starch. The history of medieval vegetables is dominated by one pair of starch vegetables and one family of taste vegetables, despite the introduction of new plants and an increasing interest in all sorts of gardening in the fourteenth and fifteenth centuries. Vegetable gardening was always a simple affair, aiming to produce a few essential vegetables. It was supremely classless, and little influenced by fashion. Most people had a vegetable patch attached to their house, where they grew the same basics, the only difference between patches being in scale and in the occasional appearance of luxury vegetables in those of the better off. Vegetable gardening has always been the humblest and least changeable of England's horticultural traditions. When Chaucer wanted to portray someone completely destitute, he said of Grisildis, in *The Clerk's Tale*, that she did not even have a vegetable garden; she was reduced to living off

> Wortes cabbages or other herbs times oft,
> The which she shred and seeth [boiled] for her living.

She had to gather her vegetables from the wilds and waysides and other people's gardens.

The vast majority of medieval Englishmen were cottagers, with little yards, attached to their cottages, at least part of which they cultivated (see illustration p. 241).

The Domesday survey lists thousands of these yards and gardens attached to cottages or to town and manor houses of all sizes. A garth or yard is the basic enclosure from which all kinds of gardens are developed, and the medievals often referred to their vegetable gardens as yards or curtilagia, their basic gardens. These might be only a few yards square, or extend to four or five acres. The main difference between cottage and big, well-to-do gardens, however, was that cottage gardens were nearly always just yards, or vegetable patches, in which fruit trees, vegetables, herbs and flowers all grew together, whereas larger gardens tended to be sectioned off, so that the vegetable patch was surrounded by more carefully arranged flower and herb patches.

The later the date and the more affluent the household, the more likely it was that the gardener would section off his herbs, fruit and flowers, leaving his vegetable patch even humbler than that of the cottager, who kept all his plants together in it. By the late Plantagenet period domestic life in the upper ranks of society was filling out, and the emergence of a merchant and administrative middle class gave evidence of its importance in the way the English middle class has always liked best: by building houses and gardens. The number and size of towns increased; there were more small estate farmers than ever before, and more households with specialized gardens.

At the same time, there were more householders with single garths. After the devastating plagues of the mid-fourteenth century, landlords found themselves without enough peasant labour to work their fields, and they leased off land to their tenants, who worked it for themselves. Smallholders enlarged their gardens and grew more plants in them. As fast as the aristocracy and middle class subdivided their gardens, the peasants expanded and enclosed theirs.

Medieval gardeners shut out the fields from which they fought to earn a living; the forests, fens and wildernesses they fought to bring to cultivation, the animals, wild and domestic, as well as thieves and neighbours. They stalwartly enclosed their garths with thorn hedges, ditches, banks of earth, fencing, paling and walls, through which the only entrance was a locked gate or door. All the tools in Alexander Neckham's twelfth-century treatise *De Utensilibus*, which lists the equipment necessary to a countryman, were as basic to palace, burgess and manorial as to cottage gardeners, and most of them were for removing all traces of wild nature from the garden, or for excluding it by means of garden enclosure:

> . . . a fork, a wide blade, a spade or shovel, a knife . . . a seed-basket for seed-time, a wheel-barrow (more often a little hand-cart), basket, pannier and trap for sparrow-hawks . . . a two-edged axe to uproot thorns, brambles, briars, prickles and

unwanted shoots, and rushes and wood to mend hedges . . .
timbers, palings, and stakes or hedging hurdles . . . he should
also have a knife hanging from his belt to graft trees and seed-
lings, mattocks with which to uproot nettles or vetch, darnel,
thistles, sterile oats and weeds of this sort, and a hoe for
tares . . .

Further on in the treatise Neckham says, 'there should be a cleaning
place where the entrails and feathers of ducks and other domestic
fowl can be removed and the birds cleaned'.

Keeping a few fowls was as basic as keeping a few herbs and
vegetables. Everyone kept a few chickens in their yard, and those
with enough room kept ducks, geese and gannets, too; the osten-
tatiously well-to-do might keep a pair of peacocks, but this was
extravagant beyond the purpose of keeping fowl, which was to have
eggs. Occasionally, kitchen garden accounts record the sale of eggs;
usually the eggs were eaten by the household and the fowls killed
and prepared for the pot by the housewife. The widow's yard in
Chaucer's *Nun's Priest's Tale*, attached to 'a narrow cottage, beside
a grove, standing in a dale', with its fowls scratching about in the
dust amid the berries, herbs and vegetables, and doubtless with its
compost heap in the corner, is the typical medieval kitchen garden.
One of the most popular medieval proverbs declared, 'A cock is king
on his own dung hill.' If a cock had a dung hill to stand on, as
opposed to a leaf compost heap, he belonged to a relatively prosperous household, for dung was precious stuff. A fork to lift dung
and compost with was one of the first tools Neckham listed for his
countryman.

His description of kitchen utensils tells us as much about the contents of the basic garth or yard as his tool description tells us about
its enclosure. 'In a kitchen there should be a small table on which
cabbage may be minced, and also lentils, peas, shelled beans, beans
in the pod, millet, onions and other vegetables of the kind that can
be cut up.' These were the basic vegetables of medieval England.
The difference between rich and poor was not that they had different
basic diets, nor that they had different basic garths in which to grow
their vegetables and herbs, but that the rich had flesh and luxury
foods like sweets and sweet fruits to add to their starch and
vegetables.

The vegetables Neckham lists were ubiquitous in kitchens and
kitchen gardens. There were very few of them, and this fact,
together with the universal popularity they enjoyed, is what strikes

one most about vegetable gardening in the medieval as compared with the modern period. For the medievals, a vegetable had to be full of either carbohydrate or flavour; it had to come near to being a cereal or a herb to justify its existence. Anything with pretensions to subtlety was a non-starter. For medieval Europe lived off cereals and relished the strongest tasting accompaniments it could find to relieve their monotony. Bread was life itself, eaten in every household at every meal.

> His bread, his ale, was always after oon [equally good];
> A better envyned [envianded, i.e. possessed of meat] man was nowhere known.

So wrote Chaucer of his wealthy franklin, putting the cereal basics of food and drink before the long list of meats the franklin indulged in.

The vast majority of Englishmen were peasants, and didn't get much further than these basics. They ate a breakfast of bread and ale at dawn. Dinner was at 9.0 a.m. and consisted of bread and ale, with cheese, fish or even meat for the better off. Supper was at 4.0 p.m., an hour later in summer, and consisted of bread, perhaps some pottage and a few vegetables, and ale. The wealthier and the aristocratic ate better, but they ate bread with the same single-minded voracity as everyone else. Two loaves[1] and a gallon of ale were everyone's daily essentials. These essentials, in all their starchy bareness, were grown in the fields.

Not surprisingly, the medieval palate longed for pungency. Medieval cookery was based on starch, but it was shot through with herbs and spices, of which the hottest, sharpest, strongest and bitterest were the best liked. All housewives used quantities of herbs in their cookery. Herbs had a culinary importance that is hard for us to grasp because we have been able to supplement our starch with a whole range of different food and tastes. They are no longer the redemptive kitchen force they once were. The only ones dealt with here, alongside vegetables, are those which we count as vegetables and which the medievals counted sometimes as one, sometimes as the other. Thus the imbalance in favour of herbs which is only to be expected in any account of medieval gardens or cooking, is righted a little towards vegetables, and towards our modern understanding.

---

1 The medieval loaf weighed approximately 3 lbs. 10 oz.

The Basic Vegetables

It was not flattering for a medieval plant to be counted as a vegetable, for a vegetable was stranded half way between the virtues of starchiness and flavour. Since starch was so much the most important item of the medieval diet, it was the more important of the two virtues, and this survey of medieval garden vegetables must begin with the ones that contained the most starch. One vegetable was so well endowed in this respect that it was often planted in the fields as a cereal crop, and only descended now and again to the status of a garden vegetable; that vegetable is the bean.

For the first ten centuries of its English life it was virtually inseparable from the pea, its field partner in starch, but gardeners nearly always distinguished the two. The medieval bean was a starchier version of our broad bean, *Faba vulgaris*, and was probably introduced into Europe at the time of the earliest Aryan migrations westwards. It was the major pulse crop of the ancient world, though a philosophical and fanatical minority mistrusted beans because of their black markings. Despite this, in ancient, as in medieval and modern England, beans were regarded as very wholesome. When the Romans left Britain the bean was already firmly established there, and its suitability to the damp English climate improved its quality. The native Celtic bean was very small, more like a pea, and the faba was the one that the Anglo-Saxons cultivated and ate in a big way.

The garths attached to cottages could never have grown enough starch to keep the labouring population alive. They had to rely on their field strips for starch, and on the meals of pottage given them by their lords, concentrating on 'taste' vegetables and herbs in their own gardens. It was the big estate gardeners who went in for beans, selecting the best ones to plant and keeping them free of vetch and weeds so that the manorial kitchens had a supply of good beans for their soups and vegetable pottages.

That most grandiose of medieval cookery books, the *Form of Cury*, begins with a recipe for 'ground benes'. This, it says, is a poor man's dish. The beans are to be taken out of their 'hulls', dried in the oven and made into broth, which was to be eaten with bacon. The second recipe in the book is for 'drawn beans', bean and onion pottage. Anyone familiar with these two recipes would have been able to hold her own in a medieval kitchen.

Nearly all medieval cookery books began with beans, and nearly all beans went into pottages; they were vegetables of substance, not personality. So basic and commonplace were they that a lot of medieval proverbs were variations of 'I don't give a bean' or 'I haven't got a bean', the latter still in use today. Kitchen gardens that were big enough to be recorded in accounts always grew more beans than anything else. These were seldom sold, for they were eaten by the householders and their labourers, and would have fetched very little on the market. They were too common to be expensive – hardly worth a bean, in fact.

The same is true of the pea. Sharing the same origins as the bean, it had such an ignominious career in the ancient world that no one even thought it worth condemning. It was probably because peas did so well in the English climate, swelling into something like the peas we know today, that the Romans kept up their cultivation in England.

Field peas were used to fatten pigs and make labourers' pottage. In cookery books they appeared alongside beans in the pottage section. The bean-pea partnership was the standard resource of the medieval housewife, much as the potato is today. It was easy, though foolish, 'to take a bean for a pease', as Gower put it in 1393, and medieval writers, literary as well as culinary, usually referred to the two together.

But peas were not altogether without their own identity or value. There were two kinds of pea: the white pea, which usually grew in the fields and made the best thick pottage, and the horticultural green pea, *Pisum sativum*, which made green pottage. 'A potful of pease', of either colour, was one of the fundamentals of Piers Plowman's life, as it was of every labourer's.

To find a strictly garden, as opposed to a field and garden vegetable, one must turn from sustenance to taste; from the essential to the most desirable; from beans and peas to the top medieval garden vegetable family and all its pungent offspring: the allium family, of which the three most important members were the leek (*Allium porrum*), the onion (*Allium cep*) and garlic (*Allium sativum*).

The allium family was everything a medieval vegetable ought to be if it was not going to be a cereal: easy to grow, hardy and, above all, strong tasting. The medieval palate couldn't get enough of its three members, the popularity of which never declined during the Middle Ages. There is little to choose between the three as far as their popularity and usefulness is concerned, but the leek was the favourite of both Anglo-Saxons and Celts even before the Normans brought their immensely leek-loving habits to England.

It began its English life under the Romans, who thought highly of it and used it to flavour their cooking. All the Celts were very fond of it. St David and his fellow anchorites lived off nothing but leeks, water, bread, and salt on feast days, in the sixth and seventh centuries. At heart they were men of the wilds, not gardeners, and the fact that the leek was the one vegetable they did often cultivate in their clearings and garths is a great tribute to the leek rampant. Manchán of Liath's vision of heaven includes a little hut and a chapel in a clearing in the wilderness where, he says, 'This is the house-keeping I would undertake; I would choose it without concealing: fragrant fresh leeks, hens, speckled salmon, bees.'

Fragrance: that is the first attraction of the leek. As soon as one pulls it from the ground one can smell the flavour. Celts, Anglo-Saxons and Norman English alike were devoted to that flavour and filled their gardens with it. The word 'leek' is Welsh and also Anglo-Saxon. Leeks were so popular with the Anglo-Saxons that their word for a kitchen garden was leek-garth (leac-tun), from which the town name Leyton, in all its variants, is derived; their word for a gardener was leek-keeper (leac-ward). They distinguished six types of allium vegetable, all six of them with '*leac*' names: cropleach – a chibolle or everlasting onion, garleac – garlic, porleac – a pot-leek, ynioleac – an onion, holleac – a vegetable leak, brade-leac – a leek. Leek was a general word for garden vegetables. This continued to be so all through the Middle Ages, new horticultural introductions and fashions notwithstanding. Thirteenth- and fourteenth-century garden accounts begin their lists of vegetables sown, bought and produced with 'leeks, onions, garlic and vegetables', almost always in that order, the 'vegetables' usually being pot-leeks. Detailed accounts sometimes distinguish still further, listing leeks, pot-leeks, poretta (pottage leeks) and vegetables, all of them leeks of one kind or another. There is hardly a single medieval kitchen garden account that does not include leeks.

The accounts of some of the Glastonbury Abbey manors for 1333-4 give us an idea of a typical manorial kitchen garden at this period. The Glastonbury gardener in 1333 was Thomas of Keynsham, who was in charge of the gardens of Mells, Pilton, Marksbury, Batcombe and four other nearby manors. His accounts show that the gardens contained beans, leeks, onions, garlic, hemp, flax, madder and herbs. The eight gardens had 23 beds of leeks between them. Most of the leeks harvested were kept in the manors and consumed by the abbot and his friends on their visits, or by the labourers; 14 lbs. of leeks were sown for the next year and a few surplus plants were sold for 7d. Such an abundance of leeks was typical. Henry de Lacy, Earl of Lincoln, was not above having a patch of leeks, onions, garlic and beans in his splendid Holborn garden. In 1357, when the Bishop of Worcester visited Eardisley and found the vicarage there so cramped and poorly endowed that the vicar had 'no room to walk, or grow leeks or other herbs', the worst fate that could befall any honest man, a bigger stretch of glebe-land was assigned to the vicar at once, so that he could plant some leeks and walk by them. Rich and poor loved their leeks.

Since flavour was the justification of medieval vegetables, they were made into soups and sauces, and cooked in hot-pots with meat or fish to flavour the heart of the meal. A standard labourers' soup consisted of peas or beans and leeks. Leeks were the pot vegetables *par excellence*. This is a fourteenth-century poem in praise of 'green porray' [pot vegetables]:

> Now leeks are in season, for pottage full good,
> And spareth the milchcow, and purgeth the blood:
> These having with peason [peas] for pottage in Lent,
> Thou sparest both oatmeal and bread to be spent.

Medieval proverbs confirmed both the value and the commonplace abundance of leeks. 'Not worth a leek's clove' was as common a derogation as 'not worth a bean'. Leek parings were used for bleaching hair and dyeing eyebrows; one could always apply some rose or violet water to cover up the smell. Leek juice and leek seeds made up several different kinds of medieval toothpaste, and were pungent enough to purge any of the colder complaints. They were stock medicine against fevers and plague, as were all the allium family, onions most of all.

Onions were often called 'ceps', from their Latin name, and were grown and eaten as widely as leeks. No vegetable patch and no decent meal was complete without them, the most popular variety for eating raw being the small strong chibolles, or chivolles, that warmed the breath of Piers Plowman on winter days, and scallions, or shallots. Pickling onions like these went into sweet and sour sauces in vast quantities. 'Fry a great portion of onions in fresh grease' is a typical opening of a sauce recipe; 'cut and pounded onions and herbs, seethed [soaked] in verjuice' is a typical medieval onion sauce recipe. Onions went into almost every soup and pottage, often in company with leeks. Like leeks, they were eaten as cold and fever cures. Chaucer's summoner was 'as hot he was, and lecherous, as a sparrow', his red cheeks and hot temper fuelled by the food he loved best: 'Well loved he garlic, onions and eke [moreover] leeks.' Onions rubbed into insect stings and bites are effective pain-killers, and have been used as such for centuries. Their skins yield a yellow dye which was used to colour household wool and cloth.

John the Gardener's section 'On the Setting and Sowing of Sedys [Seeds]' is all about seeds of the allium family, a very medieval concentration. He suggested propping the onions up with forks made of small ash branches, and said that they would be

> ripe at the full at Lammas [August 1] of Peter Apostle.
> On this manner you shall the seeds dry –
> Upon a cloth you the seeds lie,

and the rest is up to the sun. Anyone with a spacious garden could lay out his onion sets in rows, as most people do today, but few would bother, then or now, to support the stems with sticks, as John recommended. Most gardeners grew their onions, leeks and garlic in a tangled, smelly confusion. Big institutional gardeners, like monastic cellarers, grew them in separate beds, but we have no way of knowing how they arranged them within the beds. Onions and onion seeds appear in most kitchen garden accounts in quantities rivalled only by leeks and garlic.

The gar leek (Old English for spear leek, so called because of its spear-headed cloves) had a stronger flavour and used up less space, and was accordingly extremely popular. Because of its exceptionally powerful flavour and small size it was often counted as a herb, even as a spice, as well as a vegetable. In *Piers Plowman*, Piers asks a poor old lady on her way to church, 'Has thou any hot spices?' She replies: 'I have pepper and peony and a pound of garlic.'

The medieval digestion coped happily with garlic in these quantities; indeed it was miserable without it. Those with hot fevers were warned off onions, garlic and pepper, an abstinence which Chaucer's physician advocated, much to the distress of the poet. Those with colds, cold fevers and 'fevers of the head' were luckier; garlic and onions had been consistently prescribed for them since Anglo-Saxon times and still were in Chaucer's time. There was nothing like a clove of hot raw garlic to revive the system, just as a good fistful of garlic cloves made any dish worth eating.

Almost every savoury dish included garlic, and garlic sauce ranked after basic pottages and peas and beans. Fourteenth-century fried beans were made by boiling beans to pulp, adding minced onions and garlic, frying in oil or grease and serving with sweet spice powder. Goose in garlic sauce was the medieval version of the Sunday joint. Humble cooks contented themselves and their families with garlic sauce, which basically consisted of garlic, onions and vinegar.

The Glastonbury gardens looked after by Thomas of Keynsham were full of garlic to supply the abbey and the manorial kitchens. In 1333 there were 6000 cloves left over from the previous year, and 5000 cloves produced that year. Of these 11000 cloves, 3000 were kept for planting, 2000 were sent to the abbot's kitchen and 6000 to the abbey larder. The remaining 1000 were not accounted for, but were doubtless consumed on the manors. Using up garlic was never a problem.

There was always a smell of garlic in English medieval houses and gardens, where it served to obliterate less welcome odours. As one fourteenth-century writer put it: 'The stench of garlic voids the stench of dunghills.'

Pot Vegetables

The only vegetables that almost everyone grew, besides leeks, onions and garlic, were pot vegetables, of which the most important was the cabbage.

The Middle English word for cabbage was caboche and it derived, like the identical French word for cabbage, from the latin *caput*, meaning head: the cabbage was the brassica that had a head. The Old English word for cabbage was kale, which has equivalents in all the Celtic languages and is a generic name for all the brassicas, of which the cabbage was the most important. It may well have been the Celts who domesticated the *Brassica oleracea*, the ancestral wild cabbage, and brought it to Europe with them. It was a popular food with them, and they continued to grow and eat it after the Romans had left Britain. The Anglo-Saxons acquired the Celtic taste for all kinds of kale, so much so that they called February, the month when they sowed flowering kale, 'Sprout Kele'.

Kale was a pot vegetable. It was a 'porray', like leek, onions and garlic, and most of the leaves of root vegetables. Medieval vegetable gardening was largely an exercise in porray production. It has to be admitted, with regret, that the standard English method of cooking greens until they are a soggy mess is historically correct. According to one fourteenth-century cookery book, porray should be cooked from early morning until supper-time, over a good fire, and the resulting purée diluted with beef fat. On meat-eating days it should be further embellished with pigeons, hares, sausages, coots and bacon. This was a recipe for the well-to-do; the poor boiled their kale greens with bone marrow or in thick broth. Unlike today's cooks, however, they spiced them heavily with salt, mustard, garlic or vinegar; plain porray would have been unthinkable and uneatable.

All kinds of greens, or kale, continued to be a favourite Celtic food until well on in the last century, when the word 'kale' was still often used in Scotland to mean dinner, since it was such an important part of that meal. The kale yard is the traditional Scottish kitchen garden. The rentals of the Cistercian abbey of Cupar, Fife, in the late fifteenth century were assessed on tenants' 'zards' or yards, since the abbey had leased off its gardens to individual kale-yard keepers. This rental, assessed on one Dene James's zard, shows it to have been, like all the zards, planted with kale, onions and herbs:

> Dene James's zard shall furnish to the abbot and convent kale and herbs for fifteen days; it shall have two beds of herbs, such as parsley, beets, lettuce, and shall furnish to the warden each year four beds of onions, bowkale; and half the fruits growing on the trees . . .

All kitchen gardeners grew kale of one sort or another, which cannot be said of any other vegetable outside the allium family. The most popular form of kale was the cabbage. John the Gardener devoted a section of his treatise to 'The Sowing and Setting of Wurtys', just as he had done to 'The Setting and Sowing of Seeds'. His seeds had all been allium family; his 'wurtys' were all cabbages.

> Wurtys we must have,
> Both to master and to knave,

he began. The labouring poor were living off the last of their dried peas and beans and salted bacon and were glad of fresh greens for the pot in winter and in Lent, when cabbages yielded winter porray. This was hotted up by the addition of seeds: linseed, barley and knotgrass, or hot wild pot-herbs such as nettles, mallows, docks and plantain. Recipe number 100 in Richard II's *Form of Cury* is called 'Compost: a composition always to have at hand'. Compost was a mixture of parsley and onion roots, pared cabbages and rapes, pea pottage and salt, profusely spiced, with Greek wine and clarified honey, mustard, raisins and currants added. It is royally exotic, but it is still a compost, a porray pottage, an elaboration on the only acceptable way of eating cabbage.

Vegetables are social barometers. One can tell a lot about the social life of a country at any given period by looking at the way people use their vegetables. The cabbage is a perfect example of this. By the fifteenth century bourgeois Europe was treating its cabbages as individual vegetables; householders ate their garden cabbage not just in pottages but also as 'buttered wurtys', a vegetable dish in its own right; they boiled them in oil and salted water without going on to put them into meat soup. They afforded them a measure of vegetable independence, and in so doing bore testimony to their own affluence.

The most affluent way of all to eat cabbage was as a salad vegetable. By the mid-fifteenth century salads were fashionable, and usually included cabbages, though this was regarded by the conservative majority as a travesty of their true porray nature.

It is impossible to tell whether the more varied use to which cabbages were put meant that they were cultivated more widely and more selectively towards the end of the Middle Ages. Most of our information on medieval cabbage gardening comes from the Menagier, who gives the impression that cabbages were well known and loved by gardeners like himself. He grew several kinds in his kale yard. There was white or headed cabbage, which he sowed in March, thinned out and banked up, then ate in June and July. There must also have been cauliflowers, cole wortes, which had thick white coles, or stems, almost as big as their white heads. The medieval colewort was taller and less bulky than the modern cauliflower, which has reached its present shape through special breeding and cultivation. At least one medieval gardener counted it as 'a small herb'. It was not as popular as green cabbage, but was favoured by those who had the time to bank and care for it in the way the Menagier did. One fourteenth-century physician recommended those with weak heads for drink to chew raw cabbage or cauliflower stalks to increase their drinking capacity; another recommended white cabbage or cauliflower juice in vinegar as a cure for a hangover. Only a medieval constitution could have faced the prospect. Usually cauliflowers were used like every other kind of porray. The Menagier had two kinds of 'heart' cabbages growing in his kale yard alongside the cauliflowers: heart cabbage and Roman cabbage, the latter have scarcely any stems at all. Both kinds produced 'Lenten sprouts' in March, which tasted very strong and had to be boiled an extra long time. There were also 'summer greens', which sprouted five or six times a year. The Menagier gave sowing times and tips on cultivation for all these varieties. For instance, he told his wife that the best way to kill cabbage caterpillars was to spread cinders beneath the plants when it rained, and to tear off and throw away any leaves which had white grubs on the underside. If cabbages were to seed in the autumn, he said, they should be cut right down so that the stumps could produce a few more greens. French influence on gardening and cooking in Norman England was strong, and this flourishing kale yard must have had English equivalents, such as John the Gardener's wurty garden.

Caxton described 'his garden where he had set colys and wortys' in 1483. Plain coles were what we now call rape (*Brassica napus*), and were a much more common kind of kale in the Middle Ages than they are today. They had one other very popular asset, besides their porray leaves: 'Of seed of rape . . . is oil made', wrote Bartholomew Anglicus, 'and that oil is needful in many uses.' Vegetable oils were rubbed into aching joints, drunk with honey to ease coughs, added to pottages to make them richer and to baths to make them more luxurious. As for the seeds – they were always successful, being added to pottages, baths and hot medicines; they were most popular of all just as they were, chewed raw when there wasn't a clove of garlic to chew. Rapes had oil, seeds and porray leaves, and when all those were exhausted there was always the root, which could be 'scraped well, hewn small in pieces' and thrown into the pot to make the porray go further.

Turnip was also grown in English medieval gardens, despite claims by eighteenth-century propagandists that it was introduced to England in that later period. It is basically a swollen-rooted cabbage, and was grown in many a medieval kale yard. The medievals referred to turnips as 'neeps', 'nips' or 'nepts'. These were smaller than modern turnips and, like rape, were chiefly valued for their good porray tops. In the Anglo-Saxon period housewives were making porray out of 'peas and beans and neeps', the roots being boiled into soupy anonymity along with the tops. In the mid-fourteenth century 'the man in the yard pulleth neeps' and his wife put them into the pot. As root vegetables without a very strong taste, neeps were not much of a success. John the Gardener had nothing to say about them in his treatise, beyond their name. One had to be very hungry before one descended to eating a neep; hence the medieval expression: 'Not worth a withered neep'.

Pars-neeps had been cultivated in England by the Romans and were known in France and England as pasternaks, from their latin name of *Pastinaca sativa*. They were one ingredient of composts such as the one in the *Form of Cury*. According to the author of the *Pistill of Susan*, writing in about 1400, 'parsley, parsnips and porrets' were good for the pot, and indeed parsnips often did go into the pot. However, they were not primarily porray because their roots were big and sweet enough to be eaten for their own sake. They were chopped up with apples and made into sweet fritters, and those who make homemade wine, as all the medievals did, will know how good parsnip wine is. Not being good porray, they were not grown in cottage gardens. They are mentioned only in household books, which suggests that they were grown only on a very small scale in gardens and may only have survived in English gardens, after the departure of the Romans, in their native wild state.

There were plenty of porray plants that were worth such a place, and were therefore grown in kitchen gardens. One of the most popular of these was beet (white beet), which was grown for its leaves. Medieval gardening treatises advised cutting back beets to the root when they were ready to eat, so that the tops would grow again and 'give more porray'. Sometimes beets were described as spinach, since their leaves were similar to spinach leaves, and both were used as strong flavouring porray. There may have been more beets grown, under the heading of spinach, or that of porray or wurtys, than one would think from the relatively few mentions of beet under that name in the records. They are hardy and easy to grow, and had been cultivated in England since Anglo-Saxon times at least, hence their Anglo-Saxon name.

Spinach and orach (mountain spinach) were minor but appreciated porray plants. Spinach was a 'Lent porray', since it could be picked all through the winter and into Lent. It appears in some porray recipes, but doesn't seem to have been grown in England until the fourteenth century. 'Take cole . . . beets . . . and orage, and seethe them,' wrote one cook in 1440, in a set of household ordinances. The formula is familiar, and only varied in the case of orach to the extent that the sharp taste of this plant led it to be used as a herb as well as a porray vegetable. Even so, it was a porray herb.

Neither spinach nor orach was as much used as sorrel, which is native all over temperate Europe and was brought into cultivation as a porray vegetable during the Middle Ages because it improves greatly when cultivated. Its early botanical name was *Rumex acetosa*, in tribute to its acid taste. The Anglo-Saxons called it 'sure', from which its present name derives, because they put great faith in it as a purgative medicine, and probably cultivated it as a garden vegetable on some scale. According to the Menagier, the leaves of garden sorrel reach a good size and the more they are cut the more they grow, especially if one cut the big leaves and not the little ones underneath. Its acid taste made it ideal as an additive to verjuice, the green grapejuice vinegar beloved of medieval cooks. Sorrel leaves should be pounded until they had yielded all their juice, wrote the Menagier, and this could then be added to old white verjuice as opposed to dark verjuice (made from black grape juice), along with some parsley to keep the green colour bright. Sorrel was widely used as a vinegar and pot vegetable.

> With ginger the pig eaten shall be,
> And sorrel with the mutton,

declared one English household cook in 1400, keeping up the medieval tradition of salvaging any mild meal by means of a vigorous dose of herbs or strong porray. Sorrel was often classified as a herb, and this was as much because of its medicinal usefulness as its flavouring powers. It was a frequent ingredient of medieval tonic and diuretic drinks, 'hot' plasters for 'cold' wombs, cordials for the heart and for stubborn bowels. A nice strong drink for a winter's afternoon was 'sorrel, plantain and chicken meat seethed'.

Minor Pot Vegetables

For those of a hot humour who wanted to be cooled down after an overdose of 'hot' herbs like sorrel, there was another herb and porray vegetable that was appropriately purpose grown: lettuce. Its medicinal value led the author of the southern English legends to write in 1290 'a fair herb, that men call lettuce', and this fair herb was made into syrups and plasters for the cure of 'hot' complaints. Herbal plasters were made of shredded leaves, bound together with eggs or a sticky paste, and applied to the affected area of skin. Lettuce plasters, like lettuce syrups and drinks, were usually prescribed to cure liver and digestive disorders. The plants were pulled up, roots and all, to thin them out, and their seeds went into the medicine store.

Just as 'hot' seeds were a welcome product of 'hot' herbs and vegetables, so 'cold' seeds were obtained from 'plants that be in the gardens . . . lettuce and purslane', as Caxton wrote in 1483. The wife of a big medieval household had it easily within her reach to make cooling and sedative potions such as this sleeping draught: lettuce juice and seeds, white poppy and coltsfoot seeds; or this digestive drink: fennel, smallage (wild celery) and parsley roots, with endive, scariole (wild lettuce), lettuce, liverwort, maidenhair and coltsfoot seeds. If she didn't have all the plants in her garden, she had only to go into the fields and woods to find them. 'Wild lettuce that fieldmen call skarioles' was easily picked and eaten, either in porray or with bread, but it doesn't have the same narcotic properties as lettuce, and was not brought into cultivation. The Romans ate lettuces raw, with salad dressing, as we do today, but the medievals grew them primarily for medicinal purposes and secondarily as porray, particularly as an addition to pea soup.

Endive grew wild in Southern England, but was cultivated for its strong, bitter flavour. The most common variety was the broad-leaved chicory endive, which yielded 'cold' seeds in its blue flowers, and was used in the same way as lettuce in 'cold' and 'thinning' medicines. Its pretty pale blue flowers won chicory an occasional place in flower as well as herb and vegetable gardens, but it was more commonly gathered from the wilds. Wild chicory and endive were called 'succory' by the medievals, and included in 'cold' salads and bitter herbal custards and omelettes. Wild celery, known as 'smallage' or 'small ache' was used in the same way, yielding a generous amount of juice for consumption in drinks and for binding cool plasters. It didn't have enough taste to win itself a place in kitchen gardens.

Cress, by contrast, was certainly a garden plant in England by the thirteenth century, when its seeds were combined with radish roots, hyssop, licquorice and other 'hot' plants to quicken phlegmatic metabolisms. Cress gets its name from the Anglo-Saxon word *câerre*, and was one of the Anglo-Saxons' most widely used 'hot' medicinal herbs. Whether they cultivated it or used the inferior wild cress we cannot tell. Though it was much used throughout the

Middle Ages as a diuretic and sudorific, and was more common in the wilds than in gardens, cress belongs in this chapter, and in this porray section of it, because it was grown as porray in some kitchen gardens. Cress was sometimes eaten in salads, but more commonly boiled up with beets, onions and almond milk, or with garlic and salted water by the poor.

Root Vegetables

The herbs and vegetables looked at in this section are united by their medieval suitability for the pot, whatever their other uses as medicines, cosmetics and foods. Porray was popular; plain vegetables were not. There was no room for root vegetables in the kitchen garden unless they had good porray tops to them.

Compare, for instance, the medieval with the modern carrot. Carrots didn't appear in England until the end of the Middle Ages. The first mention of one dates from the fifteenth century, but John the Gardener made no mention of them in 1440-50. They had arrived in France a little before that, but were such a novelty there in the late fourteenth century that the Menagier had to explain to his wife how to recognize them in the market. He didn't suggest growing them in the garden.

Medieval carrots were not exclusively orange as we know them today; these are the product of selective breeding by mutants. They were of four kinds: purple, yellow, white and orange. The first English carrot was a purple one, of the sort still grown in some places in the East, though no longer in Europe. The yellow carrot was mainly a winter food and the white mainly cattle food, being the next most common sort after the orange, which became Europe's table carrot. The Menagier told his wife that carrots were white and orange and were sold in bunches, one white carrot to a bunch. He didn't express much interest in them. They had the unforgivable failing of nearly all root vegetables, which guaranteed them medieval contempt: a mild taste. The nearest one can find to a popular root vegetable in the Middle Ages is the radish, which was small and hot enough to be taken into kitchen garden cultivation.

The word radish was often spelt *raedic* by the medievals, who retained this Anglo-Saxon version of its Latin original *radix*, meaning root. Gardening treatises classified radishes as roots but also, inevitably, as pot vegetables; radishes hotted up pottages and sauces and, in their role as root vegetables, made a hot mouthful when eaten raw, as a change from garlic, chibolles and seeds. What they lacked in size they made up for in pungency, like garlic. Radishes and garlic were given to people with quartan fevers, if they were 'cold' fevers in need of 'hot' treatment. Being small herbal vegetables, radishes would have been planted along the borders of vegetable beds and patches, and in herb gardens. Doubtless they were left in the ground until they were outsized, fibrous and hot, but they were never a major garden herb or vegetable like garlic because the wild radish, *Raphanus raphanistrum*, is very similar to the cultivated variety and has the same essential quality of heat, though it is slightly smaller. Most people gathered and ate wild radishes; only a few grew radishes in their gardens.

Far more grew fennel, which was one of the most popular, versatile and celebrated of medieval vegetables. Its bulky root, however, was not the chief object of the celebration; fennel was used as a medicinal herb and an anisic vegetable flavouring, its leaves being particularly good for this purpose. Medieval writers more often classified it as a herb than a vegetable, and it is included in this chapter in order to illustrate the different uses that make it a vegetable today and made it a vegetable herb in the Middle Ages and, in so doing, to complete the medieval annihilation of the root vegetable as a worthwhile proposition.

Fennel (*Foeniculum vulgare*) is native to Britain and much of Europe; it was a herb garden plant and a welcome freshener in vegetable patches. Many physicians prescribed fennel juice eye-drops for sore eyes and fennel juice ointment for aching eyelids and temples, the result of that common medieval complaint, 'workings in the head'.

Despite its ocular soothing effects, fennel was a 'hot' medicine. It contains a volatile oil akin to oil of anise, which is used today to make the carminative, fennel water. The medievals crushed fennel roots for this oil, which they took not only to get rid of wind but also worms, bowel-ache, 'matter which must be expelled to the surface' and matter which fennel expelled in its capacity as a diuretic and laxative. Cooks, housewives and doctors considered its juice an ideal digestive drink after a heavy meal. Those with liver trouble took fennel, smallage, dill and parsley, roots as well as leaves, in the form of a honeyed syrup.

Fennel was put into most herbal baths, which is fair enough in view of its aromatic oil, but it also came to be put into almost every concoction against almost every kind of ache and pain; it was acclaimed as the secret of good health, the secret of eternal youth and the best way to keep witches from one's door.

But the most everyday use of fennel in the Middle Ages was to alleviate hunger. The method of alleviation was to chew the 'hot' seeds of the fennel foliage. The old lady encounted by Piers Plowman on her way to church had not only hot spices, but also 'a farthing's worth of fennel seeds; for fasting days I bought it.' Fennel seeds were allowed to mitigate the long fasts undergone on holy and penitential days. Even the Puritans, so unmedievally remorseless in their austerity, allowed themselves to take dill and fennel seeds in their handkerchiefs, to nibble during the endless sermons against appetite and indulgence, so that the seeds were nicknamed 'Meetin' seeds'.

In the later Middle Ages fennel was sometimes classified as a salad herb; throughout the period it was used as an accompaniment to meat and fish, its partnership with the latter still being favoured by cooks today. Fennel leaves gave a strong flavour to herbolades [herb omelettes], and its root blades were 'hewn small' for inclusion in pottages, which is some justification for subjecting fennel to the degradation of inclusion in the vegetable, as opposed to the herbal, chapter of this book.

Inedible Vegetables

Two plants which, by contrast with fennel, grew in many medieval kitchen gardens but hardly ever grow in modern ones, are flax and hemp. Neither are primarily edible, though flax produces edible linseeds; both were esteemed vegetables because of their fibres, which were the most vital fibres of medieval domestic and agricultural life. Both plants are outstanding examples of the varied and versatile usefulness of medieval plants.

Flax (*Linum usitatissimum*) is one of the oldest plants associated with man. It has been cultivated since Stone Age times at least, and linen made from its fibres. After thousands of years of cultivation in Mesopotamia, Assyria and Egypt, it came to western Europe with the western Aryans, and was widely cultivated despite the hard work required to make a success of it.

It was worth the work because its strong fibres could be made into cords, fish and animal nets, fishing lines, ropes, thread, bowstrings, measuring lines, sacks, bags, purses, sails and linen cloth, the latter only being displaced as the finest cloth in Europe in the eighteenth century. Flax provided the tough fibres of agricultural equipment and the cloth fibres, which could be left coarse or refined, of costume and household. It was therefore grown in cottage, manor and institutional gardens big enough to accommodate it.

There are five stages in its processing. The first is pulling, which is hard work because flax has tenacious roots. The second is rippling, when the 'bolls' or capsules are pulled off the plant and the seeds either kept for sowing the next year (but in a different patch, for one of the disadvantages of flax is that it exhausts the soil and will not do well on the same patch in consecutive years) or crushed for their oil. Linseed oil was taken in honey to ease coughs, and used by everyone from painters to physicians as a soothing agent for rough surfaces. It was a purgative, a bath oil, a lubricant for mechanical equipment such as cart wheels. Cottagers sometimes put linseed into their pottages as an oily cereal substitute. When the seeds have been removed from the flax, the stalks are tied in bundles and immersed in water, with a layer of rushes over them and a large stone or some other heavy weight on top to keep them submerged, for they are light and buoyant. They ferment for several days, and when fermentation is complete, the flax is laid in the sun to dry, still weighted down, and the rind, or membrane, comes loose from it. The flax is then 'retted', which means rolled and beaten to release the woody inner fibres. The inferior fibres nearest the rind are called 'tow', and were not much good for anything except making lamp wicks and plugging cracks in woodwork. Hence the two medieval sayings about flax, one of them enthusiastic: 'As smooth as a strike of flax', the other peeved: 'To have more tow on one's distaff', implying that one has more tow than good linen thread. The final stage of processing is scutching, which is the combing of the fibres with iron hooks to make sure all shreds of the rind have been removed.

We have an account of all this being done in a medieval garden. In 1264 the Bishop of Winchester had a new garden made on the little manor at Rimpton, five miles north-east of Yeovil. It was a big garden, nearly four acres, surrounded by a ditch and bank, on top of which was a thorn hedge. The old garden had been less than an acre big, and the Bishop wanted to step up his flax production in an area where a lot of linen was made, using locally grown flax. It was often grown around the edges of fields, where they bordered on to wasteland, for it could be moved round the edges without exhausting the arable soil; it could only be moved around in gardens if they were big or if it was grown around the edges, against the enclosing hedges or fences. That is why it was often grown in big, semi-cultivated yards, where the other things grown were fruit trees, oats (flax does well on soil where oats have been grown) or peas and beans. This was the case at Rimpton.

The first entry in the accounts there was one of 6d. paid to workmen for 'digging the ground, ready to sow flax and vegetables', which at Rimpton seem to have been peas and beans. Then 6s.6½d. was spent on 119 young plants, which were probably fruit trees. 8s.11¼d. was spent on 1 quarter 1¾ bushels of linseed[1] at 7s.4d. per quarter. The average price of seed barley, a superior cereal, was 4s.6d. per quarter in the medieval period, and the high price of linseed shows the value put on flax and its seeds.

The Rimpton garden was mainly an orchard and a flax patch. Most of the flax was allowed to go to seed. It produced 1 quarter 3 bushels (about 550 lbs.) of seed, which was added to 1 bushel (about 50 lbs.) from the previous year, presumably from the old, small garden, and 1 quarter 1¾ bushels (about 500 lbs.) of bought linseed. The seed total was therefore 2 quarters 5¾ bushels (about 950 lbs.), of which 1 quarter 2¾ bushels (about 540 lbs.) was sown and 1 quarter 3 bushels (550 lbs.) kept in store. 200 beats (bolts) of flax were produced, after the tithe had been taken, and were sold for 3s.4d.

In the following year, 1265-6, a lot of work was done on the flax, judging by the entry: 'Part of the cost of hoeing, pulling, retting and dressing the flax, 7s.4½d.' This was the year for consolidating the new garden, though the linseed yield was slightly down on that of the previous year, at 1 quarter 2 bushels (about 525 lbs.). The gardener spent 7d. on a large skep to hold these seeds, which were added to last year's surplus and kept on the manor. The 163 beats of flax were presumably made into cloth, nets, twine and so on. Garden flax was not a profit plant, as these accounts make clear.

In Thomas of Keynsham's Glastonbury gardens, where such huge quantities of onions, garlic and leeks were grown, the other plants were beans, flax and hemp, together with a little madder, apple trees and a vineyard. This was another typical flax and hemp garden: a big, rough patch, like the one at Rimpton, growing the same basics

1   about 500 lbs: enough for a very big plot.

for manorial use. But here much more of the flax was made into linen and only a little kept as seed. Fifty four beats of linen were sold in 1332 for 9s., the same amount the next year. Most of the hemp was sold too: 16 stones of it for 10s.8d. in 1332. The hemp that was kept on the manor could be made into hempen cloth for working clothes, whence the expression 'hempen homespun' for a country-man, or one who spun his own hemp into cloth.

Hemp was the poor man's flax. Rough hemp, known as 'carle', was made into shoe threads, halters, stirrup-thongs, girths, bridles and, most commonly, ropes. Finer hemp, known as 'fimble', made coarse linen that supplied humble homes with the napkins, towels, smocks and broadcloths that wealthy houses and flax experts got from their home-grown flaxen linen.

Hemp is a hardier plant than flax and requires less attention. Its native habitat is probably somewhere around the Caspian Sea, but it does well on any light, rich, fertile soil, and was cultivated in Britain very early on. The Anglo-Saxons were old hands at growing and preparing it, and English hemp had a very good name. Like flax, it has to be steeped in water and its seeds removed, to be sown or crushed for oil, or in some fashionable homes fed to caged birds; then it is retted and its fibres extracted in the same way as flax.

The rope and the canvas cloth made from these fibres was in con-stant demand. Hemp had the advantage for small gardens that it could be grown year after year in the same patch, though it was most commonly grown in big, rather primitive gardens, like the one on Cuxham manor in Oxfordshire. The vegetable patch there was sown regularly with onions, leeks, beans and hemp, and looked after by a part-time gardener. In the thirteenth century he was usually an out-sider, brought over from Oxford for a few weeks each summer; in the fourteenth century he was usually one of the manorial staff, working part-time in the garden, helped by women from the village.

Women, Their Kitchens and
Their Kitchen Gardens

Women often did the kitchen gardening. They ran the kitchens, so it was up to them to choose what they wanted supplied to them, and they worked in their gardens when they were not helping their husbands and sons in the fields at seed and harvest time. At Rimpton women planted and weeded the vegetables, at the lower rates of pay that were considered perfectly fair in the Middle Ages, women being physically weaker than men. Except, that is, for one or two women like Juliana, the gardener on the Bishop of Ely's manor at Little Downham. She seems to have been too busy gardening to marry, for she is cited in the court rolls without any mention of a husband. She fixed up a number of illicit land deals for herself, leased a fishery and several meadows from the episcopal bailiffs, and commanded a gang of village villeins who had to do a few days work in the garden each year. She kept them at it, planting peas, beans and leeks each year for consumption on the manor, and harvesting enough apples, pears, cherries, nuts, plums and vegetables, which means pot-leeks, for sale either by the steward or 'in the courtyard' on a sort of manorial produce stall. One imagines that Juliana was in charge of the sales and made a good profit out of them.

She was a tough woman: the garden was in an area of such heavy soil that in 1345, when villagers were digging a new garden there for the Bishop, they broke their spades and had to be provided with stronger ones. We do not know how much she earned and whether she was paid less, the same, or more than the man who took over from her after her death because the gardener's pay is not recorded until 1345, by which time wage levels had changed and Juliana was past working the soil and was lying underneath it.

The Menagier's wife was also a gardener, but of a more genteel kind. Unlike most women, she had servants to do the manual work for her, but she was to be in sole charge of them, organizing and checking their work. So her husband set down basic horticultural principles and some useful tips for her to learn, such as; 'If you plant out in hot weather, water the holes before putting in the plants . . . To get rid of ants, put the sawdust of oak plants over their heap, and they will die as soon as it rains, for the sawdust retains the moisture.'

Medieval vegetable gardeners were painstakingly resourceful in handling the limited resources available to them, so that a few vegetables would make a lot of pottages. Garden tools were basically the same as they are today. In 1453 the bill for garden tools at Munden's Chantry near Bridport, Dorset, was: 5d. for one spade, 2d. for one rake, 4d. for one hoe. The next year 1d. was spent on repairing the wheelbarrow. The kitchen supplied by this garden would have been equipped with a number of pots, knives and spoons, the medieval basics; vegetables that could not supply those pots were scorned as follies of insipidity.

Not all medieval vegetables were strongly flavoured, Cucumber, for instance, was one of the four 'greater cold seeds', the others being melon, gourds and citruls (water-melons or pumpkins). As the cucumber was the only one of these four that could be grown in England, and then only in warm areas under careful attention, it was much sought after. Its seeds were used against all the 'hot' complaints, but its flesh was also useful for binding cooling plasters and soothing sunburnt skin. Because of their cosmetic kindness to skin, cucumbers were grown in some fashionable gardens. They are recorded as growing in England until the 1380s, when they disappear until the reign of Henry VIII. Maybe they were a casualty of the disruptions to fashionable estates resulting from the ravages of the plague in the late fourteenth century, and then the Wars of the Roses. Or maybe they just grew on quietly, unrecorded.

Bees, Honey Drinks and Honey

Estate vegetable gardens often included a pond or well, a tool-shed, walls, hedges, fences and ditches, a gate-house, teasels and osiers, a fish-stew, poultry, rabbits, fruit bushes and trees and, on occasion, those most valuable garden servants: bees.

Beehives were usually attached to vegetable gardens, and on estates and manors the vegetable garden was farthest from the house so that the bees would not bother members of the household, who would walk for pleasure in any garden but the vegetable one.

Bee-keeping may well have been practised in pre-Christian Britain. Certainly the ancient Irish laws often mention garden bee-keepers, and there was a lot of honey produced by small hives both in gardens and in the wilds. Wales and Ireland produced a lot of honey, and their poets saw heaven as a place full of buzzing bees and dripping with honey and wine, by which many of them meant mead.

Celtic saints drank a lot of mead, which was the cult drink of Celtic Britain. Many Celtic kings exacted a vat of mead as tribute from every village in their kingdom. Mead drinkers have always been credited with the rewards of life and strength, and there were always plenty of them in medieval Britain. In the later Middle Ages first ale, then beer, began to usurp the place of mead as the favourite drink; but ale itself may originally have been a form of mead. It is made from water, malt alcohol and yeast, by the same basic process as mead, but using malt instead of honey. We even have one hint of beer being brewed in medieval England by honey fermentation. In Henry II's reign the Duke of Saxony visited England, and the Sheriff of Hampshire was allowed a quota of corn, barley and honey, Hampshire honey being particularly fine, to brew beer for the Duke. But in general honey made mead, and in Antiquity and the early Middle Ages this was the drink that was favoured, especially when it was new and extra sweet.

Even in Chaucer's time, when mead had lost some of its earlier popularity, the Earl of Derby took 24 barrels of mead with him on one of his military expeditions because nothing sustained medieval man better than hot food and sweet drinks. One fifteenth-century household book refers to 'a hot drink maked with honey', which is half way between classifying honey as a drink, of which the best sort was mead, and classifying it as a sweetener – for most medievals the only sweetener they had. It also had preservative qualities in jams. Medieval jams took weeks to make. Whatever was being used had to be soaked, boiled, poached, reboiled and turned for a long time in honey and spices. Honey was liquid and so boiled easily; it also went into syrups, preserves and drinks. Clare, made of white wine, honey, sugar and spices, and piment, made of red wine, honey and spices, were very popular. Honey was the ideal taste-killer for nasty medicines, neutralizer of excessively sour purgatives and binding agent for plasters.

It was a first-rate medicine itself, both as ointment and as drink. Innumerable medieval medicines were honey-based. The powers of honey were legion, its sweetness as soothing and restoring as sweet herbs. Honey and betony drunk after supper helped the digestion; honey and garlic eased pain; honey softened rough skin and was used, as it is today, as a skin cosmetic.

It was particularly suitable for this since almost all medieval honey was liquid. The wax was sold separately, and the honey was transported in cisterns and barrels to be bought and sold in markets and towns. The Durham monks dealt in honey from their estates in such a big way that they hired porters to carry it as far as Newcastle for sale, usually at about 3d. a gallon.

Rents were partly paid in honey where a lot of it was produced. In 1254 Geoffrey of Bagshot held the estate of Chobham, Surrey, from the Abbot of Chertsey for an annual rent which included 12 gallons of honey (worth 6s.). The vicar of Chobham paid 10s. and 6 lbs. of wax per annum for his property. In the 1900s there was still a plot of land 1¾ miles north-east of Chobham called 'the bee gard', which suggests that the Chobham bees were garden ones. 'Honey of the field' was not as common as honey from gardens, and beehives were kept on garden properties of all sizes.

Groups of smallholders shared hives between them. The Domesday survey mentions a bee-keeper (*custos apium*) on a couple of big estates, and a lot of hives (*vascula*) and wicker hives (baskets) on all kinds of properties. Wicker hives were used in Britain into this century, cloomed with lime and cow-dung to keep them warm and draught-free, and covered with hackle to keep the rain out (see illustration p. 241). *Ruscae*, which appear in some medieval records, were also wicker hives, so called because originally, before straw was used to cover the hives, they were covered with bark (*rasca*). The French word for a bee-hive, *ruche*, comes from the same root. Most of the hives in eastern England were straw skeps (*vasa apium*) of various sizes, which were probably kept under cover, often on benches. Light and easy to handle, they were popular with cottagers, but were prone to destruction by murrain (the general medieval word for animal diseases, which in the case of bees is likely to have been Foul Brood). Some bee-keepers in the eastern counties were still using skeps a few years ago. East Anglian manors at the time of Domesday had an average of two or three hives each, and there was little or no wild honey. It was more common, though still rare, in the western counties. Occasionally hollow tree trunks full of bees were carried home from the wilds and used as domestic hives. Bees were as common in medieval England as the blossoms they lived on.

At Beaulieu Abbey, in Hampshire, most of the hives had honey collected from them every year. The bees were generously fed with honey through little hollow reeds pushed through the entrance of the hive. Most of the monastic hives were in the kitchen garden, under the care of Brother John, who distributed the wax he got from them to various of the obedientaries, and sold most of the honey. Wax was much more valuable than honey and was in constant demand, particularly in monasteries, for the making of candles.

To remind us once more of the basics of the vegetable garden this chapter closes with a description of 'a noble supper', described in one of the Chester Miracle plays. The speaker is one of the shepherds from Bethlehem, who is giving his household best to Jesus and the Holy Family for their supper. He brings ale (a century earlier it would have been just as likely to be mead), hot meat, an oat loaf,

pudding (of cereal, perhaps meat, and blood), sheep's head in ale,
grain and sour milk. But the very first things he produces are the
noblest and the most vital of all:

> Here is bread this day was baken,
> Onions, garlic and leeks . . .

8

Orchard, Fruit and Tree Gardens

The garden of Eden was full of fruit trees. In the East orchards were both fruit and pleasure gardens, and appear as such all through the Old Testament. Nehemiah recalled how the Israelites won themselves a livelihood in a new land by taking possession of 'houses stocked with all kinds of goods, of cisterns ready-hewn, of vineyards and olive groves, of fruit trees in profusion'. Such trees were more than a livelihood; they were a source of delight. 'As the apple tree among the trees of the orchard, so is my beloved among the young men,' sang the bride in the *Song of Songs*. Medieval orchards and fruit trees yielded the same double harvest of fruit and delight, with the emphasis on the fruit.

Fruit was not much esteemed in the Middle Ages. It was valued primarily as a source of drink, then as material for sweet, spicy desserts, preserves and comfits, if possible dyed bright colours with fruit juice, then as a carminative, appetizer and laxative, only lastly as a food in its own right. The fruits that satisfied the most important of these preferences were naturally the ones grown in orchards and also the commonest in gardens. Those that could satisfy only the less important preferences were restricted to garden cultivation, and many were not worth the effort of cultivation, so they were left in the wilds.

Cottagers and smallholders grew one or two fruit trees in their all-purpose gardens; bigger estate and householders usually had orchards separate from their various gardens. Sometimes orchards were enclosed within the kitchen garden, in accordance with the original meaning of the word orchard, that of an enclosed garden (hortus yard, shortened to hort yard, ortyard, orchard). Whether they were gardens within gardens or separate enclosures, orchards were the purest medieval fruit gardens, because most people grew their bit of fruit in with the herbs and vegetables in their kitchen gardens, and the first part of this chapter is devoted to them.

Orchard Fruits

When medieval records refer to an orchard, they mean a fruit tree garden as opposed to a garden in which there were some fruit trees growing. Sometimes there were vines along the orchard walls, and a few patches of hemp, flax or cereals under the trees, but essentially orchards were plantations of apples or pears, enclosed by a wall or ditch. Even the biggest orchards, of nine or ten acres, were firmly enclosed so that intruders had to break or climb in or, like Sir Degrevault in the 1440 romance of that name, 'in at an orchard leap'. It is only enclosure that distinguishes primitive orchards from woods; they are the oldest and simplest form of garth.

The commonest size for manorial orchards was three or four acres. The one on the Ely Priory manor of Melbourn cum Meldreth is a typical example. It was walled, three acres in extent, and planted with apple trees. *Apul tun* is the Anglo-Saxon for apple enclosure, and appleton was a common medieval synonym for orchard. In its Latin form, *pomarium*, it appears in records throughout the period.

Orchards were a monastic speciality. Many were six or seven acres, like the ones at Lindore in Fifeshire and Haddington in East Lothian; many were famous for their fruit, like the ones at Arbroath, Warden and Westminster. Descendants of apples and pears from Arbroath and Warden are still grown today; the Westminster orchard is remembered in the street name Abbey Orchard Street, on the site of the old orchard. Monasteries had more cause than any other medieval households to cultivate orchards because they had more mouths to feed, primarily with cider, secondarily with fruit. But all big households needed these supplies, and cultivated either orchards or big gardens with a lot of fruit trees.

The king was the leading fruit grower in medieval England. He could afford to experiment with new varieties of orchard and garden fruit and, like monastic fruit growers, had the international contacts that made this possible. Most orchard owners were much humbler and more conservative. They were manorial lords who grew the stock apples, pears, cherries and nuts, and left much of the supervisory work to their wives, who had to run household orchards as well as gardens if they wanted to walk in their blossomy fragrance and eat their fruit.

If a medieval orchard was not further described, it was an apple orchard. *Avall* or *aball* is the word for apple in all the Celtic languages, and Avalon, the Celtic 'Isle of the Blessed' is also the 'Isle of Apples',

> Where falls not hail, or rain, or any snow,
> Nor ever wind blows loudly – but lies
> Deep meadow'd, happy, fair with orchard lawns
> And bowery hollows crowned with summer sea.

Even before the apple came into cultivation in England, which was probably with the Romans, the native crab apple tree was common, and it may well have been brought into cultivation by a process of gradual selection and seeding at a date too early to be traceable in the records. Both Celts and Saxons planted apple orchards, and held apples in the same regard as the Ancients and the Old Testament writers had done. Anglo-Saxon saints and Norman monks loved cider, and greatly increased its production in England. Cider was the next most common drink in medieval England after ale, only the very rich and the very poor abstaining from it, the rich because they preferred wine, and the poor when they didn't have the apples to make it.

'This Samson never cider drank, ne (nor) wine', wrote Chaucer in his *Monk's Tale*, and one has only to look at the accounts of monastic cellarers to realize how strange and ascetic the ciderless Samson must have seemed to the monk. Most of the apples grown in monastic orchards were made into cider and drunk by the community, some were eaten and any surplus was sold. The cellarer at Battle Abbey had an apple garden and his accounts include entries such as:

1359-60: Nothing from the garden this year because there were no apples.

1369-70: 55s. from the sale of 3 tuns of cider from the garden, 12 tuns having been deducted as expenses, and 20s. for the purchase of barrels and the collecting of apples.

1420-1: 3s.4d. from the sale of apples.

1512-3: 8d. spent on repairs to the cider mill.

Cider mills were for production on a large scale; smaller producers had presses that varied in size from the big horse-drawn to the small hand-worked, and often doubled as wine presses. In good apple-growing areas like Kent, Somerset and Hampshire, almost every manor had a cider press of some sort. Customary tenants like those on the manor of Crawley, in Hampshire, in 1282 had to 'collect apples in the Waltham garden and convey them to the mill, for which they get 10 apples a day and a meal,' as part of their work rent. The apples were pressed without any added sugar, and the juice drank at once if liked raw and sharp, anything up to two years later if preferred strong and sweet. The medievals liked it both ways, and often drank it strongly spiced. The Kentish cider mills were known as hob-nail mills and were already famous by Henry II's reign for producing the strong, spiced cider that the Canterbury monks began to drink instead of ale at that period.

This cider was also favoured by seamen, and stored in warehouses at the ports to supply them. Kentish cider production was a commercial, not just a manorial and garden enterprise. Thirteen of the citizens of New Romney in the mid-fifteenth century were cider sellers.

Elsewhere, the popularity of cider was regional. The Countess of Leicester's household in the late thirteenth century preferred beer, and gave the little cider it had in its stores to the poor. In Hampshire, Gloucester, Worcester, Herefordshire, Somerset and Devon cider was drunk in heroic quantities. It was popular enough to be included in all the fourteenth-century treatises on husbandry, which said that 10 qtrs. of apples or pears ought to yield a tun of cider as rent.

The best cider apples were bitter-sweets and Pearmains, the latter being also first-class dessert apples and the oldest English variety on record. An exchequer account for the year 1200 records the tenure of the petty serjeanty of Bunham, in the Norfolk hundred of East Flaff, by one Robert of Evermere, for an annual rent of 200 Pearmains and 4 hogsheads of Pearmain cider, a rent that was still being paid a century later. Both bitter-sweets and Pearmains made strong cider, and the word cider was used by preachers and poets to mean a strong drink.

The most popular medieval apple was the Costard, which made good cider and good eating. 'The Costards comely in cups be cayre (turned, gone)', wrote the *Pistill of Susan* author in 1400, and they also went into innumerable medieval stomachs just as they were, large, ribbed and juicy. As early as 1292 Edward I's fruiterer bought

300 lbs. of Costards for the royal household while it was staying at Berwick Castle, and so many Costards were bought and sold all over England that those who engaged in this commerce were known as costermongers. Costards were almost a distinct fruit in their own right. Grosseteste spoke of 'apples and Costards' in the thirteenth century, and Costard trees, like their fruit, were bought and sold for high prices. The apples often fetched as much as 1s. per 100, and in 1325 one Oxford nurseryman sold 29 Costard trees for 3s. They were good, vigorous growers, their bark yielding a red dye, and they were the national favourite until the seventeenth century. Their name, like the names of a lot of medieval apples, is probably directly descriptive, derived from the Old French *coste*, meaning rib, the Costard being ribbed and five-sided.

The Pearmain was so named because it was long and pear-shaped; the pippin, which became fashionable in the fifteenth century, because it signified any apple that grew from seed; the bitter-sweet because that is exactly what it was; 'the Pomewater and gentle Ricardons' (Lydgate) because they were respectively very juicy and introduced by Duke Richard of Normandy; the Blanksdurelle, more commonly known as the Blaundrelle or Blandurel, and now known as Calville Blanc, because it is almost white in colour.

These last were brought to England by Edward I's queen, Eleanor of Castile, who had grafts of the new variety sent over from Aquitaine to her orchard at Langley Manor, in Hertfordshire, in 1280. They must have done well and continued in the royal favour, for in 1310 William of Writtle, the royal fruiterer, began his account of supplies for the queen with this entry: 'For the queen, going to Canterbury on the Friday before the Nativity of St John [June 24], 800 Blandurels, price 6s.; 1 paigner [fruit basket] 3d; portage 5d.' He bought Blandurels for the queen all the year round. The medievals liked to store their apples in straw and let them mellow for a while before eating them.

> Her mouth was sweet as bragot [ale and mead] or the meeth [mead]
> Or hoard of apples laid in hay or heeth,

declared Chaucer's Miller.

Most of the popular medieval varieties lasted well and were eaten as late as the June after their harvest, like the Blandurels cited above. Queenings, now know as Winter Queenings because they harvest so late, lasted best of all because of their late start, and keep their red colour well, which helps to explain their medieval popularity.

There were local varieties of apple that have disappeared from the records, and have either died out or are unrecognizable under their modern names. The Arbroath Oslin or Pippin, for instance, was known medievally as the Bur Knot, and was brought to Arbroath by the Tironesian Benedictines who built the magnificent abbey there in 1178. The tree is free-growing, and was planted in a number of Scottish orchards, but never became a national variety.

The native crab apple, by contast, was known in the wilds and, to a lesser extent, in cultivation all over Britain, but it had a limited use. Crabs were too sour to compete with sweet apples like Costards and were known as 'choke apples' because of the effect they had on those who ate them raw. 'As sour as a crab' was a common medieval simile, but this sourness gave the crab its usefulness. It was the ideal complement to sweet spices in sweet and sour cooking, and crab juice made apple verjuice and sour cooking cider. In 1296 Simon de Monte of Wakefield was fined because he had failed to collect the lord of the manor's crab apples, thereby causing him to lose two hogsheads of cider. Crabs were small, hard, pickling and verjuice apples; the cultivated varieties were eaten raw to 'open the stomach' before a meal, and roasted with sugar and fennel and caraway seeds, to keep it open afterwards. Ten raw apples a day helped to keep monastic stomachs 'open' during Lent.

But if one was not over- or under-eating, the best way to eat apples was cooked and sweetened. They were sliced and dried in the sun, sealed in earthenware jars and buried under the ground, and put in honey, wine-must, brine or vinegar pickle to preserve them. They emerged from these treatments strong-tasting and in little pieces, all ready for the pot, wherein they were cooked into sweet porray for the favourite medieval desserts. Among these were apple tart, made with spices, figs, raisins, pears and saffron; apple muse (mousse), with almonds, honey, grated bread, saffron, sweet spices and salt; apple and parsnip fritters, with ale, saffron, almond milk and salt.

Raw, as they came off the trees, apples were deeply symbolic.

> An apple I took of a tree,
> God had it forbidden me
> Wherefore I should damned be,

ran a fourteenth-century lyric: 'Christ Weeps in the Cradle for Man's Sin.' The apple features in even more medieval religious lyrics as the instrument of the Fall, than it does in secular lyrics as an image of handsome health. Sacred or secular, the apple was an image that was familiar to everyone. The secular equivalent of the attractive, fatal fruit that caused Eve to corrupt Adam was the apple that was rotten at the core, probably through being kept in store too long.

Pears did not have the symbolic importance of apples because they did not have the same role in the *Genesis* story or the *Song of Songs*, where the lover sings 'comfort me with apples, for I am sick with love'. In literature pears were simply symbols of delight, pears being the next most popular medieval fruit after apples. Apples and pears were often planted, harvested, eaten and drunk together. If an orchard was not full of apples, it was full of apples and pears; failing that, nuts and pears or pears on their own. The accounts of the gardener at Norwich Cathedral Priory nearly always list apples and pears together.

> 1340: Received – 13s.4½d. for apples
> 1400: Received – 4s.7½d. for apples and pears
>   Expended – 2s.2½d. for apples for the convent
>   10d. for cloths to cover the apples
> 1402: Received – 4s.4d. for pears and nuts
>   16d. for apples
> 1403: Received – 9s. for apples and pears
> 1432: Expended – 3 combs [measures] of crabs . . .
>   2s. for cherries and apples for the convent
> 1470: Expended – 14d. for apples and pears
> 1472: Expended – 5s.9d. for apples and pears for the convent
>   4d. for apples for the frater.

Pears were marketed almost as extensively as apples, sometimes mixed in with them, just as they had come out of an apple and pear orchard, under the title 'mixed fruits'. They were eaten in the same way as apples, most popularly in tarts and pies.

The best baking pears, and the most popular altogether, were Wardens, traditionally held to have been brought from Burgundy to the Cistercian abbey of Warden, Bedfordshire, at the request of an enthusiastic monk gardener. In the West Country baking pears were still called 'wardens', and highly esteemed as winter pears, in the eighteenth century. Today Wardens are called Parkinsons Wardens or Black Worcesters; in the Middle Ages they were often called Pearmains as well as Wardens, and extensively used in cooking, the Menagier's favourite method being to lay them in a gently heated bed of hay.

They were preserved in the same way as apples, and made into sweets like Warden pies, with quinces, sugar and ginger, in 'paste coffins', and pear comfits, an alternative to roasted caraway apples, made with spiced wines, mulberries, sugar and ginger. Pears were used in cooking much more than apples because they were less suitable for making into drink and for eating raw, being what Neckham described as 'hard, cold fruits', without the sweetness and colour of eating apples.

The next most popular variety after the Warden was the Caleol or Caillou pear, so called because it was shaped like a pebble, or *caillou* in French. It may well have been as hard as a pebble too, judging from the length of time it had to be 'seethed' and boiled before eating. Like most medieval English pears, it was a French introduction, in this case imported by London sheriffs as a present for Henry III, and it was grown by householders with a lot of mouths to feed.

Henry de Lacy bought five Caillou cuttings for his Holborn orchard in 1294. In the same year he bought 3 Pesse-Pucelle cuttings, two Martin cuttings, so called because their fruit ripened at Martinmas (November 11), and two St Rule, or St Regle cuttings. These last were very expensive, costing 8d. per 100, and came from the La Rochelle district of France, which was famous for its pears. They were called after St Rule, or Regolo, the third-century Bishop of Arles, who was also the first Bishop of Senlis, and a pear connoisseur. Throughout their medieval life St Rule pears were career pears, more exclusive and expensive than the best apples, costing as much as 3s. per 100.

Among humbler pear trees, grown in numerous humble orchards and gardens, were Dreyes (3d. per 100), Sorells, Chyrfolls and Gold Knopes (only 2d. per 100). These last were a small, round variety (hence their name, knope being the medieval form of knob) that cropped heavily and steadily, especially in the north and the Scottish border country, but were of poor quality and were used to make pear porrays or pies when the Wardens had run out. Trees and fruits of all these varieties were bought by the King and London merchants from French fruiterers, but that does not mean that some of them, almost certainly Sorells and Gold Knopes at least, were not English varieties too. The wild pear is native to England, like the wild crab apples, and appears in Anglo-Saxon charters, though it seems to have been replaced by cultivated varieties more completely than the crab.

One of the few pears eaten raw was the Pear-Jenette, or Janettar, known in England by 1251, when Henry III bought some from a London fruiterer, and very common by the fourteenth century. It ripened before any of the other varieties, during the summer love-season, and was therefore the favourite fruit tree of bawdy song-writers and poets. It must have been a pear-jenette tree that Chaucer's merchant planted in his garden of delight, for when his wife wanted an excuse to climb into it and meet Damyan, her lover, in its branches, it was early summer and she said:

> I must have of the pears that I see,
> Or I must die, so sore longeth me
> To eat of the small pears green.

Most medieval pears seem to have been hard cooking pears, like the 'small pears green' on the pear-jenette tree. Since they didn't keep as well as apples, or make as good a drink, they were made into preserves, jams, puddings and, occasionally, comfits. Perry was made mainly by those who could not afford to make cider. Medieval pears being rather hard and sour, their perry was a compromise between cider and verjuice. It was pressed and fermented without sugar, like cider, and must have been very verjuicy indeed.

Perrywhite was a cheap version of perry, often mixed with cheap ale to make it go further, and sold to the poor in taverns. Official records hardly ever mention pear drinks, but confirm the impression that pears, along with apples, were widely eaten both cooked and raw, in the latter case their hard, green 'opening' properties having a strong medieval appeal.

The only major fruit that was eaten raw for preference was the cherry, orchard companion of the apple and the pear. 'Cherries were brought out of Pontus into Italy 689 years after the building of Rome, and 120 years afterward into Britain,' wrote Pliny. Unlike apples and pears, cultivated cherries did not replace the native wild species, which continued to be popular in England all through the Middle Ages. 'Cherries in the rise' (on the bramble or branch) figure in all sorts of medieval horticultural and literary records.

'Hot peascods! Strawberry ripe, And cherries in the rise! Hot sheep's feet! Mackerel, and rushes green!' were the street cries of late fifteenth-century London described by Lydgate in *London Lickapenny*.

Cultivated cherries had been sold in abundance ever since the early Norman, if not the Anglo-Saxon period. The 1236 Pipe Roll for the Suffolk manor of Clare records a receipt of '66s.5d. from pears and cider and cherries sold on the manor', all these probably coming from the manorial orchards. The Norwich Priory gardener had a cherry orchard separate from his apple, pear and nut one. In 1484 he spent 3s. on a 'windowstal for the cherry garden', which suggests that by this time it was something of a blossomy pleasance, its wall fitted with a window and perhaps a seat below that as well as an entrance door. In 1450 the gardener spent 3d. on 'mending the door of the cherry yard'. But the orchard's main medieval purpose was to produce fruit, and when it didn't produce enough to keep the community happy, the gardener had to buy some in.

> 1340: Expended on cherries – 8½d.
> 1400: Expended on cherries – 28d.
> 1427: Received for the sale of cherries . . .

The medievals liked their cherries ultra-ripe, and picked them when they were 'wine red' (1440 poem). Cherry red was next in popularity after rose red and lily white among medieval similes, and red cherries were the fruity equivalent of small, hot vegetables, seeds and spices. 'Chibolles and chervils and ripe cherries many' were the favourite summer tastes of Piers Plowman. Cottagers like Piers, who only had room for one or two trees in their gardens, often favoured the beautifully blossomed, brightly fruited cherry, and ate its fruit raw, as everyone did.

Medieval gardening treatises often recommend cherry trees as good graft stocks and their stones as good graft scions, writers later in the period being particularly keen to find ways of grafting so that cherries would grow without stones. Stones notwithstanding, 'a bob of cherries' like the one mentioned in the Towneley Mystery Plays was a common summer amusement, as were cherry fairs, or feasts held in cherry orchards at harvest time. Cherry fairs were the epitome of the sweet summer season, over all too soon after it had blossomed, and they were popular poetic symbols for transience.

The nut, like the cherry, belonged to everyone. The last of the orchard fruits considered in this chapter is the nut. Like the cherry, it was as common in the wilds as in cultivation, probably more so; it belonged to everyone, was eaten raw, but, like the apple and the pear, was preferred cooked. Nuts were categorized as great, usually walnuts, or small, usually filberts and chestnuts. Those that were simply referred to as nuts were usually the native hazel (*Corylus avellana*). The filbert (*Corylus maxima*) was so called because its nuts ripened on St Philibert's day [August 22].

'The filbert eke, that low doth incline her boughs green' (Lydgate) was a gracious tree admired by the poets, and more often grown in gardens than orchards.

Walnuts were also called walsh nuts, and were the most common variety of cultivated nut, valued for their oil, wood and dye as well as their taste. Walter of Henley estimated that a quarter of nuts ought to make 4 gallons of oil, a commodity the medievals could never have enough of for cooking and cosmetics. Walnut wood was sometimes used to make bowls, known as mazers, which were also made of maple (hence their name), and of other woods such as ash. Walnut shells contain a long-lasting black dye, which was used as hair dye. In cooking, walnut kernels were used like filberts and hazel nuts, to give some bite to fruit pies and pastes, and sweet and sour meat dishes.

'The duke bought nuts with which he seethe his meat and victuals' (1387 poem). The Menagier's wife made nut jam out of walnuts in their soft, unripe shells, which was how they were used in pickling and making nut comfits, for which they were stuck with cloves and ginger and boiled in honey. This was the most popular kind of nut dessert, raw nuts only being eaten to 'close' the stomach after a meal, or with dried fruit. Nuts and raisins were one of the favourite monastic pittances, hence the entry in the Durham Priory account rolls for 1358: '2000 walnuts at 15d. per 1000'. Walnuts were the next best thing after imported almonds, followed by filberts and hazelnuts. They were grown in nut orchards, usually in with apples and pears. The Abingdon Abbey gardener often sold some of his nuts, probably the 'small nuts', keeping the 'great nuts' for the community.

1388:   Receipts – 32s.6d. from the sale of apples and pears and nuts.
Expenses – 3s.6d. for fruit collecting.
1412:   Receipts – 2s.4d. from the sale of apples and pears, and 2s.1d. from the sale of nuts.
5s. for the sale of a nut beam [tree] sold from the garden this year.
Expenses – 4d. for apple and nut collecting.

Occasionally gardeners cultivated exclusively nut orchards. In 1403 a certain William was brought to trial at High Easter, near Dunmow in Essex, for destroying 14 walnut 'imps' (young trees) planted there.

Sweet chestnuts were probably a Roman introduction into Britain, like walnuts, though they may be native. They were not nearly as popular as walnuts, not having their oil, their carving wood or their dye. They were known as 'castaynes', and eaten both raw and roasted. Like all the English nuts except walnuts, they were common in the wilds and therefore seldom cultivated by smallholders, who gathered their nuts from the woods. Only big householders could afford the space to enclose fruit and nut trees into orchards.

Much more common habitats for fruit trees were gardens, where apples, pears, cherries and occasionally nuts were grown, by big and smallholders.

Garden Fruits

After apples, pears and cherries, the most popular fruit in well-to-do gardens was probably the quince, which is a member of the pear family. Quinces are harder than the hardest pears, much too hard to eat raw, and they were put into the pot to make sweet preserves and tarts. Their sharp, tangy taste was so much to medieval taste that it earned them forgiveness for their lack of drinkable juice, and with forgiveness, cultivation. They were grown by gardeners supplying kitchens with enough staff, honey and spices to make such things as quince marmalade which, according to the Menagier's recipe, required lavish helpings of red wine, honey and hippocras, and laboriously peeled, quartered, pipped and pulped quinces. Quince pips were stored away for use as 'cold, dry' medicinal seeds. Thriftier cooks boiled softened quince peel in sugar and water to make suc-cade, an English version of continental extravagances like marmalade. They used the flesh to make quince jelly, with grease, clarified honey, egg yolks, almond milk and saffron, or quince pastries and pies. Most quince trees grew in big, well-to-do gardens like the royal ones at Westminster, for which the King's fruiterers bought a lot of quince, pear and apple trees in 1292, the quinces costing 41s. per 100. The Tower of London were planted by the royal gardener in 1275 with:

100 cherry trees, costing 1s.6d.,
500 osier willows, costing 4s.6d.,
4 quince trees, costing 2s.,
2 peach trees, costing 1s.,
gooseberry bushes, costing 3d.,

a quart of lily bulbs, costing 1s.,
another peach tree, costing 6d.,

The peach trees were 6d. each, compared with the cherry trees, which cost less than ¼d. each. They were as expensive as quinces, and much harder to cultivate successfully in England. They appear quite frequently in literature from the thirteenth century on, usually classed with exotic fruits. Godfrey's fifteenth-century version of Palladius's *De Agricultura* advised gardeners to sprinkle their peach trees with goat's milk in order to get pomegranates from them. Only occasionally are there familiar local references to peaches, such as the one in the Tower Gardener's list or the one in the chronicle of Roger of Wendover, who reported that King John hastened his death by indulging in 'a surfeit of peaches and ale'. Peaches seem to have been royal favourites. The nearest most householders could get to a surfeit of peaches was a show of peach blossom, which might mean a few peaches at harvest time, on a tree trained along the south-facing wall of a little pleasance.

Figs too may have grown on one or two English walls, but it is not even certain that they were introduced by the Romans, and if they did survive into the medieval period, it was only in one or two places in the southern counties. If they were cultivated, they were eaten fresh and green, which is how imported figs were eaten, and were aperitive rather than sweet figs.

Medlars were sweeter and relatively common. Chaucer called them 'homely trees' and put them next to plums, pears and castaynes in the list of trees in his *Roman de la Rose* translation. The gardener at Westminster Abbey had to supply the community with 'apples, cherries in season, plums, big pears, nuts and mepsilia [medlars] if he has them in the garden'. Evidently he had some medlar trees but could not guarantee that they would fruit each year. This must have been so for quite a few English gardeners, battling with the English climate. If the trees did fail to fruit, 'a fair shoot of blackthorn, crabtree, medlar or juniper' according to a fifteenth-century treatise on husbandry, would made a useful fishing line or whip. If the trees did fruit, it was not until October, and their fruit, which resembles a small, brown-skinned apple, was stored in straw until November, when it was eaten decayed and soft, either raw or pulped into a sweet puree with honey. Neckham classified medlars with cherries and plums, all three being fruits that were to be eaten when they had ripened to the point of rottenness.

Plums were more like cherries than medlars, being easy to grow and abundant in England since Roman times. In fact they were so abundant that few people bothered to cultivate them, gathering wild plums, bullaces and sloes instead. So the very suitability of the plum to English conditions restricted its cultivation to relatively few gardens, often of the same select sort that grew peaches and medlars. Wild plums had the further advantage of tasting very sharp. This is particularly true of sloes, which were used to make dark verjuice if grapes were short.

'Get us . . . bolaces and blackberries that on briars grow,' wrote William of Palerne in 1350, and most people did that rather than cultivate the plum into domestic mildness.

Some gardeners, however, did grow plums, the Westminster Abbey gardener winning acclaim for the excellence of his. Quite a lot of Scottish monastic gardeners, who had a limited range of fruits open to them for cultivation, grew plums, or 'plowms' as they were called until the fourteenth-century, when the vowel was shortened to its present pronunciation. The Menagier had plum trees in his garden and valued them as good grafting stocks, like his cherry trees. Langland wrote about 'peescods and pear Jonettes, plums and cherries', but didn't make it clear whether the last two were wild or cultivated. As a rule they were both eaten raw, not having enough flesh on them to make stoning for cooking worthwhile.

When plums were cooked, it was in the same way as all the soft fruits: they were pulped, thickened with flour and breadcrumbs, sweetened, spiced and coloured. The resulting puree was known as a 'murrey' because it was most commonly made out of mulberries (*Morus nigra*), or at least coloured by their addition. Murrey was sweet pottage, often made more like the basic savoury pottage that no medieval could bear to do without by being reinforced with pulped veal, pork or capon and spiced until sweet and sour. A bowlful of murrey was the only alternative dessert to a pie, tart or pastry, and was usually followed by comfits and dried fruits and nuts. Murrey was also the name of a mulberry-coloured cloth.

The most popular murrey fruit was the mulberry, which gave its name to the dish. Its juice was a popular dye, ideal for brightening up medieval meals, and its taste medievally sharp. Mulberry juice and sugar was added to wine as well as pottages, to sweeten and colour it. It made an invigoratingly scarlet drink in its own right, and Henry III's clerk bought 6s.8d. worth of mulberry and raspberry drinks for the King in 1241. Mulberry juice was one of the ingredients, along with elderberry, bilberry and blackberry juice, of the blue dye turnsole, used to colour pottages and also paintings and manuscripts.

One of the twelfth-century Arthurian romances described somebody's skin as being 'black as a mulberry', and the mor-beam, as the Anglo-Saxons called the tree, seems to have been cultivated consistently, if not comprehensively, in England since its introduction by the Romans. Mulberry trees are very slow-growing and long-lived. They were planted by institutional gardeners with an eye to the future, not by hungry kitchen gardeners. There was one growing in a York garden before 1361; there was one in the Draper's Hall garden in London in the fifteenth century; doubtless there were a good many in monastic gardens.

Raspberries, elderberries, blackberries and bilberries were not cultivated because they grow quickly, profusely and bushily in the wilds, and do not reward cultivation by developing into trees or greatly inceasing their fruit. Their bright, strong juice made a good purgative, a passable murrey and a useful dye, often used to colour flower pottages. These were made out of roses, primroses, violets and hawthorn blossoms, dyed with turnsole and garnished with petals and flowers.

Strawberries also grew wild for the most part, but may have been brought into cultivation here and there because they improve so much as a result. They were popular in Anglo-Saxon times; the Countess of Leicester bought some for her household in 1265; the trend-setting Earl of Lincoln may have grown them in his Holborn garden; in 1328 Edward III's accountant recorded the purchase of 'one silver fork of strawberries'; by the fifteenth century they were so fashionable that they may have been cultivated more than the records suggest. None of the soft fruits were common in gardens, and strawberries didn't even have the sharp taste and bright dye that the others had to recommend them. But they were sweet and colourful, especially when cultivated, and were one of the increasing number of fruits cultivated by the prosperous bourgeoisie in the fifteenth century. Poems from this period display a knowledge of sweet, red strawberries such as cultivation produces:

And your strawberry lips as sweet as honey,
With rose red in your cheeks – ye have no peer!

says a fifteenth-century poem, 'The Beauty of His Mistress'. We know from Lydgate that strawberries were sold in the streets of London in the late fifteenth century. They were eaten raw more often than the other soft fruits because their taste was too delicate to make a good murrey and too sweet to need murrey treatment. Fashionable fifteenth-century cooks made them into a sort of sweet, light murrey.

There is one other berry that ought to be included in this soft fruit section. The gooseberry is native to Britain and was only occasionally brought into cultivation during the Middle Ages, for the sake of its sourness. Gooseberries were used instead of verjuice to make meat sauces, sharp broths and green pickles. Their kitchen use was entirely sharp and savoury, their kitchen garden cultivation rare. Edward I's Tower gooseberries of 1275 seem to be the only ones in recorded cultivation. Berries as a breed belonged in the wilds and offered little reward to gardeners. The Menagier told his wife that the Nativity of the Blessed Virgin (September 8) was the time to plant currant bushes, whence their leaves were picked to be infused into refreshing tisanes and the fruit to flavour and colour wine, murreys and, occasionally, pickles and sweet and sour sauces. But the garden was the preserve of tree fruits, which scented it with blossom and shaded it with leafy branches thronged with birds.

A few ambitious gardeners and a great many impractical garden theorists sought to increase the sweetness of their garden apples, pears and cherries by grafting them on to sweet varieties of the same fruits, vines and even imported fruits like pomegranates. Fruit tree grafting was the most common kind of grafting, and three different methods were evolved. The most optimistic and least common was to sow two or three pips, of pippin apples rather than the pomegranates recommended by theorists addicted to classical sweetness, and allow the strongest plant that grew up to remain, until it was ready to receive a graft. A stock grown in this way has proved itself fit; it has all its tap and anchor roots and is less liable to blow down than a transplanted tree. As the fourteenth-century proverb put it: 'A tree set in divers places will not bring forth fruit.' A pippin growing where it was sown may do. But its roots can penetrate to bad soil, and a layer of stones should be laid 18 ins. or 2 ft. below the crown of the roots to stop this happening. Expert medieval tree growers did just this, witness the elaborate series of soil and stone levels excavated in the orchard of Deer Abbey, Aberdeenshire. There was 3 ft. of rich soil on top of a paved causeway, beneath which was a bed of sand, with another paved layer beneath that, contrived so that the land was drained and the trees could not put down tap roots.

Wild apple and pear pips grown in this way grow into the most enduring trees, but very slowly. Gardeners with good soil and limited time used one of the two standard methods detailed by John the Gardener.

> In the calendars of Januar'
> Thou shalt trees both set and rear
> To graft therein apple and pear,

apples with apples and pears with hawthorns, according to John. Both these grafts are horticulturally sound, indeed conservative. John was an experienced, dourly unadventurous gardener. His grafting instructions are timelessly accurate. An apple or pear stock was to be planted and, when it had grown into a healthy young tree, grafted either by shortening the branches and inserting scions of the desired variety or cutting off the head and inserting the scions into the stem, just below where the head had formed.

Grafting had been practised by fruit growers since the Old English period at least, and some of the new varieties of apples that became popular in fifteenth-century English gardens were probably the result of consistent, careful grafting operations by men like John the Gardener. Henry de Lacy's gardener grafted scions of new varieties of pears, imported from France, on to the Earl's home grown stocks, with deliciously successful results. Grafting and pruning, the other fruit-growing skill much prized by the medievals, appear in their orchard accounts almost every year and in kitchen garden accounts very often. At Rimpton, near Taunton, an expert gardener was paid the high wage of 1s. for eight days work 'grafting new trees' in the apple and pear garden there in 1265. Grafting and pruning fruit trees were parts of a gardener's expertise. A few gardeners, notably those in charge of monastic and big manorial orchards, became grafting specialists. A few others applied their skills to fruitless trees and developed commercial tree-nurseries to provide gardeners and farmers with fencing and building timber.

Nursery Gardening

Tree gardening is the subject of the last section of this chapter, and falls naturally into two subsections: nursery gardening and pleasure grove gardening. Both are hard to detail because fruitless garden trees are not mentioned in garden accounts, and nursery trees were

The original medieval herb garden in the Benedictine monastery of
Einsiedeln, Switzerland, as it is today.

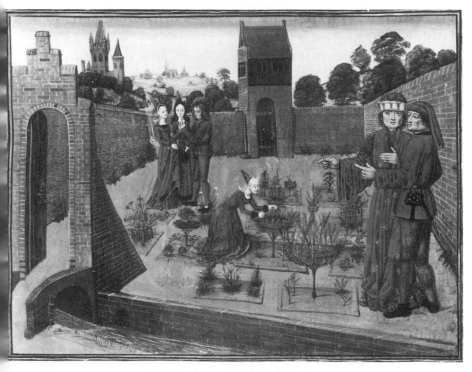

A decorative herb garden with a variety of herbs being tended by a woman
gardener and admired by her household and guests.

Cultivation of crops and gardens in a spacious 14th-century village.

A bee-keeper banging his gong to call his bees into their hives, some of which are sheltered from the elements.

often agricultural rather than horticultural, grown in coppices rather than gardens. Literary evidence is hazardous because it is often conventionally classical and only occasionally reflects reality. However, most of the trees that grew in medieval gardens can at least be identified, and a few of them detailed, by careful comparison of the different sorts of evidence. The result is that medieval nursery and pleasure gardens emerge as much more thickly but much less variously wooded than modern ones, in the same way as medieval flower-gardens were more flowery, herb gardens more herbal and vegetable gardens more densely and less variously vegetated.

Nursery garden trees were grown for sale to gardeners, farmers and estate managers, mainly for fencing and sometimes for park and forestry planting. Grafts, scions, shoots and saplings were all called 'imps', and 'impgarths' or 'impyards' were enclosed plantations of imps. In some areas, such as Durham, they were enclosures made by the planting of imps to form hedges and fences. There was an 'impcroft' at Pontefract, a town later famous for its trade nurseries, by 1215; there were impgarths at Farlam, near Brampton, in Cumberland, in 1250, and at Selby, in Yorkshire, in 1319. One of the thirteenth-century gardens at Durham Cathedral Priory was known as the impyard or impgarth. Imp as a field name compound goes back to the early twelfth century, and coppices of useful woods like hazel were planted all through the Middle Ages. It is hard to distinguish an impgarth from a field plantation or a coppice. An impgarth was a garden wood as much as it was a wood garden, full of young forest and fencing trees that would be taken out of their garth as soon as they were big enough to be useful. Impyards have a place in this chapter by virtue of the fact that they were enclosed and were therefore the same basic kind of garth as orchards.

The gardener's accounts from Norwich Priory give us a neat, detailed little summary of the contents and uses of one of these garths, this one being looked after by the gardener, which is so typical that it precludes the necessity of further impyard descriptions.

1340: Received: 28s.2½d. for faggot branches and roots [for fuel].
13s.4d. for osier rods sold [for making baskets].
9s.8d. for stamholt [stumps] and wong [crooked and broken branches sold for use as building timber].

Expenses: 6d. to a carpenter, for sawing the timber.
6d. to the Bishop's woodman, for supervising the operations.

1387: Received: 22s.3d. for fencing wood sold.
8s.6d. for walnut trees sold.
16s.6d. for osiers sold.
16s.4½d. for timber sold.

1402: Received: 18s.3d. for dry trees [deadwood] sold.
11s.3d. for faggots and astel [shavings] sold.
9d. for willows sold [for making hurdles, fences and baskets].
3s.4d. for osiers sold.
35s.4d. for trees sold to the Cellarer [for fuel or fruit production, or both].
35s.4d. for a layer of crabthorn and other things sold to the Cellarer [for fencing and fuel].
10d. for a layer of wythis [osiers] sold.

1403: Received: 8s.8d. for albele sold [white poplar, commonly planted in the Fens to form protective enclosure borders].
6s.8d. for timber sold.
15d. for faggots sold.
3s.9d. for crab-draughts and oak sold [for fuel].

1427: Received: 8s.2d. for faggots, shavings and osiers sold.

Willows and osiers, alders, poplars and aspens were the most common impgarth trees. Ash trees were also grown, because they provided good poles for hurdle-making, and hazels because their young stems were pliant enough to be made into wattle screens, hurdles, thatch frames, fences, handles, shafts, rods and crooks. Their young shoots are edible, and hazel faggots were popular as firewood. Alders were used for propping up vines. Oak trees were less common in impyards. The lord of Cuxham manor, in Oxford-shire, had three bushels of acorns planted in his orchard garden in 1316, for the building timber, shade and pig mast the oaks would provide. Walnuts are even slower growing than oaks, and were planted by nurserymen and dedicated gardeners with an eye to their nuts rather than their woody usefulness. They grew in gardens that contained trees, rather than impgarths. Tree gardens were a not un-common form of medieval pleasance, and such pleasances are the subject of the last part of this chapter.

Tree Pleasure Gardens

A garden saw I full of blossomy boughs
Upon a river in a green mead,

wrote Chaucer in his *Parliament of Fowls*, about the kind of garden
the Cistercians at Balmerino Abbey, in the Sidlaw hills of central
Scotland, must have had. At the Dissolution the names of their
gardens were 'Ward' (enclosure), 'Nutyard', 'Overmill' (the garden
by the monks' well, brewhouse and dovecot), 'Green' and
'Plumyard', making a series of tree gardens full of fruit, shade and
delight. The garden sites were identified in the last century, and the
'Ward' was found to contain a huge old Spanish chestnut, 19½ ft. in
circumference 1ft. above the ground, which was reputed to have
been as old as the abbey. The 'Nutyard' contained a large, very
ancient walnut. The 'Overmill' garden contained a Spanish chestnut
similar to the one in the 'Ward', which must have overhung the well
if it was alive in the Middle Ages. Two very large, very old beeches
were growing in 'The Green'. Nothing was left of the plum trees
that gave their name to the 'Plumyard'. The abbey gardens were a
fruity pleasance. In 1534 each of the monks had his own garden,
joined to that of his neighbour by a passageway and open to
everyone's use, its 'fruits and produce' belonging to the whole community. Each of these gardens was called 'the orchard' or the
'fruityard' or Heriot, or Barrett, or whatever the monk's name was.

Fruit, timber and decorative trees often grew together in a single
garden. In the late fourteenth century a clerk called John Henley
and an associate were summoned to court to answer to Richard
Noke, a goldsmith, who claimed they had 'broken into his close and
houses at Charring, Westminster, and felled pears, apples, poplars,
oaks, beeches, ashes, willows, thorns and trees bearing walnuts, and
carried them off.' This may have been a nursery close, plundered for
its timber, or a wooded and fruitful pleasance, broken into because of
some personal animosity between the intruders and Richard. It may
have been both.

The shade of garden trees was a source of delight to every
medieval, from the courtiers of romance to Chaucer's reeve:

His wonyng [living] was full fair upon an heath,
With green trees y-shaded was his place.

[243]

The Lord God himself had chosen to make Eden a tree garden and to walk in the cool of its shade. Some of the trees Chaucer describes as growing in the blessed part of the garden, or park, in the *Parliament of Fowls* appear in medieval garden records and were at least occasional garden trees in real life.

'The builders' oak' was a wonderful shade tree. Hermits liked to make their garths around it and shelter beneath it. Some of the more extreme of them, like St Simon Stock, lived inside the trunks of oaks. Planted by some nursery gardeners, enclosed inside gardens by people wanting shade and inside parks by huntsmen wanting a hospitable wood for deer and game, oaks were more consistently and accurately reproduced by medieval sculptors than any other trees.

'The hardy ash' was a light timber, nursery garden tree. Many place names containing the Norse *ask* or the Anglo-Saxon *aesc* commemorate ash coppices or nurseries established in the Middle Ages.

'The piler (pillar) elm' is native to Britain in the form of the wych elm which became plentiful as a forest tree in Britain in the Atlantic period, about 5000 BC, but was more usually accommodated in parks rather than gardens, because it is fruitless.

'The boxtree piper' was brought to England by the Romans and used by the medievals as a carving wood for small items such as pipes, hence Chaucer's name for it. Its Roman use as an evergreen hedge for villa gardens was not important in the medieval gardens of deciduous delight.

Still less important was the 'holm to whippes lash', a native but horticulturally uncomfortable evergreen. Holm was the medieval name for holly, which grew its spiny leaves, symbolic of Christ's crown of thorns, and its red berries, symbolic of the blood the thorns drew, in the wilds. Its white wood was used for carving chess and 'tables' boards.

The yew is also a native British evergreen, but has a stronger, if rather tangential, claim to horticultural status in the Middle Ages. Its practical use was as the wood from which the famous English longbows were carved, but its most important use was as a sacred shelter, whence it became a churchyard and a mourning tree. The Celtic missionaries consecrated yews and used them as arboreal churches or preaching places where people sheltered to listen to the word of God. Churches were built where yew trees grew, sometimes enclosing them within the walls of the church itself, always within the churchyard. The yews at Fountains Abbey are reputed to have sheltered the monks who came to build the abbey in 1132, and must have been much in need of all year round shelter on those wind-swept slopes. Yews are the trees of ecclesiastical and burial garths. Defiant of the seasons, they are dark exceptions to the medieval rule of fruit and pleasant shade for garden trees.

Evergreens had an ambivalent fascination. They defied the in-exorability of the seasons, but this only served to highlight the in-ability of deciduous plants and creatures, including man, to do likewise. This was particularly true of the laurel, the ancient symbol of victory, the sweet bay being common in medieval England. 'The fruit of the laurel tree be called bays,' wrote Bartholomew of Oxford in the late fourteenth century. Bay is the Old English word for berry, and so completely did the berries of the *Laurus nobilis* dominate practical medieval interest in the tree that it became known as the bay tree. It was popular as a symbol of evergreen constancy, and at the same time of man's failure to achieve that. Vows taken 'under the laurer which that may not fade' (Chaucer's *Complaint of Fair Anelida and False Arcite*) somehow always seemed doomed to be broken. The centrepiece of the garden that Chaucer's merchant built for his unfaithful wife was a well 'that stood under a laurer always green', the perfect centrepiece for a travesty of a paradise garden.

The single central tree, reminiscent of the central tree in Eden, with its ambivalent symbolism as the tree of knowledge and the for-bidden tree, the tree of grace and of illicit love, grew in many medieval romance gardens. The number of medieval love affairs con-summated in trees is remarkable.

> And to the tree she goeth a full pace,
> For love made her so hardy in this case,
> And by the well adoun [down] she gan [got] her dress.
> (Chaucer's *Legend of Good Women*)

The central tree usually stood next to a well, which poured forth either sanctifying grace or false worldly pleasure, depending on the Charitable or Cupiditous nature of the shade shed upon it by the tree. If romance gardens were planted in real life, and it seems that some were, their central trees were probably laurels.

If not laurels, pines, which could better bear the weight of a pair of lovers, and had been sacred to Attis, Osiris and Adonis. A British native, it has always done particularly well in the highlands of

Scotland, Ireland and the Celtic west of England, Celtic romances favouring it for their centre spot. The kernels of pine nuts made a good chew for hungry saints, soldiers and settlers in forest areas, and became a common household mouthful. Quite a few medieval recipes include pine nuts, to be used in the same way as all the other nuts, but there is no way of knowing how many, if any, pines were domesticated for their nuts.

Of the trees known to medievals, and possibly grown by them in gardens here and there, lime leaves and blossoms were used as soothing medicines and cosmetics. Maple leaves are carved on several of the thirteenth-century misericords in Exeter Cathedral. There is a perfect sycamore leaf in the stonework of St Frideswide's tomb in Christchurch Cathedral, Oxford, dating from about 1300, and there are others in the fifteenth-century misericords of St Peter and Paul's, Norwich, St Mary the Virgin, Ashford, Huntingdon-shire, and elsewhere. The plane tree, which Chaucer lists as a 'homely tree' is usually said to be the sycamore, wrongly named. But the tradition that the plane was brought to England by returning Hospitaller Knights is botanically possible, if historically unlikely. Plane trees can live to be very old. In 1582 Anthony Watson, the Rector of Cheam, reported from Nonsuch Palace that 'to the north is a wide-spreading circular plane tree, its branches supported on posts, so that many people can sit beneath it.' To have reached such a size the tree must have been at least 150 years old, which dates it back to the reign of Henry IV at the latest.

The beech migrated to the peat fens of Britain at an early date, despite Julius Caesar's statement in 43 BC, which he must have made in ignorance of the Fen beeches, that there were no beeches in Britain. Birch tree wine, fermented from the spring sap, was strong enough to be brewed as ale with only a quarter of the usual amount of malt. Thorn trees were extensively used for fence- and hurdle-making.

Hawthorn blossom made a delicate tea and pottage. The cornel (dogwood) was used for carving arrows and shafts. Junipers were chiefly valued for their seeds and berries, the former burnt as air purifiers and chewed as 'hot' seeds, the latter taken as 'hot' and diuretic stimulants. Juniper wood made a good, slow-burning fire. One of the misericords in the church of St Mary the Virgin, Ashford, has a carving of a juniper tree.

Some of these woodland trees grew in Richard Noke's fourteenth-century close, and probably in other closes and gardens where they happened to be growing when the garth enclosures were made, or were planted by gardeners who simply liked the look of them. Orchards and tree gardens varied from the artistically formal to the chaotically informal. If they were attached to institutions with expert gardening staff, such as castles, palaces, big monasteries and manors, they probably had some sort of formal lay-out, such as rows, which would facilitate the collecting of the fruit at harvest time and make wooded, perhaps blossomy walks, for their owners and visitors.

Throughout the medieval period monastic gardeners were famous for their skill in designing orchards and tree gardens, some of them for pleasure rather than fruit production, many for both. Leo, assistant gardener to Brithnod, the tenth-century Abbot of Ely, laid out 'gardens and orchards elegantly, and planted choice fruit trees there in regular and beautiful order', as well as shrubs and shady trees. Abbot Feckenham of Westminster was planting a row of elms in the abbey orchard when Queen Elizabeth summoned him to his death in prison.

Some monastic orchards, like some castle, palace and manorial orchards, were enclosed from the wilds and only gradually brought into cultivated order. The illustration on p. 256 shows a late fifteenth-century French estate, belonging to the prosperous gentleman standing in the foreground, pointing at his orchard. It is informally planted and scantily enclosed, but productive. To the right of it are two small tree gardens or nurseries, planted informally and spaciously, and enclosed by fencing. The orchard in the second illustration on p. 256 belonged to Anne of Brittany at the end of the fifteenth century. It was probably a fruit orchard, not a pleasance. Situated some distance from the palace, it is being pruned by a gardener, under the calendar page for March, for which month this is shown as a typical occupation. A woman assistant is carrying away offcuts from the pruning, which look as if they have been trimmed for use as firewood or fencing stakes. It is impossible to tell whether the trees are planted according to a pattern; they are stoutly enclosed by a brick wall, which must have had a locked door or gate somewhere in its length. Leafy trees, celebrated in poetry, recalled in the columns of decorated Gothic architecture, and planted and enjoyed in gardens and orchards, like this one, were shades of paradise. Leafless trees, revered with repentant awe in poetry and art and left alone in winter gardens to endure until spring, were emblems of the rood tree.

Winter was the dark season of holding one's own. It was the

indoor season at home, the dead season in orchard and garden, when gardeners awaited the springtime promise of work and its reward. The reward was not always everything the gardener had hoped for, from nature or from man. Nature rewarded at the whim of the Almighty, man at his human whim. This dialogue between an Englishman and a gardener at Bury St Edmunds, taken from a late fourteenth-century French conversation manual, closes the chapter with a summary of the gardener's perennial tasks and the perennial sense of reward and frustration they bring him.

> MAN: How much have you earned?
> GARDENER: . . . I have grafted all the trees in my garden with the fairest grafts that I have seen for a long while, and they are beginning to put forth green; also I have dug another garden and I have carefully planted cabbages, porray, parsley and sage and other goodly herbs. And furthermore I have pulled up and cleared away from it all the nettles, brambles and wicked weeds, and I have sown it full with many good seeds; and in it I have likewise many fair trees bearing divers fruits, such as apples, pears, plums, cherries and nuts, and everywhere have I very well looked after them, yet all I have earned this week is 3d. and my expenses; but last week I earned as much again, and I was very quick about it.
> MAN: Hé, my friend, never mind, for one must earn what one can today.

9

Vineyards

Tradition has it that the Emperor Probus planted the first vine in England shortly before his death in AD 282, at Vine, near Basingstoke in Hampshire. Almost all viticultural historians acquiesce in this tradition. There is little evidence to back it up, but it should be put in its proper context, which is that of a very brief history of vines.

The Beginnings of English Viticulture

The grape-vine (*Vitis vinifera*) is the oldest cultivated species of vine, and is descended from the wild wood vine (*Vitis silvestris*), which is native all round the Mediterranean, as far east as the Caucasus and as far north as southern Germany. It needs a long maturation period to produce good grapes, and its cultivation indicates a settled, stable society, second only to that required for the raising of cereal crops. Viticulture already had a long history by Old Testament times. According to *Genesis* 9:20, Noah planted a vineyard.

Minoan Crete had vines in abundance. The Greeks had wine-producing vines in Homer's day, and introduced them to Italy, where they did so well that Pliny described ninety-one varieties of grape, fifty varieties of wine and several methods of training vines.

French vineyards were already ancient by this time. The Phoenicians took viticulture to France in about 600 BC, with spectacularly successful results. But vineyards were only planted in France as far north as the Cevennes. When Strabo wrote, in the first century AD, it was considered impossible for grapes to ripen further north than that. It was not until the third century that vineyards were planted in north Gaul, Spain and Germany, and probably in Britain. Britain was considered by the Ancients to be too far north for viticulture. But the Romans thought of Britain as a granary, and if they decided to permit viticulture there, it was because the new crop would be of purely cultural significance. The vine was the symbol of Mediterranean civilization, and the Romans took it with them wherever they went, in literature, art and in actual plantation. They probably took it to Britain when they took it to the northern provinces, to which the Emperor Probus gave viticultural licence in AD 280. Most Roman villas were in sheltered places in the lowland, the south in particular. If the Romans did grow vines in Britain, it was in just such a place as Vine that the first vines might have been planted.

Ancient vine-stems have been found near the site of Boxmoor Villa in Hertfordshire, on a sheltered south-westerly slope. Also grape pips at Silchester and Southwark, and pips and grape skins, the debris of wine-pressing, at Gloucester, all on or near Roman villa sites. Whether the vines flourished and produced much wine, we cannot tell. They were grown on terraces, and on the peristyle and garden walls and trellised walks of the villas, in truly Roman style.

Later history of British vines shows that the climate did not prevent their widespread cultivation, though it did restrict their wine-producing potential. Consequently, Britain imported wine from the wine-producing provinces of the empire, and when the Romans departed, the missionaries who came from Gaul in the wake of St Augustine continued to import it from these districts, Gaul in particular, and carried on or revived (for we do not know what happened immediately after the departure of the Romans) the tradition of British viticulture so that they might ultimately be independent of Continental sources for their supplies of mass wine, especially when the Danish pirates began to disrupt the seaborne trade of northern Europe in the seventh century.

Bede (673-735) said that there were vineyards 'in some places' in England when he wrote, but most of Britain's wine was imported, despite Danish piracy. English viticulture led a hesitant existence in the seventh and eighth centuries. One of King Alfred's laws laid down that 'If anyone damages the field or vineyard of another, or his land, he must make compensation to him.' It sounds from this as if vineyards, like the wine trade, were in secular as well as monastic hands, though the monks were the pioneers and experts in viticulture, as they were in every kind of horticulture.

Alfred's great-grandson, Edwy, came to the throne in 955, and granted a vineyard at Pathensburgh, in Somerset, to the monks of

Glastonbury Abbey, which was one of many monasteries built on the slopes of fertile, sheltered valleys, ideal for growing vines. The tenth-century monastic expansion seems to have been accompanied by a viticultural one, headed but not monopolized by the monks. King Edgar (958-75) made one grant of a vineyard at Wycet, together with its vine-dresser, which suggests that it was a big one. An eleventh-century Anglo-Saxon calendar of the months illustrates February with vine-pruning, and the Domesday survey records the existence of thirty-eight vineyards of all sizes in England. A Danish settler called Sweyn had a large vineyard measuring six arpends[1] in Wdelsfort, Essex, which produced twenty casks of wine in good years, so at least some English grapes must have been wine-producing. But many vineyards did not produce wine; indeed some of them did not produce any grapes at all, and are described in Domesday as *non portantes* (not fruit-bearing). Those that were *portantes* produced mostly sour juice and vinegar.

Many of the Domesday vineyards had been recently planted when the survey was made and obviously the influx of Norman abbots into England after the Conquest was a great boost to English viticulture. The biggest vineyard recorded in Domesday was the one at Bisham, in Berkshire, measuring twelve arpendi, but the vineyards were of all sizes, and in lay as well as monastic ownership.

Gloucester, Worcester and Herefordshire made up the main vine-growing region of England, and the monks of the Norman abbeys that lay on the sheltered valley slopes showed some skill in planting and caring for their vines. According to the Malmesbury chronicler, a Greek monk named Constantine entered the monastery there in about 1084, and planted its first vineyard, which was terraced down the south side of a hill just north of the abbey, at Hampton, and was cultivated so well by the monks, with the help of their tenants on the adjacent moors of Doddenham and Hallow, that it was still flourishing when the chronicler wrote his account two hundred years later.

The sites of the old monastic vineyards at Worcester, Gloucester, Tewkesbury, Hereford and Ledbury were all still recognizable only a few decades ago; in the case of Hereford, on the south-west-facing slopes called 'Vinefields'. The vineyard at Ledbury was still producing red and white wine for its owner, George Skipp, in the late seventeenth-century, as it had done for Bishop Skipp before him and

---

1 All vineyards in Domesday are measured in arpendi. 1 arpend = approx 1 acre.

for Richard Swinefield, Bishop of Hereford, in the thirteenth century. Other laymen picked up the viticultural skills of the monks. There were at least four vineyards in the medieval parish of Cotteridge, Worcs. alone, and one of them survived until the seventeenth century.

Gerald of Wales was fond of vineyards, perhaps because there was one in the grounds of his family castle at Manorbier, near Pembroke. This is how he described the twelfth-century Vale of Gloucester:

> This region is more densely covered with vines than any other part of England, and they have more fleshy produce and a more delicious taste, for the wine itself does not cause the mouths of a its drinkers to twist ruefully at its bitterness, and indeed yields nothing to French wines in sweetness.

Even allowing for Gerald's local pride, the fact remains that this region was the vine and wine centre of England.

In 1288 Bishop Swinefield's vineyard at Ledbury produced seven pipes[1] of white wine and nearly one pipe of verjuice, worth £8 in all, to which he added £16 worth of imported red wine, keeping the whole lot in wooden barrels on his manor at Bosbury. It was left on tap for long periods between the bishop's visits there, and must have tasted very sour, but that didn't bother the bishop and his household, who drank anything from two to fourty-four gallons of it every day. The bishop sometimes suffered paroxysms, and found that the only thing that relieved them was a cup of wine. He valued his vineyard so highly that he gave his steward personal instructions on its maintenance and it outlived him by three centuries.

It must have been a combination of the light clay and sandy soil, the south-facing slopes and the warm summers that ripened the grapes of Gloucester, Worcester and Herefordshire into wine. There are no surviving accounts of the wine-making process used on these grapes, so we can't tell whether some kind of sweetener was added, or whether the wine was as naturally sweet as William of Malmesbury claimed. No one else seemed to think that it merited comparison with French wines. When these became available in large quantities during the reign of Henry II, English wine was treated with disdain. Henry bought some cheap English wine in Bedford, at 10s. a barrel, but it was unusual for anyone to buy English when they could afford to buy French. Most of Henry's wine came

1 One pipe = 105 gallons.

from Poitou, Gascony and Auxerre, at prices ranging from 26s. to 34s. a barrel.

But it is not true to say that the English wine-producing industry was ruined by the establishment of this Bordeaux connection. In the first place there never was such an industry: English vineyards were plentiful but English wine was scarce, only being produced in a few regions and in good years by people who could not afford French wine, and people who enjoyed making their own. In the second place, England had always imported a lot of French wine and the Bordeaux connection was only the latest in a series of wine trade links. English wine production was never a big enough business to be radically affected by the state of England's wine trade with the Continent.

Medieval English Wine

The Crown was by far the biggest buyer of wine in England all through the Middle Ages, buying for the court and its guests, and for the army and its garrisons in castles and coastal border areas; Dover castle, for example, always had huge supplies of wine in store. Rich commoners hardly ever kept bulk supplies of wine in their houses, but from the fifteenth century onwards it became common for them to meet at taverns and drink wine. The majority of the population, however, were artisans and labourers, and if they drank wine at all they drank the cheap, homemade kind, to which habitual wine-drinkers only had recourse when the Continental vintage failed.

Vintage wine and new wine were interchangeable terms, for wine was drunk at once, and sold off cheaply if it had to be kept, as it went acid and bitter. Strong wines kept best, and their harsh taste was the most popular, but they turned the sourest when left on tap, and were the cheapest of the 'old wines' sold off each September and October. Old, delicate and light wines were despised. Spices, herbs and honey were added to strong wines to disguise their extreme acidity, and the resulting compounds, known as 'piment' and 'hippocras', were great favourites.

The most common way to help English wine achieve the desired strength and sweetness was to add mulberries, which gave the wine a good colour and a much fuller taste, indeed a positively Malmsey-style one if sugar or honey was added as well. The sale of English wine that had been doctored in this way and was passed off as Malmsey or French wine was a popular ruse of tavenkeepers for which the vintners company inspectors were constantly on the look-out. When Gerald of Wales visited Canterbury Cathedral Priory in the twelfth century, he reported that what he considered to be an overabundance of cider and wine was served in the refectory:

> Piment and claret, must [fresh grape juice] and mead and mulberry and all that can intoxicate; so much so that beer, which is usually thought to be the best when it comes from Britain, and especially from Kent, has no place among these other drinks and is as little thought of as potherbs are as part of meals.

The mulberry wine Gerald mentions may have been a wine in its own right, which seems to have been the case in the monastic refectory Henry of Huntingdon described, where the different drinks were 'wine, mead, beer, piments, mulberry and cider', or it may have been wine with mulberries added, which was usually the case.

The Archbishop of Canterbury had blackberries and black-currants added to the wine made on his manors at Teynham and North Fleet. This is recorded in the vineyard accounts of these two manors. From the late thirteenth century onwards, sweet blackberry wine began to be added to the wine produced by the vines there, to satisfy from local resources the taste for sweet wines that was being catered for increasingly by imported Peninsular and Levant wines towards the end of the Middle Ages.

Elderberries were another excellent additive, and made very good dark wine in their own right. Hops, ivy leaves, hyssop, comfrey, dittany, parsley, leek seeds, rue seeds and nettles were all added to wine, but such additives were often for medicinal purposes. Sage was added to ill-smelling wine, to restore its original bouquet. Sage wine was a favourite of Henry III and his son, Edward I. Spices, sweeteners, rose and violet petals, and berries were the main additives. All kinds of homemade wine, of which the favourites were cowslip and primrose, were spiced, sweetened and coloured; red wine was often coloured with turnsole. Mixtures of spiced wine and ale were popular, and the rich drank posset, a rich, spiced pottage of milk curdled with sweetened wine, as an after-dinner treat. Spices and sugar had to be imported. Henry III had a spiced wine made for him in Gascony, with nutmeg, cubebs (peppery Javanese spice berries) and zedoary (aromatic root of East Indies curcuma plant, resembling ginger). But honey and berries were available in England, and so was one other very popular additive to wine and beer: the gillyflower, which Henry III ordered for his Christmas white wine in York.

The gillyflower was eaten, as Chaucer tells us, as an after-dinner comfit, and it was sugared and made into conserves, taken as a medicinal herb against fevers, and most commonly of all, put into drinks as a flavouring. Henry III, who seems to have been very fond of scented and spiced wines, drank white wine which was *roseata* (flavoured with rose petals), *floreata* (flavoured with petals from many kinds of flowers), and *garliofilata* (flavoured with gillyflower petals).

Decoctions of wine with flowers, herbs and sweeteners were drunk for health as well as pleasure. The quantities of wine used in these drinks were so great that health and pleasure would seem to have been considered largely coincidental, and wine to have been of great medicinal value. Drunkenness was the besetting medieval condition; belief in the medical efficacy of wine made it practically obligatory for the health-conscious.

As Neckham puts it in the *De Vinea* section of his *De Laudibus Divinae Sapientiae* (In Praise of Divine Wisdom):

> Vines are loaded with happy fruits, which are composed of good bunches of grapes. In the grape is carried the juice, and when the grape is made into wine, by the genius of nature and the work of agents, helped by the benefit of the warm air, it is happily changed into a most delicious and delightful liquid, and the heart of man is turned to rejoicing.

All the English medical writers backed Neckham in his praise of wine, which had first been expressed by the Greeks, the first Europeans to make a cult of viticulture and wine.

Hippocrates was the pioneer in applying wine to medical uses, and was followed in this by Galen, and all the classical writers on medicine, whose faith in the efficacy of wine medieval Englishmen found no reason to doubt. Both the classical and the homespun medicine of medieval England believed in the health-giving powers of wine. Hippocras was so called because it was filtered through a cloth called a 'Hippocrates' sleeve or bag', commemorating the doctor's practice of filtering vinous decoctions for medical use.

English vinous medicines were often just restatements of Hippocratic originals. He had distinguished three different strengths of wine, achieved by mixing different amounts of water with it, and the strengths were administered to suit the condition of the patient. For instance, if the blood was 'low', the patient was given a strong mixture; if his weakness was due to heat and sweating, he should take cold wine; otherwise he should take warm wine. English medical writers followed this principle.

They made numerous warm wine mixtures for 'cold' conditions, and cold ones for 'hot' conditions; purgatives 'to cleanse the spleen' and heavy, spiced wines to settle the digestion and 'comfort the liver'. Wine was the favourite relaxant, stimulant and therapy of the middle and upper classes. At the very least, it was a lubricant to social intercourse. As Yvain puts it, in his twelfth-century Arthurian romance, 'There are more words in a pot full of wine than in a whole barrel of beer.'

It was also extensively used in cooking, along with vinegar and ale. The wealthy imported wine; most people got the sour taste they wanted for sweet-and-sour recipes from verjuice and homemade wine, or pressed berries and grapes.

Medieval English Vineyards with Some Modern Comparisons

The chief difference between medieval and modern English vineyards is that the medieval ones aimed at producing wine and verjuice (grape vinegar); the modern ones aim exclusively at wine. They have the advantage of modern equipment and materials, the dubious advantages of modern pesticides and fertilizers, and the supreme advantage of modern hybrid vines which have been specially bred for northern conditions. The most successful of these hybrids, and the most widely grown in England, Switzerland, Alsace, Austria and Germany, is the Müller-Thurgau vine, which is a cross between a Riesling and a Sylvaner, and gives a Muscat-flavoured wine with a good bouquet.

What its medieval equivalent was we don't know. It seems fair to guess that if it was the Romans who brought the first grapes to Britain, they would have brought the varieties they had taken to other northern areas of Europe, such as northern Gaul. There was considerable trade between Britain and both Germany and Gaul in the Anglo-Saxon period, and after the Norman Conquest this trade became part of a strong cultural link which was crucial to the

A wealthy householder supervising the picking of his apple crop. The nearby houses have little enclosed gardens.

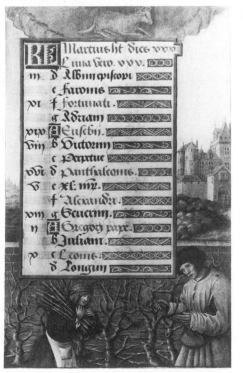

Pruning a walled orchard.

Vines being planted and harvested. They are trained up rows of stakes, or props.

15th-century labourers pruning, and possibly taking cuttings, from individually staked vines.

development of English viticulture. The vines most likely to have been cultivated in England are therefore the northern French ones, and possibly, some Rhenish ones as well. If wine was made from their grapes, it was white.

As a rule, making wine from grapes was an expensive business. Owners of vineyards hardly ever made any cash profits out of them, only the wine, verjuice and grapes harvested from them. Both wine and verjuice was important enough items in the diets of the well-to-do to make viticulture worthwhile, given suitable conditions, and a good number of people went in for it. But account rolls reveal that it took a lot of money to maintain a vineyard. The accounts of the Archbishop of Canterbury's vineyards at Teynham and North Fleet record the finances of small vineyards on chalky soil, the kind of good vine-growing soil that made east Kent the next best region for viticulture after the Vale of Gloucester.

The archbishop's vineyards were run mainly for wine production. There were vineyards at Teynham in the twelfth century, for there is a charter of that date concerning the tithe of Teynham's wine. A thirteenth-century account roll from North Fleet gives the first details of vineyard operations there: 'For peeling and manuring, digging, pruning, binding, tying up and repairing – £7.1s.8d.'

These operations required considerable labour, and were therefore expensive. Other entries account for vineyard props, palisades and hoes, workmen's wages and the repair of vineyard tools, gathering the grapes, tallow and soap for the wine press, a small hogshead 'and other vintage-time expenses'. As usual, expenses exceeded receipts. The wine and verjuice were usually consumed on the manor or sent to the archbisop, but when there was an exceptionally good harvest there was a surplus to sell: in 1273 the expenses came to £1.14s.4d., and the receipts from the sale of 3½ casks of wine and some grass mown in the vineyard came to £3.13s.10d. The work force consisted of a cultivator, an assistant, and casual labourers hired at peak work periods. At Teynham, as at North Fleet, the wine was usually consumed on the spot, but was occasionally sold for an average price of about 13s.4d. a cask, the highest it ever fetched being nearly 23s. a cask in 1278, a price worthy of comparison with the price of French wines, which were entering Britain in great quantities at that time.

Kentish wines must have been good. The vineyards produced much more wine than verjuice, which was unusual, and went on doing so, the wine being improved by the addition of blackberries and sugar, until the later fourteenth century, by which time most English vineyards had long since stopped trying to compete with Continental rivals. East Kent was already famous for its vineyards before Domesday, and in the fourteenth century the archbishopric of Canterbury alone had vineyards at Teynham, North Fleet, Copton, Barton, Chartham, Brookland, Hollingbourne and Wingham, and the bishopric of Rochester had them at North Holme, Halling, Strood and South Woodland. In 1325 Hamo of Hythe, the Bishop of Rochester, thought highly enough of the wine produced by his vineyard at Halling to send some to the King. Halling grapes were Henry III's favourites, and Henry was a connoisseur.

John the Gardener was a Kentishman, and he was also a vineyard keeper. The second section of his treatise on gardening, immediately following the section on 'Wortys', is on 'The Cutting and Setting of Vynys'. It is a short section, which John begins by saying that one should not set or bind vines when the wind is in the east. He then gives brief instructions on the setting, manuring and training of the young plants, and goes on to give instructions on the more important subjects of herbs and onions.

His mention of the east wind is interesting. East Kent is much more exposed, windy and cold than the sheltered slopes of Gloucester, Worcester and Herefordshire or the London garden suburbs of Holborn, Hatton Garden, Piccadilly, Houndsditch and East Smithfield, which all had flourishing vineyards in the Middle Ages. Exposure to cold winds can actually be advantageous to a vineyard if the winds come in April and May, because they retard the opening of the buds until the danger of all but the very latest frosts is past. Once established, vines are very tough, and are suited by the relatively dry winters of eastern England, a fact which is confirmed by the geography of present-day English viticulture, Kent being the foremost viticultural county, followed by East Anglia, which was also full of vineyards in the Middle Ages.

There were Fenland vineyards at Thorney, Ely, Spalding and Ramsey; there were vineyards at Peterborough, where there is still a Vine Street today, Bury St Edmunds, where the light, loose sand and gravel soil is perfect for vines (in 1786 one Black Cluster vine there, 36 years old, covered 44 yards of 10 ft. high wall, and produced over forty clusters of grapes), and at other places in East Anglia. The best of these vineyards were monastic. The one at Peterborough was established by one of its abbots, Martin, and the one at Ramsey by its abbot, Oswald, who had come to Ramsey from Fleury Abbey on the

Loire and was an experienced viticulturist. It was his enthusiasm and expertise that made the Ramsey vineyard a success, and the same qualities, in the person of John the Almoner, made a success of the one at Spalding Priory, where John bought and prepared land and planted orchards, gardens, and vines. The cellarer at Bury St Edmunds kept a terraced vineyard on the sunny south-east side of the town.

East Anglia was blessed with an abundance of vine-growing Norman churchmen; even more so than Kent, which had its share of them, at Canterbury in particular. Abbots and their communities were always willing wine consumers. The monastic liking for wine, which had scandalized Gerald of Wales, give rise to viticultural, winemaking and winemixing experiments on the part of monastic cellarers all through the Middle Ages. There were 'house' vineyards attached to monasteries; patent house wines, house herbal wines and spiced wines for the infirmary, and vinous decoctions for feast days. The combination of this monastic familiarity and expertise with the suitability of the climate made the east of England an area of viticultural distinction, which has again proved itself in the modern post-war revival of English viticulture.

One of the modern East Anglian vineyards is right in the heart of the Fens, on the slopes of the Isle of Ely, where there was a big vineyard in the Middle Ages. Its owner, Norman Sneesby, has written an account of its foundation in 1971, and the first two years of its life, which gives us a unique opportunity to examine the conditions under which Fenland viticulture is practised today, and to look for continuity and contrast with viticulture there in the Middle Ages. The vineyard is the 'Isle of Ely' vineyard, and it is at Wilburton, in the middle of a south slope of the Isle.

It is a small vineyard, no bigger than a small medieval one, measuring about 2.7 acres, of which a quarter of an acre is a plum orchard. This combines with a couple of houses and gardens and a sandy hill to shelter the east side of the plot from the cold east winds of spring. As we heard from John the Gardener, the medievals were also on their guard against such winds, which can be beneficial if they come early in the year, but blast the fruit blossom and keep the bees at home if they come in late April or May. The Fen 'blows', which are fierce April gales that lift all the fine black topsoil off the Fens, making work impossible and leaving devastation in their wake, are mercifully rare nowadays. In the Middle Ages the black Fen soil was much deeper, and the 'blows' more destructive; vineyards were protected from them by hedges, trees and walls. The tenants on the manors of Ramsey Abbey had to make protective hedges for its vineyard, and keep them in good repair under the supervision of the master of the vineyard, as part of their annual service rent. Many vineyard-keepers bought loads of hedge thorns each year, and paid helpers to put them into position round the edge of the vineyard.

The west side of the Isle of Ely vineyard is sheltered by an ash wood, of which there were many in the medieval Fens, along with alder woods and poplar plantations. Their drawback is that they are the home of birds, which are the vineyard's chief enemy. Modern vineyard keepers net their vines. There are no mentions of netting in medieval vineyard accounts, but some estate accounts record the hire of boys 'to scare away the crows' or 'the birds at seed time', and vineyard-keepers may have tried similar tactics.

North of the Isle of Ely vineyard is a hedge of thorn, bramble and elder, studded with tall elm and oak trees, such as surrounded many medieval gardens, orchards and vineyards. Additional shelter is provided by an orchard; in exactly the same way the monks' vineyard in medieval Ely was sheltered by an orchard to the north.

Only the south side of the modern vineyard is open, and Mr Sneesby has planted a small patch of loganberries there, aligned so that the cold, frosty air that flows down the slope (a gentle one, with a gradient of about 1 in 15 so the cold air currents are weak) can escape to the level Fen-edge clays below. Even the flat, watery Fens have their 'isles' of raised land, from which the ground slopes down to the Fen level, and some of the best medieval vineyards, like the ones at Ely and Bury St Edmunds, were terraced down these slopes. Modern, like medieval, Fen vineyards, are sited above the dark soils of the Fen level, which are liable to flood in winter, and often did so to some depth in the medieval period. The Isle of Ely vineyard is on sandy clay loam, well suited to fruit growing, though a little sticky for vines. The medieval vineyard at Ely was on this same greensand, of which the Isle is composed, and other Fen vineyards were on similar outcrops. The Kentish ones were often on chalky downlands, which are similar to the marls of the Champagne area of France.

A nice little link with the medieval period was discovered by Mr Sneesby when he was planning the drainage for his vineyard, in the shape of a chain of medieval fish-stews, indented down from the middle of the ash grove, opposite the south-west corner of the vineyard, one of them only twelve yards away from it at its nearest point. They were deep and substantial enough to be ideal for disposing of water accumulated in the upper reaches of land, and were immediately put to use in this way, so becoming a modern medieval drain.

The moisture-retaining soil of the Isle of Ely turned out to be an advantage, as it must have been to the medievals, because East Anglia is one of the lowest rainfall areas in the country (21 ins. a year, on average) and, despite the waterlogged image of the Fens, it needs all the moisture it can get. The risk of disease to vines is much lower in dry areas, and the stems and foliage do not overgrow the strength of the plant. October and November are very dry months in East Anglia, which gives the grapes a chance to ripen and the wood to begin its winter ripening without rotting.

The ripening of the grapes to full vinous maturity is the chief problem in English viticulture, and the unreliability of good summer and autumn sun to achieve it is the chief reason England has never really been a wine-producing country. Medieval records suggest that it suffered from the same climatic unreliability, possibly to an even greater extent. The only thing the vineyard-keeper can do is plant his vines north to south, facing south, which is what Mr Sneesby and his predecessors right back to Roman times have done, and train them so that they will absorb the maximum possible heat from the sun. The warm south-west bank at Denney Abbey, in the Fens, still has its medieval name, Vineyard, and the medieval vineyard at Ditchingham, in south-east Norfolk, was perfectly sited on the sheltered, south-facing slopes of the Bath Hills.

Mr Sneesby's vines are trellised straight down the slope of the Isle, in north to south rows six feet apart, the vines planted every three feet along the wire and stake rows in the Guyot system, said to have been devised by Dr Jules Guyot in the nineteeth century. But something like it was used in most of England's medieval vineyards (see illustration p. 257). One thirteenth-century Kentish vineyard account refers to 'propping up the vines with trellises'. The London Grocers Company had a new garden made in 1431 'with all the new vines and their new rails'. In fact most vines were not trained along trellis or railings, but up individual stakes, the most popular kinds of stake being willow and ash. This system of individual staking is often used nowadays, especially where the ground is steep and uneven. In 1273, 26013 'props' were bought for the Canterbury vineyard at North Fleet, and men were hired to tie the vines to them. On the Earl of Cornwall's manor of Wallingford, in 1296, two men were paid 18d. for some odd jobs in the vineyard, which included 'collecting poles to support the short vines'. Sometimes, especially if the vines were being cultivated in a private garden, there was no need to make supports; they could be trained up trees. This system has gone rather out of favour nowadays because it is hard to protect tree-trained vines from birds.

William of Malmesbury's description of Thorney in the twelfth century gives us an interesting insight into the versatility of medieval viticulturists, who were familiar with almost all the modern systems of tying and training vines: 'Here the cultivation of vines is practised . . . the vines either lie on the ground or reach up to the sky, borne on stakes. Training vines in this low manner protects the vines from exposure. It is one of the systems Mr Sneesby considered for his Isle vineyard, but rejected because low vines are extra vulnerable to cold winds.

There were probably far more vines trained up walls in the Middle Ages than there are nowadays, with viticulture tending to be commercial and vines grown in plantations rather than singly. Most of the wall vines cultivated since the Middle Ages have been in urban areas, for the simple reason that towns have a lot of walls, and the top vine town in England has always been London.

Neckham said that vines should be trained up house fronts, and the Oxford and Cambridge colleges, livery companies, monastic obedientaries, nobles, merchants and householders who could afford to build in stone often trained vines up their houses. But London had a far greater profusion of walled vines than anywhere else. Some of the south-west facing Victorian houses in Farringdon Street, Holborn, have vines growing on their walls today, where vines have been growing since the Middle Ages. Most of the London livery companies, many magnates with London houses, and many other prosperous Londoners kept vines. In Edward III's reign there were famous vines in the gardens at Hatton Garden, St Giles-in-the-Field, Piccadilly and Vine Street, Holborn, to name but a few. There were vineyards at Houndsditch and East Smithfield. In 1151 Robert of Sigillo, the Bishop of London, poisoned himself and some of his friends by eating too many grapes. He died about September 23, just at the start of the grape harvest.

The grapes of all kinds of vines were thinned before they were fully ripe, to increase the size of the ones that were left. The unripe ones were pressed and fermented to make verjuice. The ripe ones were picked and either eaten or made into wine. Occasionally medieval records mention 'little vine ladders' used in picking the grapes, but it was rare for vines to be so tall as to warrant ladder picking. Usually they were picked by the method described in the records of Abingdon Abbey and known today as the 'Italian stand-up method', which actually includes a good deal of kneeling and bending. Any fruit press can be used for pressing grapes. In the Middle Ages presses were always made of wood, and frequently doubled as cider presses. Barrels (28 gallons), hogsheads (52 gallons), pipes (105 gallons) and tuns (210 gallons) were made, cleaned and rehooped, ready to hold the wine. Big households usually drank their wine straight from these casks, without bothering to decant it, and large storerooms were required to accommodate them.

Late autumn is the busy season in vineyards, since it is not only harvest time, but also the time when the annual pruning is begun. Pruning is absolutely vital to successful viticulture and because it has to be absolutely thorough, with 90% to 95% of the growth removed to ensure a good harvest, it involves a lot of time and effort. It was one of the vineyard jobs for which extra labour was hired each year, and medieval pictures and carvings of viticulture are always either of grape picking or pruning (see second illustration p. 257).

If there is no second summer pruning, that season is taken up with hoeing and weeding, since thick weeds choke the main stems and damage the vines, though a light growth between rows can be beneficial because it protects the soil from heavy rain and erosion, and acts as a sward. Quite a few medieval vineyard keepers sold grass from their vineyards each year, which suggests that they had healthy swards.

Cuttings taken at pruning time are sheltered and kept warm during the winter and planted in March. In the Middle Ages, when it was virtually impossible to keep them warm through the winter, cuttings were usually taken in early spring. According to John the Gardener, they should be taken when the wind was in the west, and he goes on to give a perfect little outline of the medieval 'cutting and setting of vynys', which is the same as the one given by eighteenth-century, Victorian and Modern experts, and is the standard cutting propagation method:

> To be set it shall have knots three;
> Two shall be set in the ground
> And one above the ground
> In the land where it shall grow in;

It would ask to be dressed with dyng [dung].
Every year without dread
They would ask dyung about them spread.

This is the method used by John and his contemporaries, for medieval accounts include entries 'for dunging the ground for new plants', and often for sales of the cuttings.

Another method of propagation was layering. In early spring long shoots were fastened into well broken up ground, often in pots, and covered over. By autumn the new plant had enough shoots to be taken off the mother plant. Medieval vineyard accounts usually include digging and breaking up of the ground, ready for the cuttings and layers, among the jobs for which hired help was needed. The list of jobs done at North Fleet in Kent in the early thirteenth century included 'layering, digging, hoeing and propping up with trellises'. The last three could be done by any labourers under good supervision; the first, like taking cuttings, was a job for the expert. But the most expert of all viticultural and horticultural operations, the great medieval horticultural skill and pride, was grafting.

It is hardly ever an item in medieval accounts because only the vineyard-keeper, and possibly his assistant, could do it. A successful graft can transform a poor vine into a vigorous one without the expense and time involved in growing a new vine or cutting from scratch, in new root compost. The best wine grafts are those of weak on to strong wood, which lends an almost alchemical satisfaction to the achievement, and goes some way towards explaining the medieval delight in it.

There are two methods of grafting vines: the cleft method and the approach method, the first being the more difficult. In this method, scions are taken from the most productive branches during pruning, and kept in pots or under shelter until mid March, about three weeks before the vines begin to bud. However, medieval viticulturists could seldom afford the luxury of strengthening their cuttings during the winter, and often cut and grafted them straight away in spring. The scion is carefully fastened to the stock with strands of matting or hemp, and covered with moist clay. The scion often remains dormant as long as two or three months, during which time any shoots that appear on the stock must be stripped off so that all its growing power is devoted to the scion. When this has shoots five or six inches long the clay and bandage are removed.

The second method is the approach method, also known as ablactation or inarching. It is safer than the cleft method because the union is between the branches or two growing vines, and the scion is only cut off from its parent vine when that union has been accomplished after two or three months. Neither method is in general use in English viticulture today, where the chief advantage of grafting is that it immunizes plants against phylloxera, the lethal insect pest, and that exists only in mainland Europe, not Britain. So cuttings are preferred for making new vines, and grafts are not considered worth the time, care and hazards involved. Those very considerations, however, made grafting a challenge which ancient and medieval gardeners could not resist, and which presented the successful grafter with positive proof of the mysterious power of nature, his working partner.

Grafting was a horticultural operation of the utmost value. It was one of the skills attributed to the Saxon Abbot Brithnod of Ely, which earned him a reputation as a great gardener: 'In a few years the trees which he planted and ingrafted appeared at a distance like a wood,' wrote the Ely chronicler. Two centuries later, Neckham praised grafting with similar enthusiasm and that most down-to-earth of poems, the fifteenth-century *How the Ploughman Learnt his Pater Noster*, did likewise:

> He could both sow and hold a plough,
> Both dyke, hedge, and milk a cow . . .
> Of fruit he grafted many a tree,
> Fell wood, and make it as it should be.

John the Gardener was so keen on grafting that he dealt with it before anything else in his treatise. He explained the process so accurately, and in such detail, that there can be no doubt that he wrote either from first-hand experience or first-hand observation.

> Clean atwain the stock of the tree
> Wherein that they graft shall be.
> Make thy cutting of the graft
> Between the new and the old staff
> So that it be made to life [lie]
> As the back and the edge of a knife.
> A wedge thou set in midst the tree
> That every side from other flee
> Till it be opened wide
> Wherein the graft shall be laid.
> Clay must be laid to keep the rain out.
> For the showers of the rain
> Upon the clay thou shalt moss lay.

With a width of hazel tree rind
The stock fast thou bind.

Binding sometimes appears in medieval accounts as the only part of the grafting operation that could be entrusted to a skilled assistant.

Another operation that also makes an occasional appearance is peeling, or girdling. This is only done when the fruit is short of nourishment: a ring of bark is removed from the trunk or from the cane below the grapes, preventing the downward flow of carbohydrates from them, and so nourishing them more fully. The archepiscopal vines at Canterbury were peeled quite often, and seem to have thrived on it. Even so, by the end of the fourteenth century the manorial stewards, like many English viticulturists, had decided for economic reasons to concentrate on the production of verjuice.

The Abingdon Abbey vineyards in the late fourteenth and early fifteenth centuries typify the decline. They were cultivated neither extensively nor profitably. There was no vineyard-keeper, his job being done by the gardener and some assistants, yet the list of tools in the storeroom of John of Eynsham, the gardener there in 1388, included the following for the vineyard, besides all the general garden tools: a lattice; a lock; two casks; some barrels and pots; two small mesh sieves; two iron-toothed rakes; one eight-gallon liquid measure; one scales; one eight-gallon wine jar; two shears; a one-and-a-half gallon tankard; two autumn pruning hooks; one wine cask; one hook; one pipe; one mixing vessel for wine; one vat for wine and cider making; two wine pots; one length of railing; two rakes for collecting must.

As Abingdon was a fairly typical institutional vineyard, a little further study of its accounts will show how small the wine production of such vineyards usually was, and how much more important was the production of verjuice.

Only four of the Abingdon gardener's accounts survive, but they are so spaced (1369, 1388, 1412 and 1450) as to show the decline from little to no market wine production over a period of just under a century. We cannot tell how much wine and verjuice was drunk by the community since this does not appear in the accounts, but the vineyard wine was nothing like enough for them; they bought a lot of wine throughout the period.

In 1369 the gardens were mostly grass and woodland, and the only suggestion of cultivation is an expense of 2s., paid to some fruit pickers. In 1388 it was a different story; the gardener made 13s.4d.

from the sale of wine, 20s. from the sale of grapes, 2s. from the sale of verjuice and 4d. from the sale of vines. He paid 2s.9½d. to have the cases, jars and barrels purchased and repaired, and for help with grape picking, 2s. for vintaging and 4s.6d. for the propping up of vines. He also made 13s.4d. from the sale of cider and 32s.6d. from the sale of apples, wardens and nuts. He paid 3s. for cidermaking, 3s.4d. for some new cider casks and 3s.11½d. for fruit and nut collecting.

By 1415 the peak of production was well past. The gardener made no profit out of his grapes because they were sent to the infirmary to be used as verjuice there. There was no cider sold, and only 2s.4d. made from the sale of apples and pears, and 2s.1d. from the sale of nuts. In 1450 the gardener's income was almost entirely made up of rents for pieces of land leased out to tenants, though he made 10s. from the sale of fruit. His only cultivation expenses were 6d. for fruit picking, 12d. for a fruit-picking ladder, and 19d. for planting grafts, but whether vine grafts the account does not say. He spent 2s.8d. on fruit for the community, having sold the fruit from his own garden. With such a poor vineyard it is not surprising that the community had to buy its own wine. But it never bought any verjuice, and this was obviously the vineyard's main production, as it was in most vineyards.

One exception to the verjuice concentration of England's medieval viticulturists is the wine production at Windsor. Edward III spent the vast sum of £157.13s.1d. on making a new vineyard there in 1361, and hired John Roche, a French master vintner, to manage it. Roche brought vines with him from La Rochelle; he was paid the very high wage of 7s. a week; he had four expert assistants working for him, along with five skilled workmen, all of them highly paid, and over two hundred labourers. The wage bill for 1358 alone came to £139.19s.2½d. Not surprisingly, the Windsor vineyard was exceptionally productive, its wine considered good enough to be given to the Queen as a present in 1377. In 1365 it produced three pipes of red, two pipes one gallon of white wine, and the old vineyard there produced six pipes of unspecified colour. But Windsor was a royal exception.

Vineyard Products Other than Wine

Most vineyards produced only grapes and verjuice, usually enough of the latter for a surplus to be sold, despite the vast proportions in which it was used by medieval cooks. Even when there was a hot summer, with its promise of good wine grapes, some of them were picked when they were still small and green, and pressed into verjuice: no self-respecting gardener would leave the household kitchens without any. It was the one thing the unsuccessful little vineyard at Queen's College, Oxford, always managed to produce, and when the vines finally went out of cultivation in the late fifteenth century, the gardener bought crab apples and used those to make verjuice. Sorrel juice, sloe juice and the juice of almost any unripe fruit could also be used as verjuice substitute as long as its taste was bitter.

Verjuice mixed with lye (vegetable-water detergent) restored the colour to faded cloth, according to the Menagier, who also said that old, weak verjuice should be mixed with new, raw verjuice for optimum results. It was usually heavily salted, and was the standard sour ingredient of the sweet and sour dishes of which the medieval palate never tired. One of the very few simple recipes from the medieval period is for a basic version of sweet and sour sauce: vinegar or verjuice mixed with heavily sweetened rosewater in equal proportions, and poured over roast capon. Pottages, too, frequently contained verjuice, and green sauce, made up of a whole litany of herbs and particularly favoured as an accompaniment to fish, depended on verjuice for its colour and sharp, fish-brightening taste.

Green pickle to preserve fish was another herb and vinegar concoction to which spices, including whole gillyflowers, roots and all, were added. So much verjuice and spice was used in medieval cookery that it is hard to distinguish ordinary dishes from pickles; we would classify most medieval savoury dishes as either sweet and sour or pickled and most of their sauces as chutneys. Perhaps the best way of distinguishing would be to say that pickles were essentially preservative, which ordinary dishes were not. Pickling was the only medieval alternative to salting as a way of preserving food, and was one of the housewife's major autumn occupations. A pickling vat was high on Neckham's list of indispensable kitchen utensils.

Because it was a preservative, verjuice was preferred to wine in pickle cookery, and was even added to some jams and marmalade, to make sure they kept well, had a bright colour and tasted really piquant. Except for the verjuice monopoly of pickling, wine and verjuice were used in the same way in cooking, and are often given as alternative ingredients in recipes.

Sweet, spiced wines were used in sweet recipes, such as this fourteenth-century one for quince marmalade: 'Peel and quarter the quinces, taking out the pips, and the eye at the end. Boil them in a good red wine and run them through a strainer. Boil a large amount of honey a long time. Skim it and set the quinces in it. Stir well and bring to the boil until the honey is reduced by half. Add hippocras. Stir until cold, and cut into pieces to serve.' Strong stuff, medieval marmalade.

All kinds of thick pottages contained wine and vinegar, and so did many herbal and digestive drinks. It was probably added to wine drinks to make them go further, so that they were what Chaucer calls 'tempered with vinegar' – probably with a heavy hand. In medieval medicine verjuice and wine were also used interchangeably. Hippocrates and the other classical physicians had the same faith in vinegar as they had in wine, and both were used without restraint. Monastic infirmarers were always allotted some of the monastery's verjuice supply, sometimes all of it, as was the case at Abingdon. It was often put into ointments. The author of the earliest English medical treatise recommended the 'anointing' of sore nostrils with oil, vinegar and camomile, and also the application of this mixture, spread on a cloth, to an aching head. Verjuice was mixed with honey and drunk 'to soothe aching joints', an interesting medieval version of the modern cider vinegar cure for rheumatism, which is enjoying some popularity at the moment.

In true medieval style, infusions of verjuice and wine were applied to wounds and festers. John of Arderne, the eminent medieval surgeon, demonstrated the medieval fondness for prescribing the very last remedy one would choose when he prescribed this decoction for those about to go on a drinking bout: white cabbage juice, pomegranate juice and plenty of vinegar, boiled up together and drunk hot.

The thing that practically never features in medical, culinary, household or financial books is the grape. Like the apple, it was primarily for drinking, but it was not as widely grown as the apple, and never became an eating fruit as well, which the apple did. Grapes were only eaten as a fruit in their dried form, as raisins, and they were imported, not dried at home. English grapes were too small, too short of sun and too urgently needed for verjuice, must and wine, to be dried.

Must was a poor second to verjuice, since it was unfermented and therefore comparatively feeble, both in taste and in purgative effect.

Medievals drank it condescendingly or used it as a substitute for verjuice.

If the grape, pure and simple, was the humblest of the vine's esculent possibilities, there was one that could not be consumed and was therefore humbler still: vine charcoal. This was made by packing bundles of young vine roots into covered, sealed casseroles, so that the air could not get at them and reduce them to ashes, and baking them to carbon in a slow oven. The burnt sticks were used for drawing, and were sometimes ground to a powder and mixed with water for use as paints, though they only yielded a charcoal grey colour, which was nothing like as useful as black. All in all, the vine was very useful.

Medieval English Viticultural Regions and Grape Varieties

Only those who could afford meat and fish cookery, and therefore needed a lot of verjuice, and those who liked to sample their own wine or adorn their garden walls and trellises with vines, undertook its cultivation. The latter class of people grew more prominent as commercial viticulture declined in the later Middle Ages. By the end of the fifteenth century there were few big vineyards in England, but an increasing number of single vines growing up the walls of city houses and churches, and in private gardens and arbours. The *nouveaux riches* proclaimed their arrival in affluent urban society by cultivating vines, in vineyards and gardens.

The word *vinea* means vineyard, but it could also mean part of a vineyard. From 1240 to 1249 Margaret of the Vineyard had a little vinea of her own at Kingsbury Manor, near St Albans, and it was a half-acre section of the manorial vineyard where she worked. A vinea could even be a garden or part of a garden where vines were grown. Sometimes this was a little walled or railed-off section of a garden, entered through a locked gate or door; sometimes, especially in small gardens, it was a sunny corner where the vine was trained up the wall or railings. A really scratch vinea might be no more than a wall: Reginald of Durham, the twelfth-century hagiologist, saw a little church at Lixtune, in Cheshire, with vines growing up the front of it. They were almost certainly fruitless, being so far north, but Reginald declared them quite charming and the perfect adornment for a church.

Christian tradition endorsed his opinion. The vine was a central symbol of classical culture and of the Christian Church, and it remains to this day one of the best known Christian metaphors of the Church. Vineleaf was a very common decorative motif in churches and monasteries; it was carved into wood and stonework, embroidered into vestments and hangings, and illustrated in the borders of countless religious manuscripts. It was ancient, familiar, richly symbolic and attractive. It was this symbolic richness of the vine that made it such a popular decorative motif in England, and indeed in most western European and Mediterranean countries. Vineleaf and vinescroll decoration abounded in medieval England, but little of it was based artistically on English viticulture.

Minor Vines and False Vines

Although we do not know how many varieties of grape vine there were in medieval England, we do know that there were then, as now, plenty of other varieties of vine, but the grape vine is so much the most popular and renowned variety of vine that it is known simply as 'the vine'. It is because the grape vine once had a place in English gardens, and deserves to have one again, that it had a chapter in this book. The number of acres under vines, and the amount of wine being made in England is increasing, but this is a vineyard, not a garden expansion, and the modern vineyard is a far cry from the vine-garth or garden, still farther from the little corner of a garden that it sometimes was in the Middle Ages. The solitary garden vine is probably less popular now than it was before the viticultural revival.

It has been replaced by an impostor known as the Russian vine, a central Asian plant, *Polygonum baldschuanicum*, quite unrelated to the grape vine and bearing no edible fruit. It is a recent arrival in England, and has earned its name because of a fancied resemblance between its leaves and those of the vine. In fact the only resemblance between the two plants is that they are both climbers. The Russian vine is quick growing, quick dying, indelicate and domineering, devoid of all classical, Biblical and medieval associations. If English gardeners were prepared to abandon it in favour of the historic grape-vine, they would encounter difficulties, no doubt, but according to Solomon, these would contribute to their greatness. Solomon was the most quoted and best loved of all the Old Testament figures in the Middle Ages. Who are we to doubt him when he says:

> I did great things: built myself palaces, planted vineyards; made myself gardens and orchards, planting every kind of fruit tree in them . . . So I grew great, greater than anyone in Jerusalem before me, nor did my wisdom leave me.

(Ecclesiastes 2:4-10)

Bibliography

The main sources for this book are medieval manuscripts, a few of which have been printed and published in antiquarian periodicals. These, printed and manuscript, are listed in the 'primary sources' section of the bibliography.

As there are virtually no books about medieval gardens, most of the books in the 'secondary sources' section are general studies of gardening or English history which contain the odd relevant chapter or reference, and studies of related subjects such as architecture or botany. Only the major sources are listed.

Even so, many of them are obscure, and only within reach of those who have access to a first-rate reference library. I apologize for this fact, which is as regrettable as the scholarly neglect of medieval gardens which has caused it.

PRIMARY SOURCES

Abingdon Abbey, Obedientary Accounts, ed. R.E.G. Kirk, Camden Soc., 1892.

Aldgate, Holy Trinity Cartulary, ed. G.A.J. Hodgett, London Record Soc. Pubs., vii, (1971).

Ambresbury, Rentalia et Custumaria Michaelis, ed. E. Hobhouse and T.S. Holmes, Somerset Record Society, v, (1891).

ANGLICUS, BARTOLOMEUS, *"De Proprietatibus Rerum"*, ed. R. Steele in *Medieval Lore*, London and Boston 1907.

ARDERNE, JOHN OF, *De Arte Phiscali et de Cirugia*, trans. Sir D'Arcy Power, London 1922.

Barnwell, Observances in Use at the Augustinian Priory of St Giles and St Andrew, ed. J.W. Clark, Cambridge 1897.

BATESON, M., Borough Customs, 2 vols. Selden Society xviii, xxi, (1904, 1906).

Battle Abbey, Cellarer's Accounts 1275-1513, ed. E. Searle and B. Ross, Sydney 1963.

Beaulieu Abbey Accounts, ed. S.F. Hockey, Camden 4th Series, xvi, London 1975.

ST BENEDICT, *The Rule*, ed. Abbot Justin McCann, London 1952.

Bray, Estate Book of Henry, ed. D. Willis, Camden 3rd Series, xxvii, London 1916.

BROWN, C.F. ed. *English Lyrics of the 13th Century*, Oxford, 1924; *Religious Lyrics of the 14th Century*, Oxford, 1924; *Religious Lyrics of the 15th Century*, Oxford, 1939.
Bury St Edmunds, Feudal Documents, ed. D.C. Douglas, British Academy Records of Social and Economic History, viii, (1932).

CAMBRENSIS, GIRALDUS, *Opera*, ed. J.S. Dimock, Rolls Series, 1867, 8.
Carlisle, Chronicle of the Wars, 1173-4, Surtees Society, 1840, p. 77.
CHAUCER, GEOFFREY, *Complete Works*, ed. W.W. Skeat, Oxford, 1894-7.
CHOLMELEY, H.P., *John of Gaddesden and the Rosa Medicinae*, Oxford 1912.
Clerkenwell, Cartulary of St Mary, ed. W.O. Hassall, Camden 3rd Series, lxxi, London 1949.
Close Rolls, Calendar of, 1227-1485, pubd. H.M. Stationery Office.
Cornwall, Accounts of the Earldom, 1296-7, ed. M. Midgley. 2 vols. Camden 3rd Series, lxvi, lxviii, London 1942, 45.
COX, J.C., *Churchwardens' Accounts, 14th to 17th centuries*, London 1913.
Cupar, Abbey Rental Book, ed. C. Rogers, London 1879.

Domesday Book, ed. A. Farley, London 1783 (Vols 1 and 2); ed. H. Ellis, Record Commissioners, London 1816 (Vols 3 and 4).
DUGDALE, W., *Monasticon Anglicanum*, 6 vols, London 1817-30.
Dunelmensia, Gesta, ed. R.K. Richardson, Camden 3rd Series, xiii, London 1924.
Durham, Abbey Account Roll Extracts, ed. J.T. Fowler, Surtees Soc. xcic, c, ciii, (1898, 1899, 1901).

Ely, Dean and Chapter Muniments, Monastic Obedientary Accounts, Manuscripts Room, Cambridge University Library; *Episcopal Records, Manorial Accounts*, *ibid*.
Evesham, Chronicon Abbatiae ad annum 1418, ed. D. Macray, Rolls Series, 1863.
Exchequer Documents: Kings', Queens' Remembrancer Ancient Documents; Issue Rolls; Pipe Rolls, Wardrobe and Household Accounts; pubd. H.M. Stationery Office.

Fitzstephen, Chronicle, ed. J.C. Robertson, Rolls Series, 1875-83.
Forme of Cury, ed. S. Pegge, London 1780.

Gildhallae Londoniensis Munimenta, ed. H.T. Riley, Rolls Series, 1859-62.

Glastonbury Abbey Feodary, ed. F.W. Weaver, Somerset Record Society, xxvi, (1910).
Glastoniensibus, Historia de Rebus Gestis, ed. T. Hearne, Oxford 1727.
Gloucestriae, Historia et Cartularium Monasterii Sancti Petri, Rolls Series, 1863-7.
Godstow Nunnery Register, ed. A. Clark, Early English Text Society, Original Series, cxxix, cxxx, cxlii, (1905-11).
Goodman of Paris, The ed. E. Power, London 1928.
GREENE, R.L., *Early English Carols*, Oxford 1935.

HALIWELL, G.O., *Early English Miscellanies, collected for the Warton Club*, London 1855.
HENLEY, WALTER, *Treatise on Husbandry*, ed. D. Oschinsky, Oxford 1955.
Herbals: 12th century, Bodleian Ms. 130
Brit. Lib. Ms. Harleian 5294
13th century, B.L. Ms. Harl. 978
14th century, B.L. Sloane 5
B.L. Add. Ms. 22636 (xiii) (illustrated in colour)
Bod. Douce 37 (herbal medicine and distempers)
15th century, B.L. Ms. Sloane 147
B.L. Ms. Sloane 1201 (with recipes)
B.L. Add. Ms. 37786 (i).
B.L. Harl. 2407 (in English, on alchemy and herbs)
Bod. Ms. Rawl. C211, (in English, on botany)
Ms. Ash. 1481, (herbal A-Z, in English), Oxford
Trin. Ms. 905 (II.4) (in English), Cambridge.

JACKSON, K, *A Celtic Miscellany*, London 1951.
John the Gardener's treatise, Archaeologia, liv, (1894).

Kinloss Abbey Records, ed. J. Stuart, Edinburgh 1872.

LANGLAND, WILLIAM, *Piers Plowman*, ed. W.W. Skeat, Oxford 1924.
Leechdoms of the Anglo-Saxons, ed. T.O. Cockayne, Rolls Series, 1864-6.
Leicester Borough Records, ed. M. Bateson, 3 vols. Cambridge 1899-

1905; *Household Accounts & Counters*, Roxburgh Club, 1841.
Liberate Rolls, Calendar of, 1226-67, pubd. H.M. Stationery Office.
London Memorials of 13th, 14th and 15th Centuries, ed. H.T. Riley, London 1868.
LYDGATE JOHN, *Poems*, ed. J. Norton-Smith, Oxford 1966.

Magdalen College, Oxford, Notes from Muniments, ed. W.D. Macray, Oxford 1882.
Malmesburiensis Willelmi, de Gestis Rerum, ed. W. Stubbs, Rolls Series, 1887, 1889.
Medical Ms. of 14th century, from Royal Stockholm Library, pubd. *Archaeologia*, xxx (1800).
Ministers' Accounts, pubd. H.M. Stationery Office.
Ministers' Accounts for Duchy of Lancaster, pubd. H.M. Stationery Office.
MIRFIELD, JOHN OF, *Life and works*, ed. Sir P. H-S. Hartley and H.R. Aldridge, Cambridge 1936.

NECKHAM, ALEXANDER, '*De Natura Rerum*', with the poem '*De Laudibus Divinae Sapientiae*', ed. T. Wright, Rolls Series, 1863.
Norwich Cathedral Priory Gardeners' Account Rolls, Norwich Central Library.

Onions, Garlic and Pennyroyal, B.L. Ms. Roy. 17B XLVIII (ii).
Ospinge Manor and Hospital Accounts, St John's College muniments, Cambridge.
Oxford University Medieval Archives, ed. H.O. Salter, 2 vols, Oxford History Society, lxx, lxxiii, (1917 and 1919).

PARIS, MATTHEW, *Chronicon Majora*, ed. H.R. Luard, Rolls Series, 1874, 1876, 1880. 1976.
Patent Rolls, Calendar of, 1216-1485, pubd. H.M. Stationery Office.
Porkington Treatise, ed. G.O. Halliwell, London 1845.

Queens' College, Oxford, Gardeners' Accounts, 1341-1469, Queen's Library.

Rameseia Monasterii Cartularium, ed. W.H. Hart and P.A. Lyons, Rolls Series, 1884-93.
RICHARDS, T, *Early English Poetry, Ballads and Popular Literature*, London 1841.
ROBBINS, R.H., *Historical Poems of the 14th and 15th centuries*, New York 1959; *Secular Lyrics of the 14th and 15th centuries*, Oxford 1955.

Sandford Cartulary, ed. A.M. Leys, 2 vols. Oxford Record Society, xix, xxii. (1938, 1941).

Bibliography

Shrewsbury, Bishop Ralph's Household Book, 1337-8, ed. J. Armitage-Robinson, Somerset Record Society Collecteana, xxxix. (1924).
STRABO, WALAFRIDUS, *Hortulus*, trans. R.S. Lambert, Wembley Hill 1924.
Swinefield, Bishop Richard's Household Expenses, ed. J. Webb, Camden Soc. 1854.

Templars, English Records in 12th Century, ed. B.A. Lees, London 1935.

Vegetables and Herbs, B.L. Ms. Harl. 1977.

WADDELL, HELEN, *Medieval Latin Lyrics*, London 1951.
Walter of Wenlock, Abbot of Westminster, ed. B. Harvey. Camden 4th Series, ii. London 1965.
Westminster, Customary of St Peter's Monastery, ed. E.M. Thompson, London 1902-4.
Westminster Cellarers' and Gardeners' Account Rolls, Westminster Abbey Muniments Room.
Winchester Cathedral Priory Compotus Rolls, ed. G.W. Kitchin, Hampshire Record Society, 1892.
WRIGHT, T, *Popular Treatises on Science during the Middle Ages*, London 1841; *A Volume of Vocabularies*. Liverpool 1857.
WRIGHT, T. AND HALLIWELL, J.O., *Reliquiae Antiquae*, 2 vols. London 1845.

York City Freemen's Register, 1272-1358, ed. F. Collins, Surtees Soc. xcvi, (1897).
York, Early Civic Wills, ed. R.B. Cook, *Archeological and Topographical Association Records*, xxviii. (1906), pp. 827-71.
York Lay Subsidy Rolls, I Edward III, ed. J.W.R. Parker *Yorkshire Archaeological Society Series*, lxxiv (Misc. ii), 1929.

SECONDARY SOURCES

ADDY, S.O., *The Evolution of the English House*, London 1933.
ALLSOP, KENNETH, TRUST, AND JOHN FOWLES, *Steep Holm: A Case History in the Study of Evolution,* Dorset Publishing Co., 1978.
AMHERST, LADY CECILIA, *A History of Gardening in England*, London 1910.

BARDSWELL, F.A., *The Herb Garden*, London 1930.

[277]

BARLEY, B.M.W., *The English Farmhouse and Cottage*, London 1961.
BENNETT, H.S., *Life on the English Manor*, Cambridge 1965.
BENNETT R.F., *The Early Dominicans*, Cambridge 1937.
BICKERDYKE, J., *The Curiosities of Ale and Beer*, London 1965.
BLOMFIELD, J.C., *A History of the Present Deanery of Bicester*, London 1882-94.
BREWER, D.S., *Chaucer and his Time*, London 1963.
BROWN, R.A., *English Medieval Castles*, London 1954; 'Royal Castle Building in England', *English History Review*, lxx (1955).
BULL, H.G. AND HOGG, R., *Herefordshire Pomona*, Hereford 1876-85.
BUNYARD, E.A., *Old Garden Roses*, London 1936.
BURNETT, G.T., *Plantae Utiliores*, 4 vols, London 1839-50.

Caledonian Horticultural Society Memoirs, 1814-29.
CAMPBELL, JAMES, *Balmerino and its Abbey*, Edinburgh 1899.
CHADWICK, D., *Social Life in the Days of Piers Plowman*, Cambridge 1922.
CLAPHAM, A.R., TUTIN, T.G. AND WARBURG, E.F., *Flora of the British Isles*, Cambridge 1962.
CLAY, R.M., *Hermits and Anchorites of England*, London 1914; *The Medieval Hospitals of England*, London 1909.
CLIFFORD, P.A., *A History of Garden Design*, London 1966.
COATS, A.M., *Flowers and their Histories*, London 1968.
COLVIN, H.M., *Domestic Architecture and Town Planning in Medieval England*, 2 vols. Oxford 1958; *The History of the King's Works*, London 1963.
COULTON, G.G., *Chaucer and his England*, London 1909; *Life in the Middle Ages*, Cambridge 1928-30; *The Medieval Scene*, Cambridge 1939.
COX, E.H.M., *A History of Gardening in Scotland*, London 1935.
CRISP, F., *Medieval Gardens*, London 1924 (2 vols).
CUTTS, E.L., *Scenes and Characters of the Middle Ages*, London 1922.

DARBY, H.C., *A Historical Geography of England*, Cambridge 1936.
DAVENPORT, F.J.M., *The Economic Development of a Norfolk Manor, Forncett St Mary*, Cambridge 1906.
DEANESLEY, M., *A History of the Medieval Church*, London 1965.
DICKINSON, J.C., *Monastic Life in Medieval England*, London 1961.
Dictionary of Catholic Biography, ed. J.J. Delaney and J.E. Tobin, London 1962.
Dictionary of National Biography, London 1885-1912.
DRONKE, P., *The Medieval Lyric*, Oxford 1970.

Bibliography

Encyclopedia Britannica, 1911 edition.
EVANS, H.A., *Castles of England and Wales*, London 1912.

FINBERG, H.P.R., *Tavistock Abbey*, Cambridge 1951.
FLOWER, R., *The Irish Tradition*, Oxford 1947.
FOXCROFT, REV, *Excavations at Hinton Charterhouse*, Bath Natural History and Archaeological Field Club, Vol. 7 (1893).
FOX-DAVIES, A.C., *A Complete Guide to Heraldry*, London 1969.
FRASER, H.M., *The History of Bee-keeping in Britain*, London 1958.

GASQUET, F.A., *Monastic Life in the Middle Ages*, London 1922.
GENDERS, R., *The Cottage Garden*, London 1969.
GLOAG, M.R., *A Book of English Gardens*, London 1906.
GOTHEIN, M.L., *Garden Art*, London 1928.
GOUGH, R., 'The History and Antiquities of Croyland Abbey', *Bibliotheca Topographica Britannica*, iii, no. xi, (1783).
GRAHAM, R., *St Gilbert of Sempringham and the Gilbertines*, London 1901.
GREEN, V.G., 'The Fransciscans in Medieval English Life', *Franciscan Studies*, xx. (1939).

HADFIELD, M., *A History of British Gardening*, London 1960.
HALDANE, E.S., *Scots Gardens in Old Times*, London 1934.
HARVEY, J.H., *Early Nurserymen*, London 1974; *English Medieval Architects*, London, 1954; *The Medieval Architect*, London 1972.
HARVEY, P.D.A., *A Medieval Oxfordshire Village*, Oxford 1965.
HARVEY-GIBSON, R.J., *Outlines of the History of Botany*, London 1919.
HASKINS, C.H., *Medical Writings of the Dark Ages*, Oxford 1929; *Studies in the History of Medieval Science*, New York 1960.
HINNESBUCH, W.A., *The Early English Friars Preachers*, Rome 1951.
HOLMES, V.T., *Daily Life in the 12th Century*, Wisconsin 1952.
HOPE, W.H. ST J., *10th and 11th Century Castles*, London 1903; 'The Charterhouse at Mt Grace', *Yorks. Archaeological and Topographical Journal*, xviii, (1904); 'English fortresses and castles', *Archaeological Journal*, lx, (1903); *History of the London Charterhouse*, London 1925.
HYAMS, E., *English Cottage Gardens*, London 1970; *A History of Gardens and Gardening*, London 1971.

JACKSON, K., *Studies in Early Celtic Nature Poetry*, Cambridge 1935.
JACOB, E.F., *The 15th Century*, Oxford 1961.

JARRETT, B., *The English Dominicans*, London 1921.
JOHNSON, G.W., *The History of English Gardening*, London 1829.
JORET, C., *Les Plantes dans l'Antiquité et au Moyen Age*, Paris 1897; *La Rose dans l'Antiquité et au Moyen Age*, Paris 1892.
JUSSERAND, J.A.A.J., *English Wayfaring Life in the Middle Ages*, London 1920.

KATZENELLENBOGEN, *Allegories of the Virtues and Vices in Medieval Art*, London 1939.
KEMP-WELCH, A., *Of Six Medieval Women*, London 1913.
KING, E.J., *The Grand Priory of the Order of the Hospital of St John of Jerusalem in England*, London 1924.
KITCHIN, G.W.H., *Winchester*, Winchester 1891.
KNOWLES, D., *The Monastic Order in England*, Cambridge 1963; *The Religious Orders in England*, Cambridge 1948-59.
KNOWLES, D. AND GRIMES, W.E., *The Charterhouse*, London 1954.

LAWRENCE, C.H., 'The Medieval Parsonage and its Occupants', *Bulletin of the John Rylands Library*, xxvi, (1944).
LEFF, G., *Paris and Oxford Universities in the 13th and 14th Centuries*, New York 1968.
LLOYD, N., *A History of the English House*, London and New York 1928.
LOUDON, J.C., *Arboretum et Fruticetum Britannicum*, London 1838.

MACKENZIE, J.D., *The Castles of England, their History and structure*, 2 vols., London 1897.
MALLET, C.E., *A History of the University of Oxford*, vol. i., London 1924.
MALM, J.B., *L'Ordre Cistercienne et son gouvernement*, Paris 1951.
MCKISACK, M., *The 14th Century*, Oxford 1959.
MARTIN, A.R., 'The Dominican Priory at Canterbury', *Archaeological Journal*, lxxxvi, (1930); 'Franciscan Architecture in England', *British Society of Franciscan Studies*, xviii, Manchester 1937.
MOORMAN, J.R.H., *The History of the Franciscan Order from its Origins to the year 1517*, Oxford 1968.
MORETON, C.O., *Old Pinks and Carnations*, London 1955.

NEILL, P., *The Fruit, Flower, and Kitchen Garden*, Edinburgh 1845.

ORDISH, G., *Wine Growing in England and Wales*, London 1953.
Oxford Dictionary of English Proverbs, Oxford 1970.

Bibliography

Oxford English Dictionary, Oxford 1970.
PALMER, R.L., *English Monasteries in the Middle Ages*, London 1930.
PARKER, T.W., *The Knights Templars in England*, Tucson 1963.
PASSINGHAM, W.J:, *London's Markets: Their Origin and History*, London 1935.
PEGGE, S., 'The Vine in England', *Archaeologia*, i, iii, (1770, 73).
PENDRILL, C., *London Life in the 14th Century*, London 1925.
PEMBERTON, REV. J.H., *Roses, their History, Development and Cultivation*, London 1908.
PHILLIPS, H., *Flora Historica*, London 1821; *Pomarium Britannicum*, London 1821; *The History of Cultivated Vegetables*, London 1822.
POOLE, A.L., *Medieval England*, Oxford 1958.
POSTAN, M.M., *The Medieval Economy and Society*, London 1972.
POWER, E., *Medieval English Nunneries*, Cambridge 1922. *Medieval People*, London and Postan 1924. *Medieval Women*, Cambridge 1975.

RAFTIS, J.A., *The Estates of Ramsey Abbey*, Toronto 1967.
RAINE, A., *Medieval York*, London 1955.
REMNANT, G.L., *A Catalogue of Misericords in Great Britain*, Oxford and New York 1969.
RESSER, C.E., 'Very Ancient Roses'. *Annual of the American Rose Society*, 1943.
RIESMAN, D., *The Story of Medicine in the Middle Ages*, New York, 1935.
ROBERTSON, D.W., 'The Doctrine of Charity in Medieval Literary Gardens', *Speculum*, 26, (1951).
ROHDE, E.S., *Garden-Craft in the Bible*, London 1927. *A Garden of Herbs*, London 1926. *The Story of the Garden*, London 1882.

SALTER, E. AND PEARSALL, D., *Landscapes and Seasons for the Medieval World*, London 1973.
SALTER, H.E., 'Medieval Oxford', *Oxford Historical Society*, vol. c.(1936)
SALZMAN, L.F., *English Industries of the Middle Ages*, London 1964; *English Life in the Middle Ages*, London 1926.
SEWARD, B., *The Symbolic Rose*, New York, 1960.
SHEPHARD, O., *The Lore of the Unicorn*, New York, 1967.
SIMON, A., *The History of the Wine Trade in England*, 3 vols., London 1906-9.
SINGER, C., *A Short History of Medicine*, Oxford 1962.
SNEESBY, N., *The Isle of Ely Vineyard*, London 1977.
SOMNER, W., *Antiquities of Canterbury*, Canterbury 1703.

SPEECHLY, W., *A Treatise on the Culture of the Vine*, York 1790.
STEP, E., *Herbs of Healing*, London 1926.
STEPHENSON, J. AND CHURCHILL, J.M., *Medical Botany*, 4 vols. London 1831.
SWITZER, S., *The Practical Fruit Garden*, London 1742.

TALBOT, C.H., *Medicine in Medieval England*, London 1967.
TATLOCK, J.S.P., *Concordance to Chaucer*, Washington 1927.
THOMAS, G.S., *Old Shrub Roses*, London 1955.
THOMPSON, A.H., *English Monasteries*, Cambridge 1923; *Military Architecture in England During the Middle Ages*, London 1912.
THOMPSON, D.V., *The Materials of Medieval Painting,* London 1936.
THOMPSON, E.M., *The Carthusian Order in England*, London 1930; *A History of the Somerset Carthusians*, London 1895.
THOMPSON, J., *The History of Leicester*, Leicester 1849.
THRUPP, S., *The Merchant Class of Medieval London*, Chicago 1948.
TIGHE, R.R. AND DAVIS, J.E., *Annals of Windsor*, London 1858.
TILLOTT, P.M., *The City of York*, York 1961.
TOUT, T.F., 'Medieval Town Planning', *Bulletin of the John Rylands Library*, 4 (1917-8).
TURGIT, G., *Flowers Through the Ages*, London 1961.
TURNER, T., *Manners and Household Expenses*, Roxburgh Club, 1841.
TURNER, T.H., *Domestic Architecture*, Oxford 1851-9.

UNWIN, G., *The Gilds and Companies of London*, London 1908.
URRY, W.J., *Canterbury under the Angevin Kings*, London 1966.

VEALE, M., *Studies in the Medieval Wine Trade*, Oxford 1971.

WADDELL, HELEN., *The Desert Fathers*, London 1960.
WADMORE, J.F., 'The Knights Hospitaller in Kent', *Archaeologia Cantiana*, xxii, xxiv, (1897, 1905).
WALKER, J., *Essays on Natural History and Rural Economy*, London 1812.
WELCH, C., *The History of the Worshipful Company of Pewterers*, London 1902.
WESTLAKE, H.F., *Westminster Abbey*, (2 vols.) London 1923.
WHITE, L., *Medieval Technology and Social Change*, London 1962.
WILKINS, E., *The Rose Garden Game*, London 1969.
WILLIAMS, G.A., *Medieval London*, London 1963.
WILLIAMSON, J.B., *History of the Temple, London*, London 1924.
WOOD, M.E., '13th Century Domestic Architecture in England,'

Bibliography

Archaeological Journal cv. supp. 1950; *The English Medieval House*, London 1965.

WRIGHT, R.L., *The Story of Gardening*. London 1934.

WRIGHT, T., *Essays on Subjects Connected with Literature, Popular Superstitions and the History of England in the Middle Ages*, London 1846; *A History of Domestic Manners and Sentiments in England during the Middle Ages*, London 1862; *Womankind in Western Europe*, London 1869.

Illustrations Acknowledgments

1. BL. MS. 19720, f.165; 2b. BL. Cott. MS. Aug.I i, 83; 4b. BL. Harl. MS. 4431, f.376; 6a. BL. 14E VI, f.157; 9b. BL. MS. 19720, f.214v; 10a. BL. MS. 19720, f.305; 11a. BL. MS. 19720, f.80; 12a. BL. MS. 19720, f.117v. The foregoing reproduced by courtesy of the British Library Board. 2a. Trinity Coll. MS.R.17, 1 (Canterbury Psalter). Reproduced by permission of the Master and Fellows of Trinity College, Cambridge. 3a. MS. Bodley 264, f.258v; 6b. MS. Bodley Douce 195. f.26; 7b. MS. Bodley Astor A. 15, f.4. Reproduced by permission of the Bodleian Library, Oxford. 3b. BN MS. Arsénal 5064, f.151v; 8 and 11b. BN MS. Lat. 9474, f.7 and f.6. Bibliothèque Nationale, Paris. 4a. Schoengauer; Virgin and Child on a turfed seat. Ashmolean Museum, Oxford. 5. Photographs Colin Graham, with access to Steep Holm courtesy of Kenneth Allsop Trust. 7a. and 12b. Victoria & Albert Museum and Courtauld Institute of Art, London. 10b. Holkham MS. 307, f.109. Reproduced by permission of Viscount Coke and the Courtauld Institute. 9a. Museum der Allerheiligen, Schaffhausen.

Line drawings

Fig. 1. from a drawing in *Carolingian and Romanesque Architecture, 800-1200* (Conant), Penguin, London, 1959 (Pelican History of Art). Fig. 2. from a drawing by W.H. St John Hope in *Yorks. Archaeological and Topographical Jnl*, vol xviii. Fig. 3. from a drawing by John Mansbridge in *Everyday Life of Medieval Travellers* (Rowling), Batsford, London, 1971. Fig. 4. from a drawing based on one in the *Victoria County History of Yorkshire*, Vol. II, East Riding. Fig. 5. from a drawing in *Winchester* (Kitchin), Longman, Winchester, 1891. Fig. 6. from a drawing in *A Medieval Oxfordshire Village* (Harvey), O.U.P., Oxford, 1965.

Tailpieces

The chapter tailpieces are taken from the *Bury Herbal* (MS. Bodley 130) by permission of the Bodleian Library, Oxford.

Index

Index

Index

Fitz Osbern, William, Earl of Hereford, 90
Fitz Ralph, Geoffrey, 102
Fitz Solomon, Ralph, 102
Fitzstephen, William, 63, 87
flax (*Linum usitatissimum*), 23, 36, 44, 82, 204, 215-17
fleur-de-lys, 143
Florentyn, William, 102-3
flowers: variety and utility of, 139-47; useful and pretty, 147-58; beautiful, 158-64; *see also* individual flowers
Foeniculum vulgare see fennel
Form of Cury, 187, 201, 208, 210
fountains, 95, 105, 107, 133, 160-61
Fountains Abbey, Yorkshire, 244
foxglove, 142
fragrance (in plants), 139-40, 183, 203
Francis of Assisi, St, 122, 153
Franciscan Order, 53
Fraser, Simon, 148
Friaries, 53-5
'Fromond' household list, 189
fruit and fruit trees: in monasteries, 27; in London gardens, 70-1, 73, 77; uses of, 224-5; in gardens, 235-40, 243, 248; grafting and pruning of, 239-40, 248
Fulham Palace, London, 65
fumitories, 32

Galen, 255
game (for hunting), 57
garden anemone (lily-of-the-field; *Anemone coronaria*), 46
gardeners: wages, 77-8, 81, 116, 119; names, 116, 119; professional gardeners, 68, 71, 73, 76, 77, 80, 119, 219, 248; *see also* monk gardeners
garlic (*Allium sativum*), 16, 39, 81, 82, 202-3, 205-6, 214, 221, 223
garnishing, 69
Genesis, Book of, 120-21; *see also* Eden, Garden of
gentians, 193
Geoffrey of Bagshot, 221
Gerald of Wales, 92-3, 254, 259

Geranium robertianum see herb Robert
germander, 193
Gilbert of Ilkeley, 80
Gilbert of Sempringham, 42
Gilbertine Order, 42
gillyflower (pink; *Dianthus caryophyllus*), 69, 150-52, 159, 184, 255, 268
Girdlers' Hall, London, 72
gladwyn *see* iris
Glastonbury Abbey, Somerset, 20, 203, 206, 217, 251
Glatton manor, Huntingdonshire, 109
Gloucester, 63, 251
Gloucester castle, 34
Godfrey (translator of Palladius), 236
Godfric of Finchale, 53
Godspeed, John, 81
gooseberries, 78, 235, 239
gourds, 220
Gower, John, 202
grafting, 239-40, 248, 264-6
grapes, 249, 256-8, 262-3, 267-70; varieties, 271; *see also* vines and vineyards
Gray's Inn, London, 77
Gregory of Nyssa, 122
Grey of Wilton, Baron, 77
Grocers' Hall, London, 71
Grosseteste, Robert, Bishop of Lincoln, 228
ground ivy, 156
ground pine, 193
gruit herbs ('groot'), 24-5, 177, 191
Guild of Our Lady and St Thomas à Becket, 25
Guildford Palace, Surrey, 102
Guildhall, London, 76
Guthlac, St, 170
Guyot, Jules, 261

Haddington monastery, East Lothian, 225
Haddon Hall, Derbyshire, 114
Hainault, Jeanne, Countess of, 194
Haine, John (of York), 79-80
Hakluyt, Richard, 154

Index

Index

Montfort, Simon de, 95
Moorgate, London, 65
More, Sir Thomas, 195
More, Will, Brother, 34
Morus nigra see mulberries
Moslems, 126-7
Moss rose (*Rosa moschata*), 165
Mount Grace Priory, Yorkshire,
48-53
mountain spinach *see* orach
mouse-ear hawkweed (*Pilosella
officinarum*), 192
mugwort (*Artemisia vulgaris*), 141
mulberries (*Morus nigra*), 72, 237-8;
in wine, 253-4
Munden's Chantry, Dorset, 219
murrey (sweet pottage), 237-8
must, 269-70
mustard, 188

Neckham, Alexander: writes on
gardens, 33; on London, 63-5; on
fennel, 156; on lily, 162; on tools,
198-9; on pears, 231; on medlars,
236; on vines, 255, 262; on
grafting, 265; on pickling, 268
neep *see* turnip
nep (*Nepeta cataria*), 144
Nepeta cataria see nep
nettles, 110, 207, 254
Newcastle-under-Lyme, Staffordshire,
93
New Romney, Kent 227
Newstead Abbey, Nottinghamshire,
56
Neyte, Middlesex, 107-8
Nicaea, Council of (AD 325), 129
Noke, Richard, 243, 246
Normans, 20, 59, 62-3, 89-90, 150,
226; *see also* Benedictine Order
North Fleet manor, Kent, 254, 257-8,
264
Norwich, 62
Norwich Cathedral priory, 25, 29,
37-9, 230, 233, 241
Nottingham castle, 93, 97, 98
Nunburnholme, East Yorkshire, 61, 84
Nuncotton convent, Lincolnshire, 43
nurseries, 54-5, 73-4; *see also* imps

nuts, 46, 73, 109-10, 112, 233-4,
267; *see also* individual nuts

'O' days (monastic), 40-1
oak trees, 37, 242, 244
Oakham manor, Rutland, 109
obedientaries, 24, 26-7, 35, 39-41,
58
Odiham castle, Hampshire, 96, 107
Odo, Bishop of Bayeux, 90
Old Soar manor, Kent, 109
onions (*Allium cep*), 16, 27, 75, 81,
199, 202-5, 223
Ophioglossum vulgatum see adderstongue
orach (mountain spinach), 210-11
orchards: monastic, 20, 23, 39, 54,
57-8, 225, 247; in London, 70-1,
73; castle, 92-3, 95; manor,
109-10, 112; and religious imagery,
124; cultivation, 224-35; *see also*
fruit and fruit trees
Origen, 120-21
orpine (live-long), 69, 191
orris, 143
Ospringe hospital, Kent, 44
Over, Gloucestershire, 108
ox-eyes (daisies), 161
Oxford: size, 62; college gardens in,
80-3; vines, 262, 268
ox-tongue *see* bugloss

paints, 35, 155
palaces, 89-90, 97-103; *see also*
individual palaces
Palerne, William of *see* William of
Palerne
Palladius, 236
Paradise, 120-21, 123-9, 131, 137,
161
paradise gardens, 31-2; at St Gall, 16,
18; at Christchurch, Canterbury,
23; at Winchester, 31; and religious
love, 123-4; origins and
development of, 126, 135, 138
Paris, Matthew, 107
parks, 93, 97-8, 99-100, 113
parsley, 16, 75, 81, 189-90,
210-211, 254

Index

Index

turnsole (dye), 238, 254
tutsan *see* sweet amber
Tylers' and Brickmakers' Company, 72

unicorn legend, 134-5, 137

valerian (heal-all), 193
Van Eyck brothers, 137
vegetables: in diet, 27, 200; in monastery gardens, 27, 38-9; in London, 73, 75; in Oxford, 81-2; in manors, 113; cultivation of, 197-203; *see also* individual vegetables
Verbena officinalis see vervain
verjuice, 72-4, 83, 211, 229, 237, 256-7, 267-70
vervain (*Verbena officinalis*), 181
vicarages, 113
Vikings, 19-20
Vine, Hampshire, 249-50
vinegar, 269; *see also* verjuice
vines and vineyards, 15, 33, 34, 39; in London, 70, 72-4; in Oxford, 82-3, 262, 268; castle, 92-5; palace, 99; manor, 110-11; introduction and distribution, 249-53, 256-61; cultivation, 261-7; non-wine products from, 267-70; charcoal, 270; symbolism of, 271; *see also* grapes; wine
violet, 130, 148-9, 158-9, 161, 170; (petals), 254

Walafrid *see* Strabo, Walafrid, Abbot
walls; garden, 35, 58, 66, 70, 82, 105, 107, 118, 195
wallflowers, 152-3
Wallingford manor, Berkshire, 110-11; 261
walnuts, 233-5, 243
Walter of Henley, 234
Walter, Hubert, 83
Wanswell Court, Gloucestershire, 114
Warden monastery, Bedfordshire, 225, 230-31
Warkworth, Durham, 52

water, 104; *see also* irrigation; pleasances
water pepper (*Polygonum hydropiper*), 192
Watson, Anthony, 246
wax (beeswax), 27, 221-2
waybread *see* plantain
Wdelsfort, Essex, 251
wells, 95, 133, 161; *see also* irrigation
Westminster Abbey, 24, 63; infirmary gardens, 28, 175; monk gardener at, 40; at Dissolution, 55; manor (Neyte), 107-8; orchard, 225; fruits, 236-7
Westminster Palace, 63, 77-8, 99
Wherwell nunnery, Hampshire, 30, 33
Wilburton, Isle of Ely, 259
William I, King of England, 59, 90, 97
William II (Rufus), King of England, 31, 63, 91
William (Tower gardener), 77
William, Abbot of St Albans, 36
William of Auverne, 106
William of Colerne *see* Colerne, William of
William the Gardener (of Westminster), 78
William of Malmesbury, 32, 107, 252, 262
William of Palerne, 104, 237
William of Writtle, 228
willows, 242-3
Winchcombe Abbey, Gloucestershire, 156-7
Winchelsea, Sussex, 87
Winchenley, Gloucestershire, 86
Winchester, 31, 61, 83, 93, 97, 117-19
Windsor, Berkshire, 92-5, 97, 267
wine, 34, 252-7, 263, 269; production, 266-7, 271
Witham, Somerset, 47, 51
women: in nunnery gardens, 30, 42-3; in hospitals, 43; in castle life, 93, 95-7, 115; as garden labourers, 116; and medicinal herbs, 182-3; and kitchen gardens, 218-20